POPULAR
WORLD MUSIC

ANDREW SHAHRIARI

Kent State University

Routledge
Taylor & Francis Group

LONDON AND NEW YORK

First published 2011 by Pearson Education, Inc.

Published 2016 by Routledge
2 Park Square, Milton Park, Abingdon, Oxon OX14 4RN
711 Third Avenue, New York, NY 10017, USA

Routledge is an imprint of the Taylor & Francis Group, an informa business

Copyright © 2011 Taylor & Francis. All rights reserved.

All rights reserved. No part of this book may be reprinted or reproduced or utilised in any form or by any electronic, mechanical, or other means, now known or hereafter invented, including photocopying and recording, or in any information storage or retrieval system, without permission in writing from the publishers.

Notice:
Product or corporate names may be trademarks or registered trademarks, and are used only for identification and explanation without intent to infringe.

Credits and acknowledgments borrowed from other sources and reproduced, with permission, in this textbook appear on page C1.

ISBN: 9780136128984 (pbk)

Cover Designer: Kevin Kall

Library of Congress Cataloging-in-Publication Data

Shahriari, Andrew C.
   Popular world music/Andrew Shahriari.—1st ed.
     p. cm.
   Includes index.
   ISBN 0-13-612898-X
   1. Popular music—History and criticism.   2. World music—History and criticism.   I. Title.
   ML3545.S44 2010
   781.63–dc22

                                 2010022515

Table of Contents

About the Author

I became a student of ethnomusicology in 1992, having been trained in classical and jazz music (piano) since I was seven years old. I received my Ph.D. in 2001 from Kent State University in Kent, Ohio, as a specialist in the music of Southeast Asia, specifically of northern Thailand. As an instructor at Kent State, I have taught undergraduate and graduate world-music courses for more than a decade and have been active in developing online coursework for the past several years. I am fortunate to have published two books, *Khon Muang Music and Dance Traditions of North Thailand*, with White Lotus (2006), and *World Music: A Global Journey*, coauthored with Terry E. Miller, with Routledge (first edition, 2006). An audio CD of my field recordings, *Silk, Spirits, and Song: Music of North Thailand*, has been published by Lyrichord Discs and is available on iTunes.

My work as an ethnomusicologist is quite different from that of my job as a world-music instructor. As a university professor, I view my role as teacher and guide, while my career as a scholar focuses on the task of accomplishing research and disseminating it through publications, presentations, and musical performances.

Being an ethnomusicologist informs my instruction, but an effective teacher of world music does not necessarily need a Ph.D. in the field of ethnomusicology, at least not at the introductory level, such as this book is intended. In fact, I have often found that conveying too much about a subject bewilders my undergraduate students who are not music majors and leaves them disinterested. My intent with this book, *Popular World Music*, is to present the topics in as clear and simple a language as I can, with an emphasis on listening to the music. I hope you will enjoy this exploration of popular world music and use this book as a starting point for your own deeper investigation.

PATHWAYS

- **Internet:** Keyword: Kent State School Shahriari
  - *http://dept.kent.edu/music/facultypages/shahriari.html*
  - The author's bio page at the Hugh A. Glauser School of Music, Kent State University.
- **Book:** Miller, Terry E., and Andrew Shahriari. *World Music: A Global Journey*, 2nd edition. New York: Routledge, 2009.
  - *www.routledge.com/TEXTBOOKS/WORLDMUSIC/2ndEd/*
- **Book:** Shahriari, Andrew. *Khon Muang Music and Dance Traditions of North Thailand*. Bangkok: White Lotus, 2006.
  - *www.whitelotuspress.com/bookdetail.php?id=E22486*
- **Audio CD:** Shahriari, Andrew. *Silk, Spirits and Song: Music from North Thailand*. New York: Lyrichord Discs, 2006.
  - *www.lyrichord.com/index.asp?PageActions=VIEWPROD&ProdID=283*

Acknowledgments

Acknowledgments are like credits at the end of a movie. Most people skip them, unless they know their name will appear, or there's the anticipation of a funny outtake worth watching. Since I have no bloopers to make you laugh, I will start off by thanking my wife, Christina, who supports my well-being and career interests in every way. I sincerely appreciate her tireless energy that enables me to do the work that I do. I thank my parents (thanks, Mom!), sister, and my wife's family for their love and support, as well as my many friends, especially Kjersten, Preston, Kirk, Mark, Janine, Beth, and Christopher.

I am also eternally grateful to my mentor and friend, Terry Miller, who continues to provide me with guidance in my life and academic career. I appreciate his input on this book (and all my previous publications and presentations), as well as the constructive criticism and encouragement offered by my colleagues and "ethno" friends, especially Ted and Tyler Rounds, Julie Kennedy, Anne Prescott, Tang-on and Chalermpol Srirak, Priwan (Khio) Nanongkham, Wah Chiu-Lai, Sara Miller, Tom Janson, Kazadi wa Mukuna, and Denise Seachrist.

Though not the first nor the last person I mention here, I am most of all thankful for the patience and support of my editor, Richard Carlin. Richard was the original editor of the *World Music: A Global Journey* textbook that Terry Miller and I co-authored. He was instrumental in making that book a success, along with many of the publications currently available from Routledge. In writing that textbook, I realized that there was still much to be said about popular world music, and Richard agreed. I am thankful to him for having the confidence in me to accomplish this project, for even though I initiated the suggestion; I believe this book is really his brainchild. I hope he is pleased with the results. I am also grateful for his patience as I faced family challenges that distracted me from finishing sooner. He is a rare editor indeed, and I am lucky to have him as mine.

I am also fortunate to have such a professional and productive support staff at Prentice Hall. I sincerely appreciate everyone's help in completing this project, especially Tricia Murphy and Assunta Petrone. While I'm just happy to see this book in print, I hope it will be successful enough to have been worth everyone's time and energy in seeing it through to completion.

I would like to thank the following who reviewed earlier versions of this book and offered valuable comments on the text to me during its preparation.

Professor Daniel Avorgbedor, *Ohio State University*
Instructor Ronald Horner, *Frostburg State University*
Professor R Anderson, *University of Wisconsin–Madison*
Professor Paula Conlon, *University of Oklahoma*
Professor Terry O'Mahoney, *St. Francis Xavier University*

I am also indebted to Michael Bakan. Though we have only met on a couple of occasions, he has been a great inspiration to me, not only as an ethnomusicologist and fellow publisher of "a textbook," but also as a father and a human being who lives with purpose. I truly admire him and wish him well with all of his life and career aspirations.

And finally, I thank my son, Cyrus, who has been extraordinarily patient with me on a daily basis as I grapple with the challenges of being a father. Now that this book is finally done, it's all about you, Cyrus.

Preface

INTRODUCTION

World music is far too vast an arena ever to be confined to the pages of a single book. You will not find *Popular World Music* to be a comprehensive resource. Rather, this book is intended to initiate an exploration in world music by focusing on several popular styles.

Interest in popular-music studies has grown rapidly in the last three decades. What was once a pursuit scoffed at by "serious" scholars is now the centerpiece of theoretical research in music and culture. Ethnomusicologists have long held an interest in popular-music studies, focusing primarily on non-Euro-American traditions. Bruno Nettl's *Eight Urban Musical Cultures: Tradition and Change* (1978) and Peter Manuel's *Popular Musics of the Non-Western World: An Introductory Survey* (1988) still provide a foundation for scholarship on popular world music, though both are today more than twenty years old. More recent publications (see Chapter 1) increasingly focus on theoretical issues relating popular music to social and cultural studies, and well they should. There is much to say about popular music and sociocultural activity. However, we scholars often have a habit of taking ourselves too seriously. We frequently forget that learning about music, especially popular music, should be fun. At least that's *my* opinion.

Every music scholar will undoubtedly have a differing opinion as to why we study world music. But this is my book, so here is mine: We study world music to learn about people—others and ourselves. What could be simpler and yet more complex? The creative power of humanity throughout the centuries is unfathomable; the list of topics to illustrate the great diversity of the human imagination is endless. The study of music is an exploration of the human capacity to create. Music expresses intellectual, emotional, and spiritual ideals of human beings across the globe. Even the latest pop song embodies centuries of preceding traditions, and a single performance can reflect the spirit of an entire era. Knowing music is knowing life and why people live it.

Encouraging Enthusiasm for World Music

As we will see, popular music is diverse and often equally as complex as any classical or folk tradition. If we study a music that has popular appeal, the listener is more likely to enjoy it, consequently encouraging enthusiasm for further exploration of music and culture. An introductory survey of world music is like a trip to an ice cream parlor. We'll sample many flavors, and not all will be to your liking. But by the end of our visit, I hope you'll find something you want to explore in more detail.

Broadening your musical horizons has many favorable side effects. Although I don't expect you to pursue a career in ethnomusicology as a result of reading this book, if it helps you to make a friend from another culture, encourages you to travel to a foreign country as part of your life experience, prompts you to try a new ethnic restaurant, or even causes you to just pause a few minutes to watch a world-music performance on TV, then it will have succeeded. At the very least, I hope this exploration will persuade you to add some new music to your current collection or to buy a ticket to a world-music concert in your area. You may discover a new favorite music that you aren't likely to hear on the weekend Top 40. You may even attract a few inquisitors wondering "What is that music?" Having read this book, you'll be prepared to answer and share the experience with them.

Information Overload

This text provides a fundamental resource for an introduction to popular world music, but my approach is one of brevity. Too much of a good thing can lead to information overload. We'll hit the highlights so that we can recognize various world-music styles and better appreciate what they mean from the perspective of the people who create them or participate in them as the primary audience.

Each chapter will focus on specific music styles in an associated geographic area, although sometimes we will find that the genre breaks cultural boundaries and appears in many places around the globe. Representative audio examples of the major topics are included or available through specified resources on the Internet, at http://www.routledgetextbooks.com/textbooks/9780136128984/ with a few noted exceptions (e.g., the Beatles). The salient musical and cultural features associated with each genre are discussed in detail to increase our appreciation of the music. Relevant artists will be highlighted, and suggestions for further reading and listening will be offered. By the end of the book, you will be able to (1) recognize a variety of world-music styles, (2) articulate musical and cultural knowledge associated with each style, and (3) identify important artists related to the genre.

Complementing the text is an interactive Web site, which can be accessed at http://www.routledgetextbooks.com/textbooks/9780136128984/. The web site intends to stimulate further exploration. While the book focuses on each style as a distinct entity, the Web site reveals the intricate ties these musics have to one another and a great many cultural activities around the globe.

Brief definitions of important terms are provided in sidebars within the text. Refer to the glossary for more complete definitions.

AUDIENCE

My intended audience for this book is anyone who enjoys popular music and has an interest in world culture. The reader who has had limited exposure to world music will benefit the most from this introductory survey, but even specialists may find things of interest in areas they have yet to explore. Although my writing is specifically directed toward the nonspecialist with a limited musical background, I do assume that the reader has a basic understanding of music terminology, such as melody or rhythm. Since this book is primarily intended for classroom use, I presume that an instructor can aid in your understanding of the fundamentals of music without delving into great detail here or dedicating entire chapters to basic concepts, such as harmony or timbre. I give an introduction to these musical criteria in Chapter 2, but I rely on your self-initiative or your instructor to clarify necessary definitions by consulting other resources, such as a music dictionary.

SCOPE

Our focus is on music that is generally regarded as "popular world music." Ethnomusicologists are often skeptical of this term because they consider all music to be world music and describe popular music as those genres promoted primarily as a commodity—that is, produced, marketed, and sold to consumers. "Popular music of the world" seems to be the most accepted academic description of this music, but it really does no better in narrowing the focus because all music is "of the world." In casual conversation, and certainly in the realm of music marketing, "popular world music" is the label applied to the scope of music we will study, so I use it here and as the title of the book.

Traditional music, subcategorized as classical or folk, generally falls outside the scope of our discussion, unless it pertains to the direct development of a popular-music genre. Our survey of popular world music is limited to those that I consider the most prominent among world-music enthusiasts. Certainly, I expect others to disagree with the genres I have selected, but I consider this book a starting point for a person with minimal knowledge of world-music, not someone who has a specialist background in the field. I have steered away from in-depth theoretical issues of ethnomusicological interest, opting instead for fundamental knowledge of practical matters, such as history, artists, instruments, and stylistic features. Although the current trend in popular-music studies is to dismiss these aspects as rudimentary, this book assumes the reader has yet to acquire this knowledge. It is important to know the basics; you can't run if you don't know how to walk.

Many popular world-music genres are difficult to obtain via the Internet or even in hard-copy formats unless you travel to the region where they are commonly heard. Thus, in most cases, I have selected music that is easily accessible to anyone with an Internet connection and basic software, such as iTunes. I certainly recognize that not all readers will have a high-speed network connection, but today many people know how to find one. If nothing else, it is probably easier for you to find a computer with an Internet connection than a copy of an audio CD or cassette of these artists at your local music store. For example, a recording of Hibari Misora (Chapter 9) is difficult to find unless, of course, you live in Japan or you have access to an East Asian grocery that carries her music.

Another consideration regarding the scope of this book is its length. I aim to present enough information to fill a semester at a relaxed pace. I often find in my own courses that, from the very first day, I feel rushed to discuss everything I want before the end of the semester. Three hours per week to present the basic information about a music genre, play a few audio examples, show some video, and answer questions about a range of topics quickly flies by. My clock-watching students may not be aware, but I have yet to get through a semester when I didn't leave out a topic or two (or ten) simply because we just ran out of time. I could have included much more about popular world music in this book, but I feel, as an instructor, that what I have said is enough to make the semester both educational and enjoyable.

ORGANIZATION

In teaching world music, I prefer to organize my lectures according to a geographic outline, rather than a theoretical one. Not every instructor, or textbook author, agrees with this approach, but I think that a geographic orientation gives students a tangible notion of both the origins of a music and its cultural associations. Organizing our discussion according to issues such as identity, politics, or cross-cultural interaction has merit, but I find instructors using this approach often forget to talk about the music itself, which I believe is central to the discussion.

Popular World Music is largely organized around the genres themselves, but with consideration for their geographic prevalence, point of origin, or both. We will start in a particular locale, but sometimes find that the music has audiences in other parts of the world; such is the case with reggae, which has throngs of listeners around the globe. I will mention a genre's prominent artists and unique stylistic features beyond the boundaries of its place of origin, where pertinent, but I try to keep a geographic grounding for most of our discussion.

Although I use the genres themselves as an overarching outline for organization, I have purposefully avoided a rigid framework for discussing them. Rather, I approach each as if I were learning about it for the first time. I wanted to explore these musics as if I were you, reading about them with no prior knowledge and letting my own interests lead me to what I wanted to study. I let the inner topics guide themselves, rather than forcing them into a methodical itinerary.

In Chapter 1, we will define popular world music and examine some overarching issues that are unique to studying this musical style. In Chapter 2, we will review some basic music terminology and present a historical synopsis of mainstream popular-music genres, primarily from Europe and the United States (e.g., jazz). Dealing with music that is perhaps more familiar will facilitate a clearer understanding of fundamental music concepts and help us to recognize how these popular styles have had a global influence essential to the development and stylistic traits of popular world-music genres.

The remaining chapters deal with the history and musical characteristics of popular world-music genres from various geographic regions. Assuming that my primary audience is from the Western world, I move from world-music genres that are better known, such as reggae from Jamaica, to those that are less familiar, like *dangdut* from Indonesia. Chapter 3 begins with calypso, reggae, and related genres, such as mento, ska, dub, and dancehall. Chapter 4 introduces a few Latin American popular musics, such as tango, salsa, and reggaeton. Chapter 5 focuses on samba and related genres from Brazil, before we cross the Atlantic in Chapter 6 to study several traditions from Europe, including Euro-Pop, Celtic music, flamenco, fado, polka, and klezmer.

We explore many popular world-music genres and representative artists from sub-Saharan Africa in Chapter 7. This includes a survey of the musical wealth from the Republic of South Africa, introducing the traditions of *mbube/isicathamiya, kwela, marabi, mbaqanga,* and *kwaito.* We then travel to West Africa to examine the popular genres of highlife, *juju,* and Afrobeat as well as some praise-singing artists, such as Youssou N'Dour. We leave sub-Saharan Africa with a brief review of *soukous* from the central region of the continent.

The next two chapters cover the largest territory, Asia and northern Africa. In Chapter 8, we begin with the Western world's popularization of classical music from India before turning to the popular music that emanates from the country's film industry today, known as *filmi. Bhangra* is also introduced before we visit the Middle East, where popular-music artists, such as Persian diva Googoosh, have historically found it difficult to perform modern styles of music without social pressures from the general population or the government. We review the music and life of Egypt's most famous female singer, Umm Kulthum, before concluding with one of today's most popular Middle Eastern music styles, *rai* from Algeria.

In Chapter 9, we will hear music from East and Southeast Asia that is largely inspired by Western popular styles yet is mostly unfamiliar to Western audiences. We begin, however, with the widely recognized phenomenon of karaoke before discussing specific styles from Japan (*enka* and J-Pop), Hong Kong (C-Pop) and Taiwan (Mandopop) as well as China (Chinese rock). We conclude our popular world-music exploration with the music of Southeast Asia, for it is probably the most difficult to obtain in the Western world. These final genres include *phleng luk thung* from Thailand and *kroncong* and *dangdut* from Indonesia. Finally, I offer a brief afterword to encourage your continued exploration of world music and culture.

FOCUS EXAMPLES

Most of our discussion is intended to introduce you to the basic history and important artists of the popular world-music styles we survey. Obviously, we also need to understand the music itself. I have referenced dozens of examples throughout the text that I encourage you to consider for inclusion in your own music library, but I explain certain songs in great detail so that you can better understand the musical traits of the style the song represents. These are the "must-have" songs that we focus on for the purposes of better understanding each genre as a whole. I wish all our focus examples could be included on an accompanying audio CD or as free streaming audio on our Web site, but unfortunately many music labels refuse to license material for fear of piracy. Fortunately, we were able to license some of the examples in this book which are available separately on our companion website http://www.routledgetextbooks.com/textbooks/9780136128984/

The Focus Examples are outlined following a consistent format that includes a reference to the original source. Depending on the example, that is followed by an introduction to the genre, artists, and specific performance as necessary; focal points for the example; and detailed commentary of specific elements heard, referenced by time code. Please keep in mind that the time code is approximate and may vary considerably if you are listening to a different version of the song than the one recommended in the book.

FOCUS EXAMPLE
SAMPLE

"Sample," performed by Sample Artist

Sample introduction of example. May include discussion of history, style, artist, specific example, and so on.

Focal Points

Several elements are summarized, such as:

- Language/Lyrics
- Instruments
- Melody/Rhythm, and so on.

TIME	DESCRIPTION
0:00–0:00	Time codes reference the specific track, with a brief summarized description.

Detailed commentary on the listening guide is provided in the following text.

For each Focus Example, I recommend that you listen to the composition at least three times. The first time should be a passive listening approach, with the goal of familiarizing yourself with the song. The second should be with the book in hand, taking an active listening approach. Pay close attention to the time-referenced discussion in the book to better understand the important features and cultural connections. The third listening should be when you synthesize all that you have learned and internalize the music's qualities as a representation of the genre. Approaching each song in this way will help you to better appreciate the music that we study.

THREE STEPS TO MUSIC APPRECIATION
1. Familiarize.
2. Actively Listen.
3. Internalize.

PATHWAYS TO PURSUE

There are so many pathways to knowledge about world music and culture. I continually urge my students to explore the world around them by taking advantage of many of our twenty-first-century technologies. The most obvious and easiest place for today's students to start is the Internet, but I also encourage them to attend concerts, introduce themselves to international students, eat at ethnic restaurants in the area, discover ethnic festivals in their community, and ultimately travel to see other cultures as part of their life experience. Those students who do explore these pathways find them rewarding, and I frequently receive e-mails or visits from former students who were spurred to discover more about their world as a result of my encouragement.

While these first-hand experiences are great for real-world exploration, books, CDs, videos, and television programming also offer great introductions to our world. We will use the Internet often in this book. Many of my colleagues mistrust the Internet and do not allow their students to use it as an acceptable resource. My opinion is that the Internet is a valid resource, provided that students cross-check their information with other resources. Books and newspapers have misinformation, too, so entirely dismissing the Internet as a resource is misguided and a stagnant approach to research, as far as I am concerned.

In researching this book, I used the Internet extensively, particularly to download music examples, view videos of major artists, and collect basic knowledge about each genre discussed, cross-checking questionable information with traditional hard-copy resources, for example, books, encyclopedias, journals, monographs, and so forth. Filtering all this information into a digestible format was the major challenge of writing the text. To simplify matters for you, I have included a "Pathways" resource list at the end of each chapter that includes a minimized selection of resources that leads to examples we have discussed or gives access to more extensive knowledge of the subject.

Although the resources recommended at the end of each chapter are topic-specific, the pathways discussed here are fundamental resources that apply to all of our discussion.

Essential Pathways

iTunes: *www.apple.com/itunes/download/*
Napster: *http://home.napster.com*
Rhapsody: *www.rhapsody.com/*

1. **Music Access Application:** Technically known as a proprietary digital-media-player application (e.g., iTunes, Napster, Rhapsody, etc.), a Music Access application that enables you to download music from the Internet is most important for our study of popular-world music. I personally use the iTunes application, which is free and can be used on almost any computer (Mac or PC). The iTunes library includes examples of most of the music genres we discuss. It's fine to use a different application, but I have tried to limit the audio items to those available on iTunes with few exceptions where the music was unavailable. You can also access video, radio, and podcasts about world music through the iTunes interface.

2. **Search Engines:** Search engines such as Google, Yahoo!, or Bing are by far the most convenient way to locate Internet resources about popular world music. Unfortunately, they also give you a bewildering number of places to visit. Nonetheless, being familiar with search engines and their capabilities (accessing maps, video, pictures, audio, as well as written dialogue) is a ubiquitous pathway to Internet research today.

Google: www.google.com/
Yahoo!: www.yahoo.com/
Bing: www.bing.com

3. **Major Web Resources:** There are hundreds, if not thousands, of places you could start, but these few are the ones I consider most useful as starting points for exploring popular world music.

   a. Wikipedia is by far the most useful general Web site to begin your exploration of popular world music—and most any other topic. The quality of essays can be inconsistent, but many are well referenced and clearly organized. Links to related sites are often included.

   Wikipedia:
   www.wikipedia.org/

   b. National Geographic also provides a great starting point for an exploration of world music and culture. Many of the articles about world music are written by prominent scholars or journalists and are used with permission from reputable sources. You can listen to audio examples and even purchase music as well as download podcasts that include interviews of many world-music artists active today.

   National Geographic:
   www.nationalgeographic.com/

   c. Radio

   i. World Roots Radio provides an eclectic range of world-music traditions, mostly of popular artists, and works with a variety of streaming music players, including iTunes, RealMedia, Winamp, and Windows Media Player.

   www.worldrootsradio.com/

   ii. Nonesuch Radio similarly offers a variety of world-music traditions, including many popular artists, but is limited to those found in their catalog. Nonetheless, it includes some of the best world-music recordings available.

   www.nonesuch.com/

   iii. YouTube.com is an excellent repository of video clips, both amateur and professional, that provides access to a great many world-music traditions. In some cases, this is the only place to find readily available performances of international artists.

   www.youtube.com

4. **Literature:** There are numerous magazines and books dedicated to world music, but many are for specialized audiences. For general interest, the following brief list includes some of the best places to begin.

   a. *The Continuum Encyclopedia of Popular Music of the World* is a multivolume publication intended for library use. It presents the most comprehensive review of popular world music and is written by many of the world's leading scholars.

   www.continuumbooks.com

   b. *The Garland Encyclopedia of World Music* is another multivolume publication intended for library use. Most of the articles focus on traditional world music, although many essays are devoted to popular world-music traditions. The publisher, Routledge, has also produced "Concise" volumes in specific areas that are more affordable for world-music enthusiasts.

   c. *The Rough Guide to World Music* is a multivolume publication now in its third edition that is the most affordable, comprehensive general review of world music. There are also *Rough Guide* volumes dedicated to specific genres, such as reggae and salsa, and the company produces a large collection of audio recordings dedicated to world music. Each of its travel books includes some discussion of music as well.

   www.roughguides.com

   d. *Global Rhythm, fRoots,* and *Songlines* are three of the most prominent world-music magazines available. Their online resources are also good starting points for exploring world music on the Web.

   www.globalrhythm.net
   www.frootsmag.com
   www.songlines.co.uk

5. **Audio Labels:** Here, again, are a seemingly endless number of publishers dedicating part of their entire catalog to world-music artists. Although our focus is on popular world music, I also include a couple of prominent labels that deal primarily with traditional genres.

www.nonesuch.com
   a. Nonesuch Records offers an incredible array of popular world-music artists, such as Buena Vista Social Club, as well as traditional music through their Explorer series. The label also includes many recordings of other styles, such as jazz and classical.

www.putumayo.com
   b. Putumayo World Music is one of the most visible world-music labels in the United States. Their nontraditional marketing approach enables you to encounter their displays in a variety of locales, including gift shops, science centers, children's museums, clothing stores, coffee shops, and upscale boutiques as well as typical record stores and bookstores. Although the artists featured on their recordings are not always the most prominent, they provide a great variety of popular world-music styles from across the globe.

www.arcmusic.co.uk
   c. Arc Music is a prominent European world-music label that includes many popular world-music styles, such as flamenco, bhangra, and Celtic music.

http://realworldrecords.com
   d. Real World Records was founded by popular-music icon Peter Gabriel in 1989. Many of the label's artists participate in the international touring WOMAD (World of Music, Arts, and Dance) festivals that introduce thousands of people around the globe to popular and traditional world-music artists every year.

www.folkways.si.edu
   e. Smithsonian Folkways is a premier label for world music in the United States. The foundation of their catalog is based on those of the Folkways Records label founded by Moses Asch in 1948. Although popular styles such as jazz are featured, the majority of the Smithsonian Folkways catalog is based on historical recordings and traditional folk- and world-music genres.

www.lyrichord.com/
   f. Lyrichord Discs also provides an extensive catalog of traditional world-music genres, along with historical recordings of classical music.

6. **Video:** Today, many popular world-music artists can be found on video or DVD, but few labels devote much of their resources to promoting them. Although the music itself is a popular commodity, most people are more interested in seeing an artist live rather than on a video screen, and rightly so. Some of the most famous artists will offer videos of their concerts, but there are none that I would recommend. Instead, I will offer titles in the coming chapters of some of the music and the artists we discuss.

www.netflix.com
   That being said, there is one resource I highly recommend, assuming that you live in the United States: Netflix. This company offers an extensive catalog of DVDs, from the latest blockbuster releases to a great many hard-to-find documentaries and classic films from around the globe. I used this service to watch several documentaries and international films related to our studies. You do have to subscribe, but your DVD selections are delivered by the U.S. Post Office via regular mail. Furthermore, as part of your subscription the company has recently added a service by which you can stream video directly to your television, eliminating even the time it takes for a DVD to be delivered.

http://www.routledgetextbooks.com/ textbooks/9780136128984/
   Finally, I urge you to visit the textbook Web page which can be found by going to http://www.routledgetextbooks.com/textbooks/9780136128984/

The website offers many special features, including an interactive globe that allows you to explore the world music cultures discussed in the text, plus chapter review and assessment materials. Throughout the book, you will notice callouts in the margins that direct you to this website to explore these features.

CHAPTER 1

A Popular Approach to World Music

DEFINING MUSIC

Most of us probably assume that we know what music is; yet when I ask students to define it, they have a difficult time. The typical responses are either objective or subjective, such as, "Music is organized sound" or "Music is beautiful sound." Leaf through a few different dictionaries from several eras and you are likely to find similar, though more verbose, definitions.

- *Webster's New Collegiate Dictionary* (1975): "The science or art of ordering tones or sounds in succession, in combination, and in temporal relationships to produce a composition having unity and continuity."
- The *American Heritage Dictionary* (1985): "The art of organizing tones in a coherent sequence so as to produce a unified and continuous composition."
- *Webster's Dictionary of the English Language New Revised Edition* (1994): "Sounds produced in harmonious, rhythmic combinations."
- *Oxford American Dictionaries* (online-widget; 2008): "The art or science of combining vocal or instrumental sounds (or both) to produce beauty of form, harmony, and expression of emotion."

The only common element in all these definitions is sound. Whether you consider musical sound objectively (i.e., as a science) or subjectively (i.e., as an art) is important to your understanding of its value and meaning. Some musics you can immediately enjoy, but others you may appreciate only intellectually. These reactions may be based on your personal experiences with musical sounds and the manner in which you have been culturally conditioned to interpret them. All this is a roundabout way of saying that music has varying definitions, so you should not assume that the idea of music is the same for everyone, particularly when discussing people of different cultural backgrounds.

For our purposes, we will accept the often-quoted definition of preeminent ethnomusicologist John Blacking (1928–1990), put forth in his book *How Musical Is Man?*: "music is humanly organized sound." Although this definition has ramifications beyond the scope of our book, we will use concepts of melody, harmony,

PAUL · SIMON
GRACELAND

rhythm, and form as they are generally understood from the context of European music. This book is intended as an introduction to popular world music, which is strongly influenced by the musical notions of European (and American) bias (see Chapter 2). Therefore, I acknowledge that there are differing definitions of music, but we must have a point of reference in order to begin.

RECOGNIZING POPULAR WORLD MUSIC

If defining music itself is a challenge, then delineating popular music, let alone popular *world* music, from all other music is surely problematic as well. As an ethnomusicologist, I consider music as one of three categories: classical, folk, or popular. Classical music most often requires formal training and a lengthy period of practice, usually years, before a musician is considered competent. Folk music is usually learned through an informal process and, by comparison, has a relatively quick learning curve. Classical music tends to be more complex than folk music, though this is not always true. The contexts for performance can also suggest a music as being classical or folk—the former being typical of a formal setting, whereas the latter is found in more casual circumstances. But, again, this is not always true. Certainly, folk music can be performed in a formal setting (e.g., a concert stage), and some styles are extremely difficult to learn and require years of training (e.g., bluegrass). Conversely, classical music is frequently performed in informal settings, such as for personal enjoyment at home, and includes many simple pieces in its repertoire that musically astute performers can learn to play without much training.

Another observation I have made is that people without prior knowledge of a music tradition find it difficult to determine whether a music should be regarded as classical or folk, based purely on its aural qualities. Let me qualify that statement. A person with prior exposure to the folk and classical music of a particular culture can usually categorize a new piece of music as being one or the other. For example, if you were to hear a sample of Andrés Segovia playing a composition by J. S. Bach on guitar, I am confident that most listeners, assuming a Western cultural background, would recognize it as classical music, especially compared to a folk guitar performance of, for example, a Woody Guthrie song, such as "This Land Is Your Land."

((•● **HEAR MORE**
on www.mymusickit.com
Audio samples

If, however, I give an example of a Thai *piphat* ensemble performing the composition "Sathukan" and then compare it with the same ensemble playing "Lao Duang Duan," I am also confident that, unless you are from Thailand, you are unlikely to recognize the former as a classical piece and the latter as a folk tune. Although many musical qualities distinguish the two, a person unfamiliar with Thai classical and folk music will find it difficult to recognize the distinction until it is explained.

However, I have found that distinguishing between popular music and the classical/folk genres of an unfamiliar culture is less problematic. If I choose an example of Japanese Gagaku court music, you may not be able to tell me whether or not the sounds are categorized as folk or classical (the latter is correct), but you would most likely recognize that it falls outside the realm of popular music. Conversely, if I play an example of *enka* music performed by Hibari Misora, I imagine that most of you could recognize the song as a popular style.

That being said, popular world music is quite often rooted in, or at least inspired by, classical or folk music from its respective culture. We must keep in mind that most classical and folk musics were at one time the popular music of the day and, to some extent, still find a voice in popular culture. Certain music used exclusively for ritual purposes may never have been considered popular, but even so, some religious music today clearly has popular appeal, such as gospel. Popular music draws on classical/folk music in many respects, so the lines between these musical categories are often blurred.

THE BUSINESS OF POPULAR WORLD MUSIC

In the modern era, music that is classified as "popular" is driven primarily by the music business. Certainly, musicians have been in business for many centuries, trying to eke out a living in various cultures across the globe. The development of the music business as an abstract entity with the primary objective of earning money for profit, rather than for survival, is a more recent phenomenon that expanded rapidly with the evolution of recorded sound.

As the technology for capturing sounds onto recordings developed at the end of the nineteenth century, the business of making music began to take shape in the United States and quickly spread across the planet. The initial cylinder recordings created by Thomas Edison were not only a great technological achievement but also a profitable creation. So, from the very beginning, recorded sound has been largely about making a monetary profit. Maybe Edison would not have thought of it that way, but that is what the recording industry—that is, the music industry—has become: a business.

Ethnic music has played an important role in the development of the music industry since the early decades of the twentieth century. Along with the radio, the success of the Victrola (an early phonograph) made recorded music accessible and affordable for people of various social classes. By the 1920s, several record companies, including Columbia, Paramount, Okeh, and Victor, recorded and marketed a variety of ethnic music. So-called race series were created to present African American music—namely, blues, gospel, and jazz—while the music of many ethnic groups found in the United States, particularly from Eastern Europe (e.g., polka), was also marketed to select audiences.

Also important to the future of ethnic music recordings was the work of John Lomax (1867–1948) and his family, particularly his son Alan (1915–2002). Beginning in 1933, father and son began traveling throughout the United States to record musicians of various ethnic groups, particularly African Americans. Their initial intent was to preserve music that they considered endangered; along the way, they discovered American music legends, such as Huddie "Leadbelly" Ledbetter (1888–1949). After the elder Lomax passed, Alan continued to record musicians from the United States and throughout the world, particularly those from Europe and the Caribbean, until the final years of

⦿➤ **EXPLORE MORE**
on www.mymusickit.com
Visit the Alan Lomax page.

Alan Lomax playing guitar on stage at the Mountain Music Festival, Asheville, North Carolina, ca. late 1940s.

Paul Simon's Grammy-winning album, *Graceland* (1986).

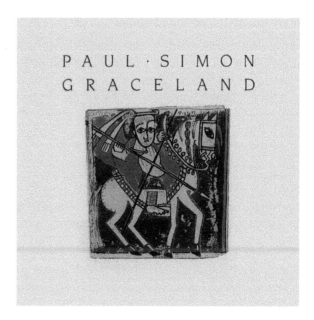

his life. Other entrepreneurs, such as Moses Asch (1905–1986), founder of Folkways Records, also took an interest in recording ethnic music, with the aim of preserving and helping to promote it to a wider audience.

Certainly, some international genres had found mainstream success during earlier periods of the twentieth century, such as tango, salsa, bossa nova, and reggae, but the concept of a world-music market blossomed only in the late 1980s. Its popularity was due in large part to the enormous success of the album **Graceland** (1986), by American popular-music icon Paul Simon. The album featured music from the Republic of South Africa and was a major impetus for motivating record-company executives and other music industry leaders to agree upon a single moniker, "world music," to promote their growing catalogs of international popular artists, which had previously been described with varying terminology, such as "world beat" or "ethno-pop."

The label "world music" has its critics, but the term has come into common usage to describe international artists of popular, folk, and classical genres outside the Euro-American mainstream. For today's average consumer, "world music" refers to the ever-increasing volume of popular world-music artists whose recordings are generally more prominently promoted than those by artists of international folk and classical music styles. Though the latter was the primary concern of music scholars for more than one hundred years, this trend has changed over the last two decades (since the term *world music* was adopted) so that now popular music from the international arena is a central focus of academic research in the field of ethnomusicology.

PORTAL TO WORLD MUSIC AND CULTURE

Though hundreds, if not thousands, of books and other media explore popular world music, they are mostly fragmented into discussions of specific styles or designed as catalogs of information without an expressed pedagogical intent. I envision this book, *Popular World Music*, as a portal to pathways of knowledge that can lead you to further

GRACELAND

• Grammy: Best Album of the Year
• Grammy: Song of the Year, "Graceland."
• *Billboard* Top 200: Highest Position #3
• *Rolling Stone* magazine's 500 Greatest Albums of All Time: #81
• *Time* magazine: Voted one of the all-time greatest albums

exploration according to your interests. We will examine several popular world-music traditions with the objective of learning about their history, relevant artists, and prominent stylistic features. My hope is that you will find these introductions appealing and be encouraged to discover new artists and musical styles beyond those mentioned in this book.

An important supplement to *Popular World Music* is the Internet. Today, the Internet is an essential tool for nearly every college student in almost any area of study. We will capitalize on this technology and explore popular world music by using this book as a means of accessing online music, videos, and literature to supplement traditional formats of knowledge acquisition (books, CDs, DVDs, etc.). The preface lists the essential starting points, as does the end of each chapter.

Aside from teaching "the basics" of popular world-music history and style, I also have the underlying objective of exposing you to other cultures through music study. Learning about music is learning about culture. When we learn about another culture and the people who live in it, we end up learning much about our own cultural values and ourselves. Let me offer a brief anecdote to demonstrate my point.

In 1997, I had an opportunity to lecture about ethnomusicology to a group of students at Zhejiang University in Hangzhou, China. Throughout the presentation, a young woman raised her hand several times to ask questions. At one point during the lecture, I was discussing how a national anthem reveals much about a nation's values. When the young woman asked me to elaborate, I asked her to sing her national anthem. Suddenly, she grew quiet and looked at her desk. After an awkward pause, a young man sitting next to her raised his hand and explained: "Sir, when we sing the national anthem, we must *all* sing."

My response: "OK, let's hear you." Without hesitation, the entire class of more than seventy students stood up in near unison and sang the Chinese national anthem with deafening gusto. I was astounded. When everyone sat down again, the inquisitive young girl, her face beaming with pride, asked me to sing my national anthem. I hadn't anticipated that, either. Stopping, somewhat embarrassed, after the first line, the class was gleeful that I had made the effort, perhaps interpreting my lack of confidence as being due to performing without the support of a group, rather than my meager vocal skills.

This anecdote illustrates how Chinese culture thrives on group effort. To stand out from the crowd—to sing the national anthem without the support of the class—is to counter a basic philosophy of Communism. American culture, in contrast, encourages individual achievement to a greater extent. For example, it is common to attend a baseball game and listen to the national anthem being sung by a single person on a microphone, with little or no audience participation. Americans highly value such individual achievement and show their group support of the performer and the teams of athletes through the uproar of applause that inevitably accompanies the last phrase of the song, "and the home of the brave."

I have often wondered how that same young Chinese woman might interpret the performance of the national anthem at an American baseball game. Many people do not sing during its performance. Others sing poorly, and many do not even know all the words! She might interpret such seeming lack of interest by the participants as an absence of pride in their nation, even as disrespect. Such an interpretation would be clouded by her own cultural values, rather than an understanding that individualism is a fundamental aspect of American cultural values. Neither cultural value system is better, just different. Recognizing how our own background shapes our value system is an important step forward in better understanding others and ourselves.

SUMMARY

LEARN MORE
on www.mymusickit.com
Chapter summary and
exam

In this chapter, we defined *music* as a general concept and clarified what we mean by *popular world music*. Our discussion also illustrated the role of technology and the music business in the development and dissemination of music. Finally, I outlined the basic intent of our study and the use of this book as a portal to further exploration of world music and culture.

Pathways

- **Internet: Keywords:** Edison national sound
  - Historical information and audio examples of Edison recordings.
  - *www.nps.gov/archive/edis/edisonia/sounds.html*
- **DVD:** Kappers, Rogier. *Lomax: The Songhunter*. PBS, 2006.
  - Documentary about Alan Lomax and his life's work.
  - *www.pbs.org/pov/pov2006/lomax/*
- **Book:** Taylor, Timothy D. *Global Pop: World Music, World Markets*. New York: Routledge, 1997.
  - Review of the rise of the world-music industry and related issues.
  - *www.routledge.com/books/Global-Pop-isbn9780415918725*
- **Book:** Carlin, Richard. *Worlds of Sound: The Story of Smithsonian-Folkways*. New York: Harper Collins, 2008.
  - Historical review of Smithsonian-Folkways Records and its founder Moses Asch (1905–1986).
  - *www.folkways.si.edu/explore_folkways/worlds_of_sound.aspx*

Keywords for Additional Music Examples

- Segovia
- Woody Guthrie
- Sathukan
- Lao Duang Duan
- Etenraku
- Gagaku
- Hibari Misora
- Folkways original vision
- Graceland remastered

CHAPTER 2

A Review of Fundamental Terminology

INTRODUCTION

This chapter presents an overview of the major Western popular music genres that have influenced popular world music around the globe and reviews fundamental music terminology that will be used throughout the book. By *Western*, I mean mainstream popular music genres emanating from the United States and Europe, primarily Great Britain. This emphasis reveals my cultural bias; however, the American popular music industry has been the most influential on modern musical creations since the twentieth century. Jazz, rock, and hip-hop music are powerful forces that have fueled the development of many popular world-music genres, such as reggae, salsa, *kwaito*, *bhangra*, *dangdut*, and many others, as we will discover.

Although detailing the history of these Western genres is beyond the scope of this book, a basic review of musical characteristics, instruments, and artists will serve us well in learning about popular music from the non-Western world. I will assume that most readers have at least some prior exposure to these musical styles and a basic knowledge of musical terms, such as *melody*, *harmony*, and *rhythm*. Nonetheless, let's refresh our memory of the prominent Western popular music genres by using these styles to review some of the fundamental terminology that appears throughout this book.

Fundamental Music Terminology

- **Melody**—a succession of pitches forming a musical idea
- **Harmony**—a blending of three or more different pitches
- **Rhythm**—the organization of the duration of musical sounds
  - **Beat**—a regular pulsation implied or articulated in a music performance
  - **Meter**—the grouping of a specific number of beats
  - **Tempo**—the speed of the beat in a music performance
- **Text Setting**—the number of pitches per syllable of sung text
  - **Syllabic**—one pitch per syllable
  - **Melismatic**—more than one pitch per syllable
- **Timbre**—the quality of a sound
- **Ornamentation**—an embellishment of a melody or musical sound
- **Improvisation**—spontaneous musical performance
- **Form**—the underlying structure of a musical performance over time

POPULAR SONG

⊙→ **EXPLORE MORE**
on www.mymusickit.com
Chapter objectives

A simple place to start is with song. Using the term *song* suggests singing, that is, musical vocal utterances. Song appears in every known human culture in both spiritual and secular contexts, though it is not always referred to as such by those who perform it. Some scholars consider it likely that singing developed simultaneously with, or even prior to, the human capacity for speech as a form of communication. Song is featured in folk, classical, and popular categories of music around the globe and is varied in its performance practice.

The act of singing is considered song, although many people use the term more colloquially to refer to any music performance, whether or not the voice is included. Instrumental performances are more accurately described as *instrumentals*, and frequently the more generic term *composition* is used. For example, it is more correct to describe an instrumental jazz performance as a "jazz instrumental" or an instrumental classical performance as a "classical composition" than as either a "jazz song" or "classical song." If the voice is the primary focus of a composition and the instruments serve only to accompany the performer, then using the term *song* is more often the norm.

One category of popular song is a form common to France known as *chanson*, typically a solo vocal performance with or without instrumental accompaniment. *Chansons* are usually sung in French and frequently performed in cabarets (nightclubs or restaurants that feature live entertainment). They are particularly lyrical compared to other European popular music, which is often more dance oriented, and their lyrics often dwell on themes of romance and the challenges of daily life.

Premier among chanson singers of the twentieth century is Edith Piaf (1915–1963), affectionately known as "The Little Sparrow." Piaf's life has been the subject of several biographies and was most recently depicted in the multiple-award-winning movie *La Vie en Rose* (A Life in Pink), in 2007. She spent much of her life as a performer, initially as a street singer, before finding success as a cabaret performer in the mid-1930s. Her fame spread throughout France during the 1940s, and internationally after World War II, when she toured the United States and Europe. She appeared in several films dur-

French chanteuse
Edith Piaf.

ing the late 1940s and 1950s and recorded hundreds of songs in French as well as in English until the year of her death, in 1963. She is widely regarded as France's greatest popular singer.

FOCUS EXAMPLE
FRENCH MODERN *CHANSON*

"LA VIE EN ROSE," PERFORMED BY EDITH PIAF

"La Vie en Rose" was Piaf's signature song. After first popularizing it in 1946, she performed the song at many of her concerts and even recorded an English version. We will limit our focal points of this example to help you better understand some fundamental music terminology and methods for recognizing musical style in later chapters.

((• **HEAR MORE**
Download the iTunes playlist link on MyMusicKit

Focal Points

- **Instruments:** Orchestral accompaniment. Note the absence of percussion.
- **Vocalist:** Single Female (Artist: Edith Piaf).
- **Language:** French.
- **Melody:** The vocalist sings the melodic line, with the instruments providing supporting harmony.
- **Tempo:** Fluctuates, in accordance with the singer's lead.

TIME	DESCRIPTION
0:00–0:13	Introduction by orchestra. Note the clarinet solo appearing at 0:07.
0:14–0:26	Voice enters. Note the fluctuating tempo.
0:27–1:30	Main melody appears. Note the return of the opening melodic phrase at 0:51 and 1:18. Also, note the slowing tempo at 1:10–1:17.

In analyzing a music example at an introductory level, whether popular music or otherwise, don't overload yourself with too much information. Start with the basic qualities and progress to the more complex aspects to help you recognize a musical style and better understand its key components.

The first thing to note in this and almost any composition is the *medium*, or what produces the sounds you hear. In this example, the performance begins with just instruments. If you can identify the instruments, all the better; if not, try to estimate the size of the ensemble. This example includes a small classical ensemble (an orchestra).

When vocals are present, you should identify two things about the medium: the number of vocalists singing and their gender. In this case, there is a single female voice. Chansons can be sung by men or women, and they are most commonly solo performances.

Language is another extremely important marker of a musical style. Certainly, one cannot expect to recognize every language you encounter in world music. But the more exposure you have to different languages, the easier it will be to recognize some basic characteristics.

This version of "La Vie en Rose" is sung in French, a Romance language. If it were sung in Spanish or Portuguese, you might have a difficult time recognizing much difference (unless, of course, you speak one of those languages). If it were sung in German, Arabic, or Japanese, you can become familiar enough with the common phonemes of those languages to differentiate among them, even without knowing how to speak them. If you can make a best guess what language is being sung, that information may help to provide a geographic orientation that can lead to the recognition of a musical style.

Although the voice has already entered, the main melody doesn't appear until 27 seconds into the song. **Melody** is an important concept to most music, particularly with popular world music. The key element of our definition of melody is the notion of it as a musical idea. Melody comprises both pitch and duration (rhythm), but these elements define the organization of the sounds you hear. By considering one or the other or both, the pitches and their durations can form a creative "thought," or musical idea.

Leaving our example briefly, ask your instructor (or do so yourself) to play a descending major melodic scale of one octave on any instrument, say, C to C on a piano (the white keys). In this manner, the pitches are organized in succession, with equal duration. For most listeners, this sequence is entirely uninteresting as a melody; there is no real thought or idea involved that makes the succession of pitches sound interesting or memorable. Now, play the pitches in succession again, but this time changing the rhythm to follow the "Joy to the World" melody commonly heard around the winter holidays in the United States and abroad. Same pitches, but the addition of a varied rhythm creates a memorable musical idea, that is, a melody. Similarly, the rhythm requires the correct variations of pitch to produce a melody—just using one pitch would not sound like "Joy to the World."

In our example of "La Vie en Rose," the primary musical idea is first articulated at 0:27 and reappears several times throughout the performance. Melody is used as a unifying element throughout the piece. The core feature of French chansons is melody as an expression of the lyrics. The singer's idiosyncratic interpretation of the melody is what makes each artist and every performance unique. Compare Piaf's English version of "La Vie en Rose" with that of American trumpeter Louis Armstrong (1901–1971); though overall there are many obvious distinctions in style between the performances, the subjective interpretation of the melody by each performer changes the emotional character of the music. You might also compare Piaf's French and English versions; even though both recordings are by the same person, she expresses the melody much more effectively in the French version, her native tongue, than in the English-language recording (in my opinion).

Listen through the remainder of the performance and note the points when the main melody reappears. The repetition of this "musical thought" helps make the song memorable for the listener. Most popular songs utilize the repetition of a melody to ensure its recognition; in the music business, they call this a "hook." From a cynical profiteering perspective, the use of a melodic hook is to embed the melody into your everyday thoughts, so that you are motivated to purchase the song or product that the tune is advertising. Even a simple three-note phrase, such as NBC's "peacock" chimes or Nestlé's "Hot Pockets" jingle, can be curiously unforgettable. Television and movie themes also capitalize on the repetition of a memorable melody to encourage you to watch.

Chansons are only one category of popular song throughout the world. We will encounter others, such as Portuguese *fado* or Japanese *enka*, that have many similarities of style. Many of these styles draw inspiration from folk or classical genres; others are influenced by popular song artists from Europe, such as Piaf, and the United States, such as Bing Crosby (1903–1977) or Frank Sinatra (1915–1998).

BALLROOM DANCE

Ballroom dance is one of the world's most popular social activities accompanied by music. Ballroom dances are typically choreographed couples dances, although several styles include larger groups of people to encourage socialization, such as the quadrille, a precursor to the folk style known as *square dance*. People all over the world from all social classes participate in ballroom dances for social interaction, exercise, therapeutic

---

Melody   a succession of pitches forming a musical idea

objectives, and their own entertainment. In China, for example, a visit to one of the many parks in major urban areas reveals hundreds of people exercising in the morning: some are jogging; others practice martial arts such as Tai Chi; many play physical games such as basketball; and still more dance waltzes or fox trots, with or without musical accompaniment. Latin ballroom dance trends, such as tango, mambo, and cha-cha, were international crazes decades before rock and hip-hop music became global forces.

Competitive ballroom dance is a prominent subculture in Europe, the United States, Asia, and elsewhere. In 1958 martial-arts icon Bruce Lee (1940–1973), for example, was crowned Cha-Cha King of Hong Kong. Local, regional, national, and international competitions draw thousands of global participants and are often broadcast on television and the Internet. In recent years, regularly televised ballroom dance competitions, such as the BBC program *Strictly Come Dancing*, have been enormously successful, spawning international versions in more than twenty countries, including *Dancing with the Stars*, which premiered in the United States in 2005. Ballroom dance is a regular feature of theatrical productions and the movie industry as well. Actors are often expected to have proficient ballroom dance skills and may spend hours learning dance routines with as much rigor as when learning the choreography of an extended fight scene.

The accompanying music of ballroom dance can be a variety of styles, such as classical, jazz, or rock. Although a ballroom dancer considers the style of music during their interpretation of a dance, the core elements of the choreography remain the same. These core elements are based primarily on features of the rhythm, namely beat, meter, and tempo. To better understand these music terms, we will focus on one of the most popular types of ballroom dance: the waltz.

Our excerpt is from the film *The Story of Vernon and Irene Castle*, from 1939. Vernon (1887–1918) and Irene (1893–1969) Castle were dance celebrities during the early twentieth century who helped to adapt and popularize many dances, including American ragtime dances, the vaudevillian fox trot, and the Argentine tango. The Castles appeared on vaudeville stages, in Broadway shows, and in motion pictures and wrote a dance instruction manual, *Modern Dancing* (1914), which is regarded as a fundamental resource on social dance of the period.

Fittingly, the Castles were portrayed in the film by legendary motion-picture icons Fred Astaire (1899–1987) and Ginger Rogers (1911–1995). Each was successful

Ginger Rogers and Fred Astaire in
The Story of Vernon and Irene Castle, 1939.

as an actor individually, but "Fred and Ginger" are best remembered for performing together in several films during the 1930s as well as in the 1949 musical *The Barkleys of Broadway*. Performing more than thirty dances in these movies, Fred and Ginger became international stars and further enhanced interest in ballroom dance among all social classes.

FOCUS EXAMPLE
WALTZ

LEARN MORE
Visit MyMusicKit to connect to video resources for this excerpt.

"THE MISSOURI WALTZ," EXCERPTED FROM THE MOVIE
THE STORY OF VERNON AND IRENE CASTLE,
STARRING GINGER ROGERS AND FRED ASTAIRE (1939)

Focal Points

- **Beat:** The dancers' footsteps correspond to the beat (pulse) of the music.
- **Meter:** Triple meter, or three-pulse groupings of the beat.
- **Tempo:** Moderate to fast to slow changes in tempo mark three distinct sections in the performance.

TIME	DESCRIPTION
0:01–0:11	Introduction. The orchestra enters just before Ginger Rogers says, "Oh, Vernon."
0:12–0:53	The beat is grouped into a triple meter at a moderate tempo.
0:54–1:18	Fast tempo.
1:19–1:21	Tempo slows in transition to third section.
1:22–2:12	Slow tempo.
2:13–2:19	Tempo slows at the concluding phrase.

Rhythm   the organization of the duration of musical sounds

Your first objective in discussing **rhythm** should be to identify the beat, or regular pulsation of the music. Popular music typically has a recognizable beat, although the absence of a consistent pulse (known as *free rhythm*) is frequently found in folk and classical music. In popular music genres, a percussion instrument, such as a kick drum and snare combination, will often sound the music's basic beat. In Western classical music, percussion is frequently absent, so the conductor articulates the basic beat by waving a baton. In this example, there is minimal percussion and the conductor cannot be seen. Consequently, you must listen carefully to hear the basic beat.

Beat   a regular pulsation implied or articulated in a music performance

The **beat** is most easily identified at the point where Fred and Ginger begin to dance. The upper stringed instruments play the melody while the bass sounds on the initial beat, followed by the woodwind instruments (flutes and clarinets) sounding on the follow-up beats (**1** 2 3). Watch the dancers' feet and notice that each step touches the ground on the beat. This is easiest to see with Fred's choreography, as Ginger's feet are sometimes hidden by her dress. The dancers maintain this steady adherence to the beat throughout the first section of the music until just before the transition (0:51) to the second section.

Meter   the grouping of a specific number of beats

After identifying the beat, the next feature to recognize is the meter. **Meter** can be difficult to discern for the non-musician, but, fortunately, most popular music uses groups of two, three, or four beats. Those groupings of two or four are described as having a *duple* (divisible by two) meter, whereas those with three have a *triple* (divisible by three) meter. Of course, sometimes the meter groups the beats into numbers divisible by either (e.g., six beats) or neither (e.g., seven beats) two or three, but this happens infrequently in popular music compared to duple- and triple-metered music.

In waltz music, the beats are grouped into multiples of three (triple meter). Each grouping is referred to as a **measure**. When the first section begins (0:12), the first two pitches of the main melody supplied by the upper strings sound on the "1" beat. The melodic phrase continues to emphasize where this "1" beat is throughout the performance. The lower strings also articulate the first beat, followed by the woodwinds sounding on beats two and three: 1 – (2 – 3 –), 1 – (2 – 3 –), and so on. This continues through the first section, with minor variation as the piece progresses.

Measure a unit of time corresponding to a set number of beats

Again, it is helpful to observe the dancers' movements in conjunction with the meter. The basic waltz choreography includes three steps corresponding to the three beats of the meter. A full step leads into the first beat, and two shorter steps articulate the second and third beats. Watch the variation in stride length of Fred and Ginger as they move around the dance floor. They cover more floor space on the steps that fall on the "1" beat than those of the follow-up beats.

Although the triple meter is maintained throughout this performance, a clear rhythmic feature during each of the three melodic sections is the variation in tempo. **Tempo** refers to the relative rate of speed between beats. Tempo can indicate a mood of a musical performance, with faster tempos often suggesting happy or lively feelings and slower tempos frequently indicating a sad or calm expression. Other times, tempo is merely a musical feature used to present contrast within a performance or to reinforce aspects of the overall form, as in this example.

Tempo the speed of the beat in a music performance

After finding the beat (and meter) in our example, listen through the entire performance and note where the tempo changes (0:54, 1:22). The progression is from a moderate to fast to slow tempo. Clap your hands to the beat throughout the performance and you will more easily note the differing tempos. You can also fast-forward or rewind to different points in the selection to compare the tempo of the beat, particularly to contrast the first and third sections (moderate versus slow tempos).

Also, notice the change in Fred and Ginger's movements from one section to the next. In the first section (0:12), the pair consistently follows the basic choreography of a waltz, stepping on each beat and following the long-short-short step pattern that corresponds to the meter. Note that their feet stay close to the floor throughout this section.

During the middle section (0:54), the tempo increases and the dancers' movements correspondingly quicken. The couple seems to bounce around the floor as their feet more frequently leave the ground, in comparison to the opening section. The final section is marked by a transition (1:19) to the slowest tempo in the performance (1:22). The dancers move beyond the basic steps of the waltz to interpret the music more creatively. Fred frequently lifts Ginger off the ground as they spin serenely around the dance floor, concluding with a near-kiss to typify the loving emotion that fills the scene.

Dance and music are closely connected, with the latter expressing emotion through sound and the former through movement. Popular music genres around the world are frequently linked to social dance, be it ballroom or other styles. Recognizing the basic features of the rhythm, particularly the beat, meter, and tempo, is usually vital to correctly performing the associated dances. Sometimes dance is merely a catalyst for audience participation, emotional release, or both and need not correspond closely to the music (as occurs in moshing). In other instances, dance is not considered appropriate, for the music is primarily intended for listening. Even in these cases, however, identifying the music's basic rhythmic elements can enhance your enjoyment and understanding of a musical style and its performance.

JAZZ

The term *jazz* encompasses a great variety of styles that have flourished in the United States and abroad since the late nineteenth century, particularly during the so-called Swing Era, between 1935 and 1946. Many of the most prominent popular world-music genres, including highlife (Ghana), salsa (Cuba-Puerto Rico-New York), bossa nova (Brazil), Calypso (Trinidad), Afrobeat (Nigeria), klezmer (Eastern Europe), among many others, have been influenced by jazz music. Jazz itself is in many ways a popular world music in that it blends musical traits from Europe, Africa, Latin America, and the United States into a unique style.

LEARN MORE
on www.mymusickit.com
View the Jazz Timeline.

Though the early history of jazz is rooted in African American music of the late nineteenth century, primarily ragtime and blues, European Americans and Latin Americans have made invaluable contributions to its development and dissemination. Many jazz musicians recognized the foolishness of racial segregation long before the civil rights movement of the 1950s–1960s, integrating their ensembles and welcoming audiences of any racial background or social class, despite frequent resistance from club owners, law enforcement, and government officials. Europeans, particularly in France, were entranced by the "exotic" American sounds and invited many ensembles to perform, with little consideration for their ethnic descent; they were Americans, that's all.

Among the greatest jazz icons was trumpet virtuoso Louis "Satchmo" Armstrong. Born in New Orleans, Louisiana, the heart of jazz music in the United States, Armstrong developed his talent at an early age, listening to ragtime bands and singing on street corners with his friends. He began performing professionally on the cornet in his teenage years and was mentored by another jazz great, Joe "King" Oliver (1885–1938), composer of our Focus Example, "West End Blues." Armstrong earned a reputation playing with riverboat bands and for high-society functions in New Orleans before accepting Oliver's invitation to join his highly successful Creole Jazz Band in Chicago in 1922. Within a few months, Armstrong made a name for himself and soon left Oliver's band in search of greater financial reward. He had a brief stint playing in New York City before returning to Chicago to perform under his own name with his groups Louis Armstrong and His Hot Five and, later, Louis Armstrong and His Hot Seven, which consisted primarily of musicians he had played with during his early years in New Orleans.

During the 1920s, Armstrong and his bands made several influential jazz recordings, such as "Hotter Than That" (1927), "Potatohead Blues" (1927), "West End Blues"

Louis Armstrong's Hot Five, Chicago, 1925. Left to right: Louis Armstrong, trumpet; Johnny St. Cyr, banjo; Johnny Dodds, clarinet and sax; Kid Ory, trombone; Lil Hardin Armstrong, piano.

(1928), and "Weather Bird" (1928), that featured his improvisatory skills as well as his characteristically gruff vocals. These recordings solidified his growing stature as an innovative and prodigious musician. Although the Great Depression of the 1930s took its toll on many jazz musicians and performing venues, Armstrong was able to keep earning a living playing in Los Angeles dance clubs for Hollywood celebrities. He expanded his vocal repertoire and appeared in many films and television programs through the 1940s and 1950s. By the time rock music supplanted jazz as America's popular music focus in the late '50s and '60s, Armstrong had already established his legacy. He continued to perform at concerts and to appear in television broadcasts until the final years of his life. He was posthumously awarded a Grammy Lifetime Achievement Award in 1972 and featured on a commemorative U.S. postage stamp in 1995 as one of the legends of jazz.

LEARN MORE on www.mymusickit.com Watch a documentary on Armstrong.

For more than five decades, Armstrong performed throughout the United States, Europe, Africa, and Asia, exposing thousands of people to jazz music. Many of his most famous recordings, such as "Ain't Misbehavin'" (1929, 1938), "Hello, Dolly!" (1963), and "What a Wonderful World" (1968), feature not only voice but also his legendary trumpet improvisations. His 1920s recordings also highlight both of these talents and showcase the other musicians who performed in his ensembles. We will focus on one of his most famous recordings from this period, "West End Blues," to better understand the fundamental concepts of timbre, improvisation, and ornamentation.

FOCUS EXAMPLE
JAZZ

"WEST END BLUES," PERFORMED BY LOUIS ARMSTRONG AND HIS HOT FIVE (1928)

Focal Points

- **Timbre:** Each instrument provides a unique quality of sound (timbre). The ensemble includes trumpet, trombone, clarinet, piano, banjo, and wood block.
- **Improvisation:** The trumpet, trombone, clarinet (with voice), and piano each perform a spontaneous solo inspired by the main melody and accompanying harmony.
- **Ornamentation:** Each solo utilizes melodic ornamentation distinctive to the capabilities of the instrument.

TIME	DESCRIPTION
0:00–0:12	Introductory trumpet solo.
0:13–0:14	Band enters.
0:15–0:49	Main composition begins with trumpet playing the lead melody, accompanied by remainder of the ensemble. Listen for the main melodic motive, i.e., musical "thought," from 0:15–0:19.
0:50–1:23	Trombone solo improvisation. Piano and banjo play accompaniment on the beat along with percussion (wood blocks).
1:24–1:58	Clarinet solo with responding vocal scat improvisation. Piano continues accompaniment.
1:59–2:32	Piano solo improvisation.
2:33–2:56	Full band returns with variation of main composition.
2:57–3:04	Piano break with descending melodic flourishes.
3:05–3:16	Closing phrase with full ensemble. Wood block ends the performance.

Timbre   the quality of
a sound

Timbre is the fundamental property of sound that helps you to identify an instrument type. The other sound properties include pitch, duration, and volume, all of which are nonspecific with regards to the recognition of an instrument or voice. If, for example, I play the pitch C at the same volume with the same duration on a piano, guitar, trumpet, violin, sitar, mbira, panpipe, xylophone, or any number of other instruments from around the world, the only distinguishing property would be the timbre of the sound produced.

Recognizing the timbre of an instrument or voice is based on familiarity. If, for example, you receive a phone call from your mother, the quality of her voice is more easily recognizable than that of someone you have only just met. The more often you listen to Louis Armstrong sing, the easier it will become to identify his voice, based on its timbre, when you encounter it in other recordings. I strongly encourage you to listen repeatedly to the music found in this book, because recognizing the distinctive qualities of an instrument or voice is often enough information to identify a genre. The other elements of music—melody, rhythm, and form, for example—can support your conclusions but are not always necessary for recognition.

Recognizing the timbre of a musical instrument or voice can become second nature, although describing it in words is often difficult. We use a variety of nonspecific terms to describe timbre that people often interpret differently. The timbre of the trumpet might be described as having a "brassy" sound, which makes sense since the instrument is made of brass. The trombone (0:50) is also made of brass, so describing its timbre as "brassy" might also be used, but that description does not distinguish it from the timbre of the trumpet; the term is nonspecific. Perhaps "deep and brassy" would help to qualify the timbre of the trombone, but, again, there are many instruments that can be described as "deep."

I believe it is important for each person to use his or her own terminology to describe the timbre of a musical sound. We generally describe timbre by relating it to prior experiences with similar sounds. If you hear a sound and think, "Sounds like a trumpet," in this case you would be correct. But if you hear the sound of a conch shell played by a Tibetan Buddhist monk, you might say the same thing. From an ethnomusicological standpoint, you would be correct; both instruments are classified as trumpets. Visualizing the latter, however, would prove difficult if you had never before seen the instrument. Imagining a Western-style trumpet played in the context of Tibetan Buddhist ritual music would be grossly inaccurate, but comparing the qualities of sound can be helpful for aural recognition.

In popular world music, we encounter many traditional instruments that you will be unlikely to recognize until you become accustomed to their timbre and appearance. We will also hear many Western instruments, such as the trumpet, that are probably more familiar. "West End Blues" features several musicians, so I encourage you to listen through the example and describe in your own words the timbre of each instrument performed.

Following Armstrong's dramatic solo trumpet introduction, the remainder of the performance highlights the improvisational skills of each of the melodic performers, except the banjo. **Improvisation** is a common practice in many world music traditions and often featured in popular music genres as well. Rhythmic improvisations are quite common, but we will focus on melodic improvisation as is heard in this example.

Improvisation
spontaneous musical
performance

Improvisation allows a musician to display his or her technical skills and creativity through singing, the performance of an instrument, or both. Melodic improvisation can be entirely spontaneous, but more frequently it is inspired by a melody or theme (a musical idea) that has been previously heard in the same performance. In jazz music, the main theme is typically stated near the beginning and end of a performance, with one or more musicians improvising a variation of the melody between these statements. The opening phrase is usually the unifying melodic element and can be heard several times throughout the performance.

In our example, the main melodic "thought" occurs from 0:15 to 0:19 and is played by the trumpet. The **motive** is only three pitches sounding through six beats of the meter, with the extended pitch (third to sound) falling on the downbeat (first beat of the meter): 4–1–2–3–4–1–. (The trombone slide heard in the background signals the end of the motive.) This opening motive acts as a melodic question that is answered by a variation of the motive and extended resolution that closes at 0:26. Although there is more to the melody, this brief musical thought is the essential unifying element to identify as the piece progresses.

Motive a short rhythmic or melodic idea

The opening motive of the trombone solo at 0:50 varies this musical thought, meaning that the musician improvises, taking advantage of the instrument's capability to slide between pitches. This technique is known as **portamento** and is a unique melodic capability of the trombone that is more difficult to accomplish on other instruments. The main melodic motive is recalled directly when the clarinet appears at 1:24, followed by an imitation by Armstrong's voice. The **call-and-response** exchange between the two musicians reinforces the rhythmic component of the main musical thought, with the clarinet adhering to the three-note phrase but altering the pitches. Armstrong expands the melodic content with his own vocal improvisations, using nonlexical (i.e., meaningless) syllables, a practice in jazz known as "scat" singing.

Portamento a continuous progression from one pitch to another through all of the between frequencies

Call-and-response an antiphonal music passage that includes a lead part (the "call") followed by a answering part (the "response")

A key feature of Armstrong's scat singing is a technique known as **ornamentation**. Rather than repeating the clarinet phrase exactly, he embellishes the motive by adding additional pitches, or ornamentations. Compare the first couplet with the second: In the former, Armstrong matches the clarinet, but in the second he adds an additional pitch. He follows his own interpretation of the main theme for the rest of the duet exchange, sometimes answering and other times overlapping with the clarinet phrasing. The use of ornamentation to expand a melody or rhythmic pattern occurs frequently in musical improvisation. The ornamentations are not generally considered part of the main melody, but more as "decoration" of it.

Ornamentation an embellishment of a melody or musical sound

The piano improvisation (1:59–2:32) diverges dramatically from the main melodic theme because the musical idea of the three-note motive has already been well established. The opening phrases are filled with many ornamentations, obscuring the original composition to such an extent that the underlying harmony is the primary reminder of the earlier musical content.

Armstrong opens the final chorus (2:33) with a return to the main motive, using pitches an **octave** higher than the original melodic idea. The last note of the motive, a high B-flat, is sustained for fifteen pulses, a significant challenge for most trumpeters. Note that the clarinet also sustains its pitch for the same length. The remainder of the conclusion also displays Armstrong's virtuosity before arriving at a short piano break (2:57) and the final melodic phrase.

Octave an interval of two pitches with the same name, but sounding at different frequencies

Jazz music, such as "West End Blues," has been a staple of America's musical culture for more than one hundred years. Though its popularity in the United States has waned since the advent of rock music, performers of its various styles can still be found the world over. Jazz musicians, such as Armstrong, Glenn Miller, and Dizzy Gillespie, have often served as ambassadors for the United States on State Department–sponsored tours or performing overseas for military troops. Amateur jazz ensembles, often from American colleges and high schools, frequently tour internationally to countries where jazz musicians are less common, continuing to spread the popularity of the genre abroad. Numerous secondary and higher education programs in the United States have jazz ensembles that perform standards of the jazz repertoire, along with newly composed music. Even though the recording industry has retracted much of its support due to sagging sales, jazz continues to be a vibrant part of America's musical legacy.

ROCK

Rock music has been a dominant force in popular music around the world since it first appeared in the United States during the 1950s. The term is broadly used to label a variety of substyles, including rockabilly, folk rock, soul, funk, punk, bubblegum pop, disco, heavy metal, and alternative, among others. Rock music reflects the ideals and interests of youth subculture around the globe. Young adults in Japan, South Africa, Germany, Brazil, Australia, Great Britain, and elsewhere have embraced it as a means of channeling their angst, affections, admirations, and energy into distinctive musical styles that could easily be discussed as a book in itself. The United States, however, still provides the central influence on rock music styles around the world through the international mass media, Internet, and concert tours of some of the most popular artists.

LEARN MORE
on www.mymusickit.com
View the Rock Timeline.

As the birthplace of rock music, the United States provides a wellspring of young rock music icons with each successive generation. Many are bred by the music industry to conform to a marketable image in hopes of reaping great financial rewards for themselves and their associates. The majority of rock musicians, however, toil away hours and hours in garages, dive bars, and grueling mini-tours for gigs (performances) that earn them little money or notoriety. Some do it for the love of the music, others in hopes of being discovered by an industry A&R representative who will offer them a lucrative recording contract, and some, quite frankly, for lack of much else to motivate them.

The underlying spirit of these underground rock musicians is one of rebellion. This sentiment may be expressed in lyrics, music, appearances, or the physical actions of the performers onstage. Some musicians may consciously encourage defiance against social norms, whereas others regard their activities as typical of rock culture. They may tackle social issues with visible anger and intense stage performances or reveal their passions with seemingly innocuous songs about love or relationships. Preceding generations to the "now" youth culture are largely unaware of the latest rock idols and innovative music styles. That is the nature of popular music in general: It changes. The trends of today are the nostalgia of tomorrow. Young and old alike may enjoy the music of a variety of earlier periods, but the latest fashions of popular culture are considered the property of the most current generation of young adults and teenagers.

Such was the scenario during the 1950s, when the children of the World War II period were coming of age. Jazz had been the most prominent popular music in the United States since the 1920s, but the Swing Era was coming to a close as the number of big bands diminished after the war. Jazz ensembles grew smaller and innovative musicians became more experimental, creating music meant for listening, rather than dancing. As twenty- and thirty-something beatniks were creating an intellectual counterculture, teenagers wanted something more visceral. They wanted to dance!

Certainly, there was plenty of dance music to be found, but it was nostalgic and considered old-fashioned for the youngsters. Television was surpassing radio as the media outlet of choice. As the economy picked up steam in the postwar years, the automobile industry was booming and modern appliances were becoming affordable for more people. Many families had disposable income for the first time since the Great Depression, and teenagers—now freed from needing to help contribute to the family income—were finding they had more free time on their hands.

This situation was true for most Americans, no matter their ethnic background. Many African Americans had left the rural areas of southern states, such as Mississippi, Alabama, and Georgia, and moved to cities in the north, especially Detroit, Memphis, Cleveland, and Chicago, to work in factories or find other jobs. Musicians followed their audiences and adapted rural styles, namely the blues, to the modern urban context. Icons of blues music, such as Muddy Waters (1913–1983), Howlin' Wolf (1910–1976), and B. B. King (b. 1925), created electrified versions of well-known country blues songs and wrote new music that drew droves of patrons to juke joints and nightclubs in ever-increasing numbers. Some jazz band leaders, such as Louis Jordan (1908–1975), downsized the big bands to play new styles, such as boogie-woogie, stride, and jump blues.

The catchall phrase "rhythm and blues," often shortened to R&B, came into vogue as a way to label all the new music emerging from the African American communities in these urban settings. By the time Cleveland DJ Alan Freed (1921–1965) began describing the rhythm and blues music he played on his late-night radio broadcasts as "rock and roll," the music had already begun to filter to white audiences throughout the country. Independent labels, such as Chess Records in Chicago and Atlantic Records in New York City, signed many young black artists and quickly mounted competition for the larger white-dominated record companies.

Although white teenagers and young adults became interested in the rhythm and blues records, their parents were generally displeased with the controversial new sound and its origins from working-class African American communities. Racism in America was still overt, and segregated schools, restaurants, buses, bathrooms, and drinking fountains remained an everyday reality. Rhythm and blues artists during the early 1950s, such as Fats Domino (b. 1928), Chuck Berry (b. 1926), Ray Charles (1930–2004), and Little Richard (b. 1932), sold records but often met with racial discrimination during their concert tours.

Fortunately, times were changing in the United States. The landmark Supreme Court decision in *Brown* v. *Board of Education of Topeka, Kansas,* in 1954, deemed as unconstitutional the "separate but equal" rulings of previous courts. The new ruling effectively sanctioned the racial integration of public schools and initiated a watershed of open protest against segregationist policies throughout the country. Youth culture's interest in rhythm and blues music reflected these social changes.

As white artists such as Bill Haley, Elvis Presley, and Jerry Lee Lewis began to record their own versions ("covers") of the songs produced by black rhythm and blues artists, the new "rock and roll" label became a useful means of reaching a wider market. Naïve white teenagers were generally oblivious that the phrase "rock and roll" was African American slang for having sex; instead, they interpreted it as a reference to dance. Adults at the time were largely unfamiliar with the lingo of youth culture, as tends to be true of each generation, so the white artists were able to distance themselves from the racial stereotypes of R&B music by describing their music as "rock and roll." The new name also allowed African American artists greater opportunities to sell and perform their music for white audiences and the mainstream media.

Although the music and its performers met with continued controversy, by the end of the 1950s rock music became mainstream and proved lucrative for the music business. American entertainment icons Ed Sullivan (1901–1974) and Steve Allen (1921–2000), among others, welcomed rock and roll performances on their television

(1928), and "Weather Bird" (1928), that featured his improvisatory skills as well as his characteristically gruff vocals. These recordings solidified his growing stature as an innovative and prodigious musician. Although the Great Depression of the 1930s took its toll on many jazz musicians and performing venues, Armstrong was able to keep earning a living playing in Los Angeles dance clubs for Hollywood celebrities. He expanded his vocal repertoire and appeared in many films and television programs through the 1940s and 1950s. By the time rock music supplanted jazz as America's popular music focus in the late '50s and '60s, Armstrong had already established his legacy. He continued to perform at concerts and to appear in television broadcasts until the final years of his life. He was posthumously awarded a Grammy Lifetime Achievement Award in 1972 and featured on a commemorative U.S. postage stamp in 1995 as one of the legends of jazz.

For more than five decades, Armstrong performed throughout the United States, Europe, Africa, and Asia, exposing thousands of people to jazz music. Many of his most famous recordings, such as "Ain't Misbehavin'" (1929, 1938), "Hello, Dolly!" (1963), and "What a Wonderful World" (1968), feature not only voice but also his legendary trumpet improvisations. His 1920s recordings also highlight both of these talents and showcase the other musicians who performed in his ensembles. We will focus on one of his most famous recordings from this period, "West End Blues," to better understand the fundamental concepts of timbre, improvisation, and ornamentation.

LEARN MORE on http:// www.routledgetextbooks.com /textbooks/9780136128984/

FOCUS EXAMPLE
JAZZ

"WEST END BLUES," PERFORMED BY LOUIS ARMSTRONG
AND HIS HOT FIVE (1928)

Focal Points

- **Timbre:** Each instrument provides a unique quality of sound (timbre). The ensemble includes trumpet, trombone, clarinet, piano, banjo, and wood block.
- **Improvisation:** The trumpet, trombone, clarinet (with voice), and piano each perform a spontaneous solo inspired by the main melody and accompanying harmony.
- **Ornamentation:** Each solo utilizes melodic ornamentation distinctive to the capabilities of the instrument.

TIME	DESCRIPTION
0:00–0:12	Introductory trumpet solo.
0:13–0:14	Band enters.
0:15–0:49	Main composition begins with trumpet playing the lead melody, accompanied by remainder of the ensemble.
	Listen for the main melodic motive, i.e., musical "thought," from 0:15–0:19.
0:50–1:23	Trombone solo improvisation. Piano and banjo play accompaniment on the beat along with percussion (wood blocks).
1:24–1:58	Clarinet solo with responding vocal scat improvisation. Piano continues accompaniment.
1:59–2:32	Piano solo improvisation.
2:33–2:56	Full band returns with variation of main composition.
2:57–3:04	Piano break with descending melodic flourishes.
3:05–3:16	Closing phrase with full ensemble. Wood block ends the performance.

FOCUS EXAMPLE
ROCK

Focal Points

- **Harmony:** Uses three chords, i.e., harmony: I (root), IV (subdominant), V (dominant).
- **Form:** Follows a standard 12-bar blues progression.

TIME	DESCRIPTION
0:00–0:17	First verse following a 12-bar (i.e., measure) blues harmonic progression.
0:00–0:06	Opening "Hound Dog" line. Listen for the bass pitches outlining the root, or "home," harmony (I).
0:07–0:09	"Hound Dog" line repeats. Harmony changes to the "fourth" above the root, or *subdominant* (IV).
0:10–0:12	Harmony returns to the root (tonic–I).
0:13–0:14	Harmony changes to the "fifth" above the root, or *dominant* (V), then moves to the "fourth" (subdominant–IV).
0:15–0:17	Drum break. Only the root pitch is sounded, with the implication that we have returned to the home chord (tonic–I).

Understanding harmony is probably the most challenging aspect of Western music study. Music majors spend a solid year (or more) learning the basics, for it is the foundation of the composition of Euro-American music, classical or otherwise. Because of the influence of European and American culture on popular world music, harmony exists in almost all forms of popular world music styles.

Although understanding the complexities of harmony is worthwhile, it is more important to recognize it when you hear it. Simply put, **harmony** is the blending of three or more different pitches. We call this unit of three pitches a *chord*. Myriad chords can be created, but only two basic types are referred to in Western music: *major* and *minor*. Each includes a root pitch, a higher pitch at an interval of a third (either major or minor third) above the root, and the highest pitch at an interval of a fifth above the root (e.g., C–E–G). When the pitches change, the harmony changes. At this point, our objective is to recognize this occurrence.

Harmony a blending of three or more different pitches, as in a chord

In our Focus Example, listen carefully to the bass (lowest-pitched instrument) as it continually repeats the three pitches of the basic harmony. Although these pitches are not sounded simultaneously, they are played in succession to form a single unit. This practice of outlining the chord is referred to as **arpeggio**. To find these pitches, it is useful to find the basic beat of the music, which follows a four-beat meter. The root pitch (C) sounds on beat one (at the moment when Elvis sings the word "hound"), whereas the third (E) and fifth (G) pitches above sound on the third and fourth beats, respectively. This arpeggio pattern occurs throughout the performance to outline each of the chords in the harmony.

Arpeggio a chord whose pitches sound in succession rather than simultaneously

This harmony remains the same for sixteen pulses, four groups of four beats (i.e., four measures); this solidifies the **tonal center** of the performance. Establishing a tonal center is important in most melodic music, because it gives the performance a point of reference. The tonal center, or root harmony, is considered the point of relaxation,

Tonal center the "home" pitch or harmony, i.e., *tonic*

whereas other pitches or harmonies create tension to make the music interesting. By moving away from the home harmony, or tonal center, the musicians increase the tension; by returning, they release the tension. In most popular music, the composition will conclude with the root, or home, harmony, also known as the *tonic*, which is symbolized with the roman numeral for one (I).

After the first four measures (at 0:07), the arpeggio pattern played by the bass creates a different chord, indicating a new harmony. This new harmony is known as the *subdominant*, symbolized by the roman number for four (IV), because the interval of the chord is a "fourth" above the tonic (home chord). The subdominant (IV) continues for two measures (eight beats) before returning to the tonic (I) at the moment Elvis sings the word "time" (approximately 0:10).

After two measures of the tonic, the harmony shifts to the *dominant* (roman numeral V), which is a "fifth" above the root. This sounds for one measure (four beats) and is followed by a transition to the subdominant (IV) for another measure before the closing of the verse on the tonic (I) at 0:15, which is marked by the snare drum solo break.

Admittedly, following all of this "talking" about the harmonic progression can be confusing. Musicians do not read such verbose dialogue as they perform. Certainly, many musicians are able to read staff notation, but the vast majority learn to play by ear, that is, without notation. Oftentimes, however, writing out the fundamental chord changes will remind them of what pitches to play. In so doing, they articulate the form of a harmonic progression.

"Hound Dog" follows a harmonic progression known as a "12-bar blues," so named because it comprises twelve measures (frequently called "bars") before repeating; though not exclusive, it is common to blues music. Harmonic progressions are also known as **form**, so we can describe this as a 12-bar blues form. *Form* is defined as the underlying structure of the music over time and can refer to a section of the performance, as in this case, or describe the piece in its entirety. Our discussion describes this 12-bar blues form in detail, but it is much simpler to write the progression as follows:

Form   the underlying structure of a musical performance over time

I	I	I	I
IV	IV	I	I
V	IV	I	I

Key   the prevailing harmony of a composition or improvisation

A capable musician can use this outline of the harmony to play in any key. In musical terms, a **key** refers to the prevailing harmony of a composition, typically indicated by the tonic ("home") chord. "Hound Dog" is in the key of C (major), as indicated by the tonic (I) chord of C. Each measure is four beats, and there are twelve measures to complete the form. This is repeated several times, with the vocalist singing different lyrics or the guitar performing a melodic solo. Listen through the entire performance and follow the points when this 12-bar blues form repeats after each drum solo break (0:18, 0:34, 0:50, 1:07, 1:55), as well as at the end of the guitar solos when there is no drum break (1:23, 1:39). The progression is played a total of eight times.

The term *form* is also used to describe what happens throughout these repetitions of the internal 12-bar blues progression. Some types of compositions, particularly in classical music, are identified by this adherence to a form (e.g., sonata). Popular music exhibits a tendency toward forms based on lyrical content, such that you have verse sections, in which the lyrics change, and refrain or chorus sections, in which the lyrics are the same each time they are played. The latter typically include the melodic hook.

In our Focus Example, each repetition of the 12-bar blues progression indicates a section of the overall form. The form might be written as follows: Chorus–Verse–Chorus–Solo (Guitar)–Verse–Solo–Verse–Chorus. Note that in this example, the verse lyrics are the same for each repetition, though normally they would change. Certainly, much pop music has more complex form than this performance by Elvis, as we shall see next.

Elvis is a key figure in the development of rock music and continues to be much beloved today. In addition to his musical success, he acted in more than thirty films, performing many of his hit songs as part of the storyline. Although his acting prowess earned him mixed reviews, such films as *Jailhouse Rock* (1957), *G.I. Blues* (1960), *Blue Hawaii* (1961), *Girls! Girls! Girls!* (1962), *Viva Las Vegas* (1964), *Clambake* (1967), and *The Trouble with Girls* (1969) helped him to sustain his visibility throughout the 1960s, even as younger musicians usurped his domination of the popular music charts.

After his 1968 television comeback special, *Elvis*, Presley focused on his stage performances, playing many of his hits as well as numerous gospel songs, for which he was highly regarded; he even won a Grammy award in 1974 for his version of "How Great Thou Art." His extended engagements in Las Vegas were highly successful and his 1973 "Aloha from Hawaii" concert, to support the Kui Lee Cancer Foundation, was the first satellite broadcast of a live concert, airing to millions of viewers worldwide. The rhinestone-covered white jumpsuit he wore on stage became a lasting image of Elvis in his later years.

Although Elvis's career was again flourishing during the 1970s, his personal life suffered. He became increasingly withdrawn after his divorce from his wife, Priscilla, in 1973, and his health gradually deteriorated as his dependence on prescription drugs escalated. His stage performances suffered in his final years, and he lost interest in recording new material. He died at his estate, Graceland, in Memphis, Tennessee, on August 16, 1977. Elvis's music remains popular today and his image has become iconic around the world; his legacy is rivaled by few individual artists in rock music history.

Among Elvis's most visible fans were the Beatles, who established a musical and cultural legacy arguably greater than that of "The King." The "Fab Four," as they are commonly known, consisted of John Lennon (1940–1980), Paul McCartney (b. 1942), George Harrison (1943–2001), and Ringo Starr (b. Richard Starkey, 1940). The quartet grew up in Liverpool, England, and became popular during the early 1960s, performing original music and covers of popular American rock musicians, such as Carl Perkins (1932–1998), Little Richard, and Chuck Berry.

"Beatlemania" swept the globe from 1963 to 1966 as many of the Beatles' records dominated the popular music charts around the world. They had sixteen No. 1

The Beatles' landmark "concept" album,
Sgt. Pepper's Lonely Hearts Club Band, (1967).

singles during this period, including "I Want to Hold Your Hand" (1963), "She Loves You" (1963), "Can't Buy Me Love" (1964), "A Hard Day's Night" (1964), "Eight Days a Week"(1964), and "Help!" (1965). Their 1965 No. 1, "Yesterday," is cited by the *Guinness Book of World Records* as having the most recorded cover versions of any song in popular music history. They made two self-satirizing films, *A Hard Day's Night* (1964) and *Help!* (1965) that were quite successful and strengthened their international appeal. The group gave concert tours throughout Europe and the United States, as well as Asia, and appeared on numerous television broadcasts, such as *The Ed Sullivan Show* in 1964. The Beatles were awarded the prestigious MBE (Member of the Order of the British Empire) by the Queen of England in 1965 and received several Grammy nominations and awards from the National Academy of Recording Arts and Sciences.

LEARN MORE on www.mymusickit.com Watch the Beatles documentary.

The Beatles stopped touring in 1966, preferring instead to focus their energies on studio recording. In 1967, they released their album *Sgt. Pepper's Lonely Hearts Club Band*, widely regarded as their most seminal work. *Rolling Stone* magazine described it as the "most important rock and roll album ever made" and ranked it No. 1 on their list of the 500 greatest albums of all time. Our Focus Example, "A Day in the Life," is the final track on the album and highlights two additional aspects important to an understanding of harmony and form.

FOCUS EXAMPLE
ROCK

"A DAY IN THE LIFE," PERFORMED BY THE BEATLES

Focal Points

- **Harmony:** Both major and minor keys are used to present contrasting sections of the song.
- **Form:** The underlying structure includes three sections (ternary) with extended transitions and conclusion (ABA).

TIME	DESCRIPTION
0:00–0:11	Introduction. Beginning is masked by applause from the previous track.
0:12–0:43	First verse emphasizing an E minor harmony. (Form: A)
0:44–1:10	Second verse with closing variation. (Form: A′)
1:11–1:47	Third verse with closing variation. (Form: A′ with extended "I'd love to turn you on" ending.)
1:48–2:14	Transition to next section marked by extended orchestra **crescendo**.
2:15–2:48	Middle section emphasizing an E major harmony. (Form: B)
2:49–3:17	Interlude: harmony changes quickly, avoiding a tonal center.
3:18–3:51	Return to opening musical content emphasizing E minor harmony for final verse. (Form: A′ with extended "I'd love to turn you on" ending.)
3:52–4:20	Concluding extended orchestra crescendo.
4:21–5:03	Piano ends song on E major chord.

"A Day in the Life" is a complex song to analyze in terms of harmony and form. The creative use of major and minor chords, variation of melodic content, transitions utilizing orchestral **crescendo** and the "circle of fifths" harmonic progression, as well as

Crescendo   increasing volume of sound

the infamous extended final chord (approximately 42 seconds), is intriguing for a theory scholar from a musical standpoint, not to mention the controversial aspects of the song's lyrics that initially prompted the BBC and other broadcasting companies to ban it from radio airplay. We, however, are less concerned with the complexity of detail in the piece than with the more overt features that explain additional aspects of harmony and form.

In our previous Focus Example ("Hound Dog"), our primary objective regarding harmony was to recognize when a chord changed, for example, from I to IV to V, and so on. We could use the basic beat to find this as the chord changes followed a basic 12-bar blues chord progression (see previous explanation). In this focus example ("A Day in the Life"), our objective is to recognize the difference between the sound of a major chord and one that is minor.

As mentioned previously, a chord has three or more pitches that sound as a unit, either simultaneously or in sequence (that is, arpeggio). Major and minor chords use nearly the same intervals, namely a root, third, and fifth. The distinction between them is a half-step difference between the pitch referred to as the "third."

To better understand this concept, it is helpful to have access to a piano. If on the piano you play a root pitch, say, C, the major third is four half-steps above this pitch (E). (Ascending from one piano key to the next constitutes a half-step.) If you label the root pitch as the 1 key, then the E would be labeled the 5 key, ascending on both the black and white keys of the piano. If you continue to the fifth scale-degree (G), then you ascend three more half-steps to the piano key that would be labeled 8, again counting both black and white keys. These three pitches together, C–E–G, create a major chord.

Major chord
on piano

Following the same procedure as above to find the root and fifth, the only pitch that changes to create a minor chord is the third, which is a half-step lower (E-flat), or would be labeled 4 if you count piano keys starting with 1 as the root.

Minor chord
on piano

It is important that you can aurally distinguish between major and minor chords such as these, because music compositions in the Western tradition, be they classical, folk, or popular, utilize these two types of harmony to express differing emotions. Broadly speaking, you can describe these emotions as either "happy" or "sad," with *major* representing the former and *minor* the latter. Certainly, you can use major and minor harmonies to represent a host of other emotions, but happy/sad suffice as a general reference.

Although major chords are heard throughout the introduction and verses of "A Day in the Life," the opening verses emphasize E minor chords (E–G–B) at several points (0:16, 0:20, 0:28, 0:35, etc.). The use of minor suggests a sad feeling that persists

HEAR MORE
on www.mymusickit.com
Major and minor chords

throughout the section and is articulated by the vocalist (John Lennon) in the lyrics, such as "And though the news was rather sad" (0:25–0:29).

In the middle section (2:15–2:48), the mood changes to a happier feeling, which is reinforced by a shift in the harmony to emphasize E major chords (E–G-sharp–B). While the lyrics do not specifically express happiness, they have shifted topic to the daily morning routine of the vocalist, which has changed to Paul McCartney. The clearest lyrical indication of a happy mood is at the end of the verse, "I went into a dream" (2:47), which suggests a pleasant feeling.

After the interlude, Lennon returns to present a vocal timbre contrast, and the opening musical content again emphasizes the E minor harmony (3:18–3:51). In this case, the change in tone signifies boredom, rather than unhappiness, as the central character in the song reads the newspaper. The lyrics "Four thousand holes in Blackburn Lancashire" (3:24) is a cultural reference to local authorities that were asked to count the number of potholes in a road. Lennon wryly proposes that those holes could fill the Royal Albert Hall, a premiere arts venue in London, suggesting that reading the newspaper was a waste of his time, just as counting potholes was a pointless activity for the government workers.

The contrast of minor to major to minor harmonic emphases changes the mood of each section but also provides an underlying structure of how the piece progresses over time, that is, form. In our previous Focus Example ("Hound Dog"), our objective was to hear the internal form of the 12-bar blues progression, which was repeated several times throughout the piece. In this Focus Example, our objective is to understand form as it relates to the entire song.

Our initial description of the song outlines the basic form: Introduction–A (repeated with variation)–transition–B–transition–A–conclusion. In art music terms, this is described as a "ternary" form because it has three basic sections: ABA. The form of a popular song usually follows an even simpler form, as with "Hound Dog," which just repeats the same musical material (A) throughout. Other times there is an alternation between the musical material of the verse and that of a repeated chorus. Composers of popular music frequently use a stock form such as these to write songs, merely supplying new melodies and lyrics. The Beatles did so in their early career but began experimenting with form on many of the albums that preceded *Sgt. Pepper's*. With this album and subsequent ones, the band consciously broke from the standard forms to expand their musical creativity and propel popular music into uncharted territory.

The triumph of the *Sgt. Pepper's* album heralded a new age of popular music in Western culture. Although creating dance music was still the primary objective for most rock artists, the Beatles helped to legitimate rock music as more than just a passing trend. Their exploits, image, and attitudes greatly affected popular culture throughout the world. They represented a counterculture in Europe and the United States at a time when institutionalized authority was greatly mistrusted by the masses, particularly by the so-called baby boomer generation that came of age during the 1960s. After the band broke up in 1970, each of the Beatles remained prominent figures in rock music and its continued development. The band's legacy remains a lasting influence on popular music artists around the world today.

HIP-HOP

The most recent global force in popular music is hip-hop. It emerged among disenfranchised urban youth from the Bronx in New York City who grew up in the post–civil rights/Vietnam era of the 1970s. African Americans and Latin Americans in the city's poverty-stricken ghettoes considered themselves culturally marginalized and sought a means to express their angst. The severely underfunded schools offered little inspiration, cutting special programs such as sports or the arts to conserve financial resources. Many teenagers joined street gangs, which offered protection, structure, and financial rewards as well as a sense of belonging.

As the gangs grew in numbers, they increasingly used graffiti to mark their turf (territory). Some graffiti crews began decorating the dilapidated buildings and walls of their neighborhoods with creative stylized writing, portraits, and landscapes. They used subway cars as their canvases and aerosol cans as their paintbrushes. Their work became the visual expression of what was later to be known as "hip-hop culture."

The physical expression of hip-hop culture during its early years was a dance style known as *breakin'*, or more colloquially as *b-boying* or *b-girling*. The style is physically demanding and employs choreography inspired by jazz dances, gymnastics, and martial arts. The style's many unique moves, such as the windmill ("mill," for short), body wave, various handstand and headstand spins, poppin', and freezes (quick-stop poses) characterize break dancing, which sustained its initial popularity during the 1980s. Street performers in New York City and Los Angeles would blast songs such as Herbie Hancock's *Rockit* (1983) from their boom-box portable cassette players and perform on a makeshift dance floor made from flattened cardboard boxes or linoleum tiles.

As with b-boy/girling, hip-hop music, like rock and jazz before it, drew from many previous musical styles to develop into a distinctive genre. The key musical features include MC-ing (emceeing) and DJ-ing (deejaying). The MC (master of ceremonies) is responsible for the vocal content, and the DJ (disc jockey) provides the musical component. Other musical instruments common to the jazz and rock music genres may be added, as well as additional vocalists, but the focus is on the lyrics of the MC and the dance beat provided by the DJ.

The distinctive vocal characteristic of hip-hop is the spoken-style delivery of the MC, known as *rap*. The roots of this style can be traced back to West African praise singers, although its direct influence is the Jamaican practice of **toasting**, in which a rhyming narrative is delivered with or without musical accompaniment. The typical musical accompaniment to toasting was either a simple rhythmic beat on a bass/snare drum combination or a recorded rhythm, often made by the performer. DJs in Jamaica modernized this tradition, toasting, shouting, and chanting verse over previously recorded ska, rock steady, and reggae songs that had been stripped of the vocals to emphasize the music's bass and rhythmic elements, a practice known as *dub* (see Chapter 3).

Toasting a rhyming narrative tradition from Jamaica

Hip-hop DJs took a similar approach, using prerecorded music to emphasize the rhythmic "break" of a song. Jamaican-born DJ Clive "Kool Herc" Campbell (b. 1955) is considered the inventor of this practice, inspired by the dub DJs he had heard as a young teenager in Jamaica. The rhythmic break in songs, such as James Brown's "Give It Up or Turnit a Loose," were popular for the dancers at his parties, so he would use two turntables to cue the records in alternation (called "merry-go-round") and thereby extend the "break-beat" section. Kool Herc and others, such as Grandmaster Flash (b. 1958), expanded this idea by linking the break sections of different songs and "scratching" the records (quickly reversing the turntable to emphasize a short rhythmic/melodic segment or to create a new rhythm).

The DJs or an accompanying MC would rap (speak/chant rhythmically) during these breaks, improvising rhyming lyrics or shouting out to encourage a response from the audience. As the new sound caught on, DJs began to record their own music, with an emphasis on the rhythm and bass, while the MCs included more poignant social commentary in their lyrics. By the end of the decade, these innovators were in high demand at dance clubs and attracting the attention of young adults outside the inner-city social circles.

Disco clubs, which had proliferated earlier in the decade, were losing patrons as criticism of disco music mounted. R&B artists and a new wave of punk musicians were

DJ Kool Herc performing in Brooklyn, in 2008.

agreeable alternatives, but these genres were already familiar to suburban teenagers. The b-boy/girl crews, such as Rock Steady Crew, would bring in large crowds eager to watch the "battle" dances between groups, which encouraged interest in the music. Rap, as the public generally described hip-hop music during this early period, offered a fresh sound and reflected the spirit of rebellion that other popular music no longer provided.

"Rapper's Delight" (1979), by the Sugarhill Gang, provided an ideal introduction for introducing hip-hop to a wider audience, for it utilized the bass/rhythm section of the No. 1 hit single "Good Times," by the R&B–disco group Chic. It reached No. 36 on the U.S. pop charts and No. 4 on the U.S. R&B charts later the same year, making it the first hip-hop song to find success in the music industry mainstream.

Of those who took notice of the hip-hop trend was the increasingly popular new wave band Blondie, whose single "Rapture" (1981) referenced Sugarhill Gang's DJ, Fab 5 Freddy (b. 1959), as well as the DJ pioneer Grandmaster Flash. The song's music video was one of the first to air on the newly established MTV network in 1981 and included a cameo by Fab 5 Freddy and prominently featured the art of graffiti pioneers Jean-Michel Basquiat (1960–1988) and Lee Quinones (b. 1960). Not only was this song important for encouraging the mainstream success of hip-hop, it also illustrates that the genre's earliest performers intended for hip-hop to be racially inclusionary.

Hip-hop continued to find growing audiences across the country throughout the 1980s. A few movies, such as *Wild Style* (1982), *Flashdance* (1983), and *Beat Street* (1984), as well as the PBS documentary *Style Wars* (1983), further encouraged its visibility. Run-DMC's album *Raising Hell* (1986), with its hit single "Walk This Way," performed with the song's composers, Aerosmith, was the watershed release that solidified hip-hop's place in the mainstream market. It was closely followed by the controversial *Licensed to Ill* (1986), by the Beastie Boys, a white group from New York City, which received much criticism from both black and white pundits for usurping the style even though the group was already accepted on the New York hip-hop scene and was one of the acts opening for Run-DMC on their *Raising Hell* promotional tour. The album sold more than five million copies and spent seven weeks at No. 1 on the U.S. Billboard Charts.

After the success of these two albums, the opportunities for the genre's artists opened dramatically. The 1980s produced a bevy of hip-hop stars from around the country creating new substyles. Performers such as LL Cool J, Public Enemy, 2 Live Crew, Dr. Dre and Ice Cube (both from the group N.W.A.), along with female artists such as MC Lyte, Queen Latifah, and Salt-N-Pepa, became superstars for a new generation of young adults. The videos of pop hip-hop artists like DJ Jazzy Jeff and the Fresh Prince (Will Smith), MC Hammer, and Tone-Loc aired regularly on MTV. By the end of the decade, hip-hop culture was an international phenomenon. Since then, the music has permeated all popular music styles common to commercialized media today.

Hip-hop has always incorporated a variety of music styles, sampling bass riffs, break rhythms, and melodic phrases from rock, jazz, soul, funk, classical, and even traditional world music genres. As the genre proliferated during the 1980s, many artists performing in established styles updated the music by incorporating hip-hop elements. Modern R&B artist Mary J. Blige (b. 1971) has been especially successful in syncretising the sultry sounds of soul music with the heavy beat of hip-hop.

Partnering with former Wu Tang Crew member Method Man (b. Clifford Smith, 1971), Blige presents us with our Focus Example, "I'll Be There for You/You're All I Need to Get By," which takes its main theme from the 1968 classic version by Motown artists Marvin Gaye (1939–1984) and Tammi Terrell (1945–1970). The song showcases many of the elements characteristic of hip-hop, but our focus is the contrasting vocal delivery of the two singers, Blige and Smith.

FOCUS EXAMPLE
HIP-HOP

"I'LL BE THERE FOR YOU/YOU'RE ALL I NEED TO GET BY" (EP VERSION), PERFORMED BY MARY J. BLIGE AND METHOD MAN (1995)

((⦁ HEAR MORE
Download the
iTunes playlist link on
MyMusicKit

Focal Points

- **Text Setting:** The two vocalists present contrasting styles; Blige (female) uses a predominantly melismatic text setting, whereas Smith (male) uses a syllabic text setting.

TIME	DESCRIPTION
0:00–0:32	Main theme ("You're All I Need to Get By") is introduced. Back beat starts at 0:23.
0:33–1:23	Male vocalist sings verse with a syllabic text setting. Female vocalist improvises nonlexical syllables in the background with a melismatic text setting.
1:24–1:43	Lead female vocal improvises with a melismatic text setting.
1:44–2:03	Lead female vocalist sings verse with a syllabic text setting.
2:04–2:40	Lead male vocalist returns, singing with a syllabic text setting. Female voice continues to improvise with a melismatic text setting.
2:41–5:09	Main theme repeated until end. Contrasting vocal delivery continues. Note the prominent use of melisma in the female voice at 3:49.

Text setting   the
number of pitches per
syllable of sung text

Syllabic   one pitch per
syllable

Text setting refers to the number of pitches sung per syllable of text. Everyday speech is syllabic, using just one pitch per syllable. Speech that includes a change in the inflection of the voice, as frequently occurs in tonal languages, is still considered syllabic. In our example, the text setting of the male vocal is **syllabic** throughout the performance.

The singing voice can also utilize a syllabic text setting. Again, when only one pitch per syllable is sung, the text setting is syllabic. In our example, the female vocal emphasizes a syllabic text setting at 1:44, when she sings the verse beginning "Like sweet morning dew." Blige does add some ornamentation to her melody at the end of the verse on the word "you" (2:04). Such ornamentation is referred to as **melisma** because she is singing more than one pitch per syllable of text.

Text Setting Continuum

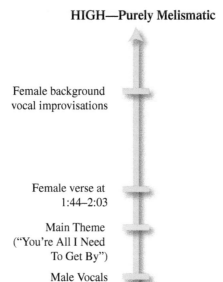

HIGH—Purely Melismatic

Female background
vocal improvisations

Female verse at
1:44–2:03

Main Theme
("You're All I Need
To Get By")

Male Vocals

LOW—Strictly Syllabic

Melisma/Melismatic
more than one pitch per
syllable

If a vocalist frequently uses melisma, then the text setting of his or her vocal delivery is described as **melismatic**, meaning that more than one pitch corresponds to each syllable of text. Characterizing a vocal performance as melismatic is somewhat subjective, usually describing the degree to which melismatic singing occurs. Think of the text setting in a vocal performance as a continuum, with strictly syllabic singing at the bottom and purely melismatic singing at the top. In our Focus Example, the "rap" of the male vocalist falls at the very bottom (i.e., syllabic). You might describe this as having "zero degrees" of melisma.

((•● **HEAR MORE**
on www.mymusickit.com
Melismas

When the female vocalist sings the verse at 1:44, the text setting would also fall at the bottom, until the last word ("you"), where she adds melisma. The degree of melisma is slightly higher for this section of her performance; it is still largely syllabic, but not strictly. As Blige continues to improvise on the text "You're all I need to get by," she adds more melisma, which contrasts with the vocal delivery of her male counterpart. This is also true of her background vocal improvisations throughout most of the performance. The contrast can be most clearly heard in the first verse (0:33–0:52) when the percussion provides the only accompaniment to the two vocalists. Blige's vocal improvisations have a higher degree of melisma, but she does not ornament the text on every syllable.

Finally, we hear the main theme, "You're all I need to get by," repeated at several points during the song. Each syllable of the phrase corresponds to an individual pitch of the descending melody (i.e., syllabic), until the last word, "by," which corresponds to a repetition of the first pitch followed by a second pitch below (i.e., melismatic). Again, the degree of melisma is minimal, but enough to note.

Identifying the melismatic degree of every utterance in a vocal performance is unnecessary, but recognizing the overall tendency of the singer is often useful for distinguishing styles of music. For example, rap performances include little to no melisma, whereas gospel singers frequently add ornamentations to the end of their vocal phrases (colloquially known as "runs"). This song is essentially a mixture of these two styles. With world music, popular or otherwise, vocalists have a tendency toward either syllabic or melismatic text settings, based on their cultural background and musical training.

Classical singers from India, for example, spend years studying specific vocal ornamentations (i.e., melisma) to make their improvisations more interesting. In contrast, European classical singing tends to be more syllabic, due in part to the minimal use of vocal improvisation. Determining the degree in which melisma is utilized can suggest the cultural origin of a music; Indian music tends toward a high degree of melisma, whereas European music tends toward syllabic text settings.

Hip-hop represents the most recent music style to influence popular world music. The commercialization of the genre has disseminated hip-hop culture to many countries, although critics often bemoan its superficial use in global mass media. The sounds of hip-hop permeate the advertising industry, television programs, movie productions, and radio broadcasts. The music appears in video games and cartoons aimed at adolescents and small children, inciting reactions from many parents who continue to hold negative stereotypes of hip-hop, believing that the music encourages violence, misogyny, and sexual promiscuity. Such discrimination deafens listeners to its positive social aspects—encouraging peace and unity, denouncing poverty and racism, promoting lasting family and love relationships (as expressed in our Focus Example), and rebelling against social and political injustice.

Hip-hop's worldwide success has inspired related popular world music styles, such as *kwaito* (South Africa) and *reggaeton* (Caribbean and Latin America), which continue to carry the genre's original spirit as a medium for social commentary. Young adults throughout the world improvise freestyle raps in their own language and sound beatbox (vocal percussion) rhythms into amplified microphones for house parties and dance hall events that feature b-boys/girls displaying remarkable acrobatic choreography. The biggest hip-hop stars of the United States and elsewhere tour internationally with great success and reap huge financial rewards. Like popular song, ballroom dance, jazz, and rock before it, hip-hop has established itself as a fundamental component of the world's popular music soundscape.

SUMMARY

In this chapter, we defined basic music terminology necessary for a better understanding of the popular world music genres explored throughout this book. The fundamental terminology included *melody, harmony (major/minor), rhythm (beat, tempo, meter), text setting (syllabic/melismatic), timbre,* and *ornamentation* as well as other key terms, such as *improvisation* and *form.*

Our review of these terms also introduced the major popular music genres from the United States and Europe that have had a global influence on popular world music styles. We used examples of popular song, ballroom dance, jazz, rock, and hip-hop to clarify our definitions of music terminology through active listening. This brief introduction to these Western styles will help us to recognize their appearance in the popular world music we study in the remaining chapters.

LEARN MORE
on www.mymusickit.com
Chapter summary
and exam

Pathways

- **DVD:** *The Story of Vernon and Irene Castle* (1939)
  - *www.amazon.com/Story-Vernon-Irene-Castle/dp/B000H6SXTM/ref=sr_1_3?ie=UTF8&s=dvd&qid=1251658772&sr=8-3*
- **DVD:** *La Vie en Rose* (2007)
  - An award-winning film about French singer, Edith Piaf.
  - *www.edithpiafmovie.com/*
- **DVD:** *Jazz* (2001)
  - A film series for PBS by director Ken Burns covering the history of jazz.
  - *www.pbs.org/jazz/index.htm*
- **DVD:** *American Roots Music* (2001)
  - A film series for PBS covering a variety of American folk music traditions.
  - *www.pbs.org/americanrootsmusic/*
- **Internet:** *www.elvis.com*
  - Official Web site of Elvis Presley
- **Internet:** *www.beatles.com/*
  - Official Web site of the Beatles
- **DVD:** *The Freshest Kids: A History of the B-Boy*
  - A documentary about hip-hop culture focusing on breakin' (break dancing).
  - *www.imdb.com/title/tt0361638/*
- **DVD:** *Scratch vs. Freestyle*
  - A two-part documentary about hip-hop culture focusing on the art of "turntabling" and the improvisatory oral narrative, known as "freestyle."
  - *www.palmpictures.com/film/scratch-vs-freestyle.php*
- **Internet:** *www.grandmasterflash.com/*
  - The official Web site of Grandmaster Flash, Deejaying pioneer.
- **DVD:** Hip-Hop Films
  - *Wild Style* (1982)
  - *Flashdance* (1983)
  - *Beat Street* (1984)
  - *Style Wars* (1983)

Keywords for Additional Music Examples

- "Joy to the World" performed by Nat King Cole
- "La Vie en Rose" performed by Louis Armstrong
- Louis Armstrong: The Complete Hot Five & Hot Seven Recordings
  - "Hotter Than That" (1927), "Potatohead Blues" (1927), and "Weather Bird" (1928)
- Louis Armstrong—Additional Recommendations
  - "Ain't Misbehavin'" (1929, 1938), "Hello, Dolly!" (1963), and "What a Wonderful World" (1968)
- Blues Artists
  - Muddy Waters
  - Howlin' Wolf
  - B. B. King
  - Louis Jordan
  - Robert Johnson (Country Blues)

- Early R&B/Rock and Roll Artists
  - Big Mama Thornton
  - Fats Domino
  - Little Richard
  - Chuck Berry
  - Ray Charles
  - Bill Haley
  - Jerry Lee Lewis
  - Carl Perkins
- "That's All Right," performed by Arthur "Big Boy" Crudup
- Sun Records Artists (Jack Brenston, Rufus Thomas, Rosco Gordon, etc.)
- "Blue Moon of Kentucky," performed by Elvis Presley
- The Beatles catalog is not currently available online. Visit *www.beatles.com/* to purchase their music or do an Internet search for music available online.
- "Rockit," performed by Herbie Hancock
- "Give It Up or Turnit a Loose," performed by James Brown
- "Rapper's Delight," performed by the Sugarhill Gang
- "Rapture," performed by Blondie
- *Raising Hell*, by Run-DMC
- *Licensed to Ill*, by the Beastie Boys
- Hip-hop artists from the 1980s
  - LL Cool J
  - Public Enemy
  - 2 Live Crew
  - N.W.A.
  - MC Lyte
  - Queen Latifah
  - Salt-N-Pepa
  - DJ Jazzy Jeff and the Fresh Prince
  - MC Hammer
  - Tone-Loc
- "You're All I Need to Get By," performed by Marvin Gaye and Tammi Terrell
- Classical singing from India
  - Search by: India Kriti
- Classical singing from Europe
  - Search by: Opera Arias

Caribbean Music: Calypso and Reggae

INTRODUCTION

Few popular world musics have achieved the extent of international visibility as reggae. Synonymous with Jamaican popular music, reggae flourished in the 1970s and early 1980s thanks in part to the global success of Bob Marley (1945–1981), the genre's international icon, and continues to be one of the world's most popular music genres. Yet the roots of reggae, the message of its musicians, and the spiritual underpinning that has inspired many of its best-known artists are largely overlooked by most people acquainted with the "reggae sound." In this chapter, we will explore some of the predecessors and genres related to reggae, including Trinidadian calypso and *soca*, as well as Jamaican *mento*, ska, rock steady, and the more recent musical developments of *dub* and dancehall.

COLONIALISTS AND CARNIVAL

The Caribbean islands are the birthplace of many of the most successful popular world-music genres. This chapter focuses on two prominent locales: Trinidad and Jamaica. Both islands were visited by Christopher Columbus (1451–1506) during the fifteenth century and consequently claimed for the Spanish empire. Indigenous populations, the Arawak and Carib, were found on both islands and soon suffered as slaves in the quickly developing agricultural industry established by the Europeans. In addition, enslaved labor from Sub-Saharan Africa was imported to work on the increasing number of plantations appearing on the islands, particularly in Jamaica, which became the world's leading exporter of sugar during the early 1800s.

Trinidad and Jamaica came under British control during this period: Jamaica in the mid-seventeenth century (ca. 1655) and Trinidad in the late eighteenth century (ca. 1797). The slave trade was abolished in 1807, although slavery continued through the 1830s. To compensate for the loss in manual labor from Africa, the British colonialists imported indentured servants from China and India, which has resulted in the diverse ethnic makeup of the islands' populations today.

Although Jamaica and Trinidad share similar colonial histories, the century-later occupation by the British of Trinidad allowed

French colonists a refuge following the revolutions in France and Haiti during the late 1700s. Of the many cultural customs the French brought with them was the annual celebration of *Carnival*, a festival that precedes the period of Lent in the Roman Catholic Church. During Lent, Catholics are expected to fast and abstain from "pleasures of the flesh" for the forty days before Easter, the day celebrating the resurrection of Jesus Christ. Carnival, a secular event, is considered a "farewell" celebration to such pleasures. The festivities therefore include indulgences in music, dance, food, drink, and other revelry.

Pre-Christian celebrations are believed to be early sources for some of the Carnival activities, but the modern event is considered to have originated during the thirteenth century in Italy; it soon spread to France, Spain, and Portugal. The celebrations in Venice, Italy, included the wearing of masks, which became a hallmark of the event in Trinidad and has evolved into the spectacular costumes commonly associated with modern Carnival today. Although Carnival is celebrated today in many countries, the event is a critical cultural component of Trinidad's musical development.

POPULAR MUSIC FROM TRINIDAD

Calypso

Trinidad's most prominent musical contributions to the global soundscape include calypso and *pan*. The latter refers to the variety of steel drums, made from 55-gallon oil barrels, that have become a trademark of Caribbean music. Trinidadian's take great pride in this instrumental invention, which first appeared among Carnival revelers during the late 1940s. Pan orchestras have great community support throughout the island and play a variety of musical styles, including classical, jazz, rock, and popular song.

Many composers and players of pan, such as Lennox "Boogsie" Sharpe (b. 1953), Ellie Mannette (b. 1926), and Ray Holman (b. 1944), earn a living by traveling the globe composing and performing as guest artists with a growing number of overseas orchestras that are affiliated with community and educational programs, particularly those in the United States. Many of their compositions include original calypso music or orchestral arrangements of popular calypso songs. These instrumental versions of calypso standards, such as *Marianne* (1945) or *Pan in A Minor* (1987), remain staples of the pan orchestra repertory.

The international promotion of pan has encouraged the popularity of calypso in its original format as a popular song genre. The origins of calypso can be traced to the call-and-response-form singing of African-descended slaves in Trinidad. The leader of such songs, known as a *chantwell* (derived from the French, *chanteur*, meaning "singer"), became an important means of disseminating local news and entertaining revelers during Carnival celebrations after emancipation in 1834. The chantwell singers frequently challenged each other in song duels to the accompaniment of stick bands or small brass bands. The vocalists were prized for their witticism and improvisational rhyming skills, similar to today's freestyle rap battles found in the United States and elsewhere (see Chapter 2). By the 1880s, many of these performances occurred in large tents during the Carnival celebrations, a context that remains important to calypso competitions today.

The term *calypso* derives from a West African exclamation commonly romanized as "Kaiso!" Audience members would frequently shout, "Kah Iso!" (akin to "Go on!"), to encourage the chantwell singers during their performances. By the 1910s, the vocalists were referred to as *kaiso* singers, which became *calypso* by the 1920s. By this time

Lord Invader,
ca. 1946.

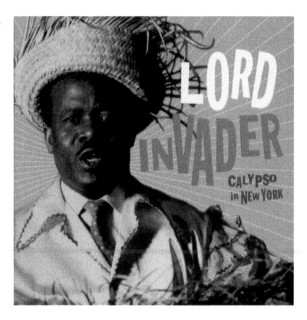

music-business entrepreneurs had begun recording musicians in the Caribbean, encouraging international interest in the genre. In 1934, two of calypso's most prominent performers—Rafael de Leon (1908–1999), aka "Growling Tiger," and Raymond Quevedo (1892–1962), aka "Attila the Hun"—traveled to New York to record some of the earliest standards of calypso music, including "Ugly Woman" (1934) and "Fire Brigade" (1934). Such recording trips became an annual event for the era's most famous calypso artists as interest in the music grew throughout the decade.

In 1940, the United States established a naval military base in Trinidad to try to benefit from a productive oil industry and the island's geographic location at the southern front of the Caribbean Sea. The American presence greatly affected Trinidad's economy, politics, and culture. Calypso singers incorporated the changing conditions into their lyrics, lambasting local officials who profited from the foreign visitors and lamenting the debauchery of the island's women. These circumstances presented a pivotal moment in Trinidad's musical history, not only for the invention of the steel drum (pan) but also for increased international interest in calypso music.

During the 1940s, local calypso musicians and touring USO (United Service Organizations) troupes from the United States provided entertainment for the American soldiers stationed there during World War II. In 1943, the song "Rum and Coca-Cola" became a local hit. Its melody was based on a familiar tune popular in traditional Caribbean music, and its lyrics were inspired by the American soldiers' penchant for drinking rum with Coca-Cola (instead of plain soda and rum, as was typical of Trinidadians). The song's lyricist, Rupert Grant (1915–1961), aka Lord Invader, used this drink as the central idea in the song to comment on the "American social invasion," as he perceived the U.S. presence in his country.

FOCUS EXAMPLE
CALYPSO

"RUM AND COCA-COLA," PERFORMED BY LORD INVADER (1946)

Focal Points

- **Instruments:** Small group, including guitar, clarinet, drum set, and maracas (shaken rattle).
- **Language/Lyrics:** English lyrics, with witty social commentary on local circumstances.
- **Melody:** Memorable melodic "hook" that emphasizes the song's title.
- **Text Setting:** Syllabic throughout the performance.
- **Harmony:** Predominantly major key to express a happy mood.

TIME	DESCRIPTION
0:00–0:11	Introduction, with clarinet lead playing the melody of the vocal verses.
0:12–0:25	Male vocalist enters with first verse:
	And when the Yankees first went to Trinidad
	Some of the young girls were more than glad
	They said that the Yankees treat them nice
	And they give them a better price
0:26–0:39	"Rum and Coca-Cola" chorus, with backing vocals.
	They buy rum and Coca-Cola
	Way down Point Cumana
	Both mothers and daughters
	Working for the Yankee dollar
0:40–0:51	Backing vocals repeat the chorus.
0:52–1:04	Second verse.
	Now look, I had a little chica the other day
	But her mother came and took her away
	Herself, her mother, and her sisters
	Went in a cab with some soldiers
1:05–1:18	"Rum and Coca-Cola" chorus repeated.
1:19–1:30	Backing vocals repeat chorus, with clarinet solo break.
1:31–1:43	Third verse.
	They have some aristos in Port of Spain
	I know a lot, but I won't call name
	And in the day they wouldn't give you a right
	But you could see them with the foreigners late at night
1:44–1:56	"Rum and Coca-Cola" chorus repeated.
1:57–2:07	Clarinet solo.
2:08–2:20	Final verse.
	I know a couple who got married one afternoon
	And was to go to Miami on their honeymoon
	But the bride run away with the soldier lad
	And the stupid husband went staring mad
2:21–2:37	Final chorus, with slowing tempo at the end.

The instrumentation of calypso is ever-changing, keeping up with current trends in popular music. This example uses instruments reflective of the World War II period (1940s). There are no electric instruments, which become most significant in the rock music era (late-1950s). Also, there is no pan (steel drum), which is commonly featured in Caribbean music today but was yet to be featured in calypso music when this recording was made (1946). A clarinet lead was common to jazz styles of the swing era and has therefore been added to give the ensemble more popular appeal. The percussion instruments are minimal, but it is important to note the use of maracas, originally from West Africa and found frequently in Caribbean music genres.

Calypso is a male-dominated genre; women vocalists were rarely heard until the 1980s. Also, its focus is lyrical content, although the singer here, Lord Invader, follows a melodic line. Popular music that emphasizes a story line tends to have syllabic text settings so that the audience can understand the words. The language used is English, and, with the reference to Trinidad in the opening line, the text clearly indicates the genre's geographic origin.

Bacchanal a slang term in Trinidad for a calypso singer's critical commentary

The text also introduces the topic of Lord Invader's **bacchanal**, a term used by Trinidadians to describe a calypso artist's witty, often controversial, commentary. Note that "Yankee" is a mildly pejorative term for Americans. The singer specifies the American soldiers' presence in the next verse and suggests that Trinidadian women found them friendly. He also uses one of the calypso singer's most powerful weapons, **double entendre**, meaning a word or phrase having more than one interpretation. By saying that "they" (the women) give "them" (the soldiers) a better price could be taken to mean that the soldiers pay less for goods such as food. Calypso, however, is usually much more risqué. A naïve American audience of the 1940s was unlikely to consider the "better price" a reference to services offered by the island's prostitutes, which a Trinidadian audience was more apt to recognize as the intent in the singer's witty lyricism.

Double entendre a word or phrase having more than one interpretation

The first appearance of the chorus (0:26) makes reference to the American soldiers' preferred drink choice, rum and Coca-Cola, which further suggests that the story's setting occurs during leisure activities (actually, "a bathing resort," or beach resort, as Lord Invader remarks in the pre-performance), rather than the marketplace. He again gives a local reference, "Point Cumana," which locals knew to be a popular beach where the American soldiers would meet Trinidadian women. The reference to "Mothers and daughters/Working for the Yankee dollar" suggests that the women accompanying the soldiers were more interested in the Americans' money than the men themselves, another allusion to prostitution.

The second verse reveals Lord Invader's frustration with the military presence on the island. He tells about his *chica*, a Spanish slang term for a beautiful woman, being taken away, along with her sisters, by their mother to go and meet soldiers, but does so in a humorous manner. Calypso often deals with serious social subjects, but presents them in a satirical way. Although the artist may be making a social statement, he also wants his audience to have fun and enjoy the performance. This approach contrasts with reggae music, which tends to present social commentary with more serious and often confrontational lyricism.

The clarinet solo (1:19) seems to intrude into the response of the backing vocalists, who drop out after the instrumental improvisation begins. This suggests that the lead clarinetist may have been added to the group for this particular performance, which was for an American audience in New York City.

In the third verse, Lord Invader again indicates the geographic locale of the song's story through a reference to Port of Spain, Trinidad's capital. He also criticizes the island's social elite ("aristos," or aristocrats) for discriminating against the common folk, unwilling to give them a "right" (a handshake) while socializing regularly with the American military.

The final verse again makes light of a serious situation, relating a story about a newlywed who left her husband for an American soldier. The audience may find this commentary amusing and critical of the soldiers who steal away the local women, but Lord Invader slyly faults the "stupid" husband for losing his bride and going "staring mad" (crazy). This addresses a stereotypical image of male calypso singers, and Trinidadian men in general, who consider themselves sexual predators, not easily seduced by a woman. Invader's insult of the husband *sans humanitae*, ("without mercy"), suggests that the man was foolish for marrying in the first place.

Although Lord Invader and his partner, Lionel Belasco (1881–1967), are credited with writing "Rum and Coca-Cola," the song was copyrighted by American actor-comedian and radio personality Morey Amsterdam (1908–1996), who is best known for his part in the 1960s television series *The Dick Van Dyke Show*. Amsterdam heard the song while visiting Trinidad in 1943 and rewrote some of the lyrics to better suit an American audience. Movie starlet Jeri Sullavan then performed his version for live shows with moderate success, even making a film "soundie" in 1945, before the Andrews Sisters recorded it later that year.

The Andrews Sisters' version of "Rum and Coca-Cola" became a big hit throughout the United States, despite being banned by the major radio networks for its free advertising of the Coca-Cola soft drink, as well as for its reference to rum and allusions to lurid activities. Sheet music of the tune sold in the thousands, prompting Lord Invader to file a copyright infringement lawsuit against Amsterdam, which he eventually won. The lawsuit, along with the song itself, spurred a greater interest in calypso music, which enabled calypso performers to travel more frequently to the United States for concert engagements.

In 1956 American singer Harry Belafonte (b. 1927) recorded *Calypso* (1956), the first full-length recording by a single artist to sell more than one million copies. Though not a

Harry Belafonte's *Calypso* album, released 1956.

calypso singer himself, Belafonte evoked the romantic spirit of the Caribbean isles with such folk songs as "Brown Skin Girl," "Jamaica Farewell," and "Day-O (The Banana Boat Song)"; this last continues to be a staple song of American popular culture. The album spent thirty-one weeks at the top of the U.S. popular-music charts and prompted greater interest in Caribbean music. Many folk artists were attracted to the music, which sprung a host of enthusiasts, including the Kingston Trio, whose name is taken from the capital city of Jamaica.

Although a few calypso artists, such as Slinger Francisco (aka "The Mighty Sparrow," b. 1935), and Aldwyn Roberts (aka "Lord Kitchener," 1922–2000), found moderate success with international audiences, the advent of rock music curtailed American interest in overseas genres. By 1963, the American military had left Trinidad, instigating an economic decline that endured throughout the remainder of the decade. Calypso artists maintained local interest, but international audiences were disinterested in the plight of the country's circumstances, which were commonly featured in its music.

Soca

By the mid-1970s, Trinidad's economic situation was improving as increasing oil prices helped to drive the country's major export. Tourism also picked up, especially around Carnival festivities, which attracted hundreds of visitors each year. These prosperous times encouraged new musical developments in calypso that reflected the interests of its local and international audiences. External and internal influences also affected the style as musicians incorporated the steel pan as a solo instrument and adapted their sound to modern trends from the United States and elsewhere.

Disco, R&B, and soul music became popular styles in night clubs, along with Indian *filmi* (film songs) imported to Trinidad via the large population of East Indians (see Chapter 8). Some calypso artists, such as Garfield Blackman (aka "Lord Shorty," 1941–2000), feared their music would lose its relevance if they did not consider the change in the attitudes of their patrons, who were more interested in dancing and frivolity than bemusement from the witty lyricism that characterizes calypso. Persistent drum machine rhythms, electric synthesizers, and funky bass lines became the central focus, and the vocalist's main role was to provide a melodic hook to instigate a group response. The lyrical themes shifted from pointed social criticism to more general themes about partying, dancing, and casual love affairs. By the end of the decade, "soul-calypso," or *soca*, had emerged as the dominant music of Carnival season.

The most successful international soca hit to date is "Hot, Hot, Hot," (1982) by Alphonsus Cassell (aka "Arrow," b. 1954). Because Arrow was born on the island of Montserrat and not Trinidad, the song was refused entry into the Carnival competitions. Nevertheless, after enjoying success in the United Kingdom and United States, "Hot, Hot, Hot," has become an unofficial anthem for international partygoers to Trinidad. It was adopted as the official anthem of the 1986 FIFA World Cup, which exposed soca to a worldwide audience. Since then it has been covered by several artists, most notably David Johansen (as his "Buster Poindexter" persona), from the former punk rock group the New York Dolls, in 1987.

FOCUS EXAMPLE
SOCA

"HOT, HOT, HOT" (1982), BY ALPHONSUS CASSELL
(AKA "ARROW," B. 1954)

Focal Points

- **Language/Lyrics:** English lyrics focus on party themes.
- **Instruments:** Modern Western instruments such as electric bass and guitar, as well as synthesizer, are used throughout. Brass and percussion are also present.
- **Rhythm:** Fast tempo in a duple meter, with a steady rhythm played on a "brake" drum, typical of steel pan orchestras.

TIME	DESCRIPTION
0:00–0:16	Brass introduction, with "brake drum" and conga drums.
0:17–0:23	Group cheers, "Ole! Ole!"
0:24–0:39	"Hot, Hot, Hot!" chorus.
0:40–3:30	Song continues with party-themed verse and variations of the chorus.

The instrumental opening establishes the tempo and introduces the melody and hook phrase ("hot, hot, hot") to prime the audience. The "brake" drum is, literally, a brake drum from an automobile; it is commonly used as a percussion instrument in steel drum (pan) orchestras to provide a loud and steady driving rhythm. Many local popular music songs will incorporate this characteristic sound, no matter the genre, as a symbol of Trinidadian musical identity.

Soca music encourages group participation, particularly on the melodic hook phrases. The "ole! ole!" chants serve this purpose, followed by the "hot, hot, hot!" chorus. The "funk" bass is common to soca music of the 1980s and 1990s and still appears in many hits. Soca music thrives because of the performer's ability to keep up with contemporary trends in popular music.

Many soca songs have lyrics with more depth than these; nevertheless the majority focus on having fun, dancing, drinking, partying, and the like. The remainder of the song reflects this sentiment. By contrast, calypso places much more emphasis on lyrical content and a diverse range of topics, typically those relating to local circumstances. The success of "Hot, Hot, Hot" is perhaps due to its elimination of social commentary and its focus on participants having a good time, a theme with no specific cultural or social association.

Today, soca continues to play a major role in Carnival celebrations, though its popularity recedes during the rest of the year. Soca singers work hard to have the big hit of the season in hopes of reaping financial rewards, though most enjoy only fleeting fame. Calypso artists still perform for limited local audiences, becoming most visible at the tent performances that are a fixture of the Carnival competitive events. *Extempo* competitions, in which calypso performers battle using improvisatory ("extemporaneous") lyrics, have become another avenue for these artists to demonstrate their ingenuity and oratory skills.

Chutney music follows in the calypso and/or soca style but is more frequently sung in East Indian languages, such as Hindi. This style also has a significant following throughout the year, particularly at Carnival time. It frequently incorporates Indian classical instruments, such as the sitar and tabla, and closely follows the trends of Indian filmi music. Some Trinidadian artists, such as David Rudder (b. 1953), have infused modern soca music with more meaningful commentary, whereas others, such as chutney-soca singer Rikki Jai (n.d.) or ragga-soca singer Bunji Garlin (b. 1979), create fusions of the various popular music styles of the island and elsewhere in the Caribbean. The great diversity of music that Trinidad offers continues to draw thousands of tourists each year to join in the festivities of Carnival.

POPULAR MUSIC FROM JAMAICA

While the audience for calypso and soca from Trinidad has remained primarily local, Jamaica's popular world-music contributions are among the most globally recognized genres on the planet. Reggae and dancehall music pounds out of nightclubs and karaoke bars from Jamaica to Japan. Red, green, and gold Rasta colors adorn the stage sets of reggae musicians throughout the world, and portraits of Bob Marley (1945–1981), the genre's eternal icon, and other memorabilia can be found in street stalls and clothing shops in even the remotest areas of the planet. The sound of reggae is one of the most recognized popular world-music styles in the international music industry.

The Evolution of Reggae: Mento → Ska → Rock Steady → Reggae

Jamaican popular music has seemingly always had a recognizable sound. An "upbeat" articulation, usually provided by a guitar or keyboard, contrasting with a missing or low-range instrument "downbeat," has characterized the earliest recordings of *mento* to classic (or "roots") reggae to much of today's hip-hop ragga-dancehall bands from the island. The popularity of calypso throughout the Caribbean during the first part of the twentieth century was influential on the lyrical development of Jamaican music as well, contributing to the evolution of toasting, which is akin to the oral improvisations of the Trinidadian chantwell and kaiso performers. Though the Trinidadian performers have had Carnival as an annual outlet for voicing their social criticisms, because of stricter British governance of the island Jamaican artists have historically had fewer opportunities to vent their frustrations. This more restrictive atmosphere led to the more serious tone of reggae, compared to its Trinidadian musical counterparts.

Mento

Reggae's roots are found in the Jamaican rural folk genre known as mento. Like calypso, this style focuses on witty, often bawdy, lyrical content and an ad hoc collection of acoustic instruments, normally banjo, small hand drums (e.g., bongos), and a bass lamellophone (known as a rumba box) derived from similar instruments found in Africa. A bamboo saxophone, fife, or homemade flute is sometimes included as well. Throughout the 1930s, Jamaican musicians often modeled their sound on popular calypso music imported from Trinidad. Consequently, early recordings sometimes refer to mento as "Jamaican calypso" or the more generic label "Jamaican folk song."

Today, rural mento is regarded as the root of Jamaican popular music. Few recordings of traditional early-twentieth-century folk songs are available, but several groups, such as the Jolly Boys, recorded rural mento styles during the 1950s and early 1960s, when foreigners held a fascination with Caribbean folk songs. As reggae became the predominant musical style emanating from the Caribbean in the 1970s and 1980s, independent labels and world-music enthusiasts in search of the music's roots traveled to Jamaica and rediscovered mento. Our Focus Example, "Woman's Smarter," performed by the Jolly Boys, comes from this later period but still exemplifies the traditional rural mento.

FOCUS EXAMPLE
MENTO

"WOMAN'S SMARTER," PERFORMED BY THE JOLLY BOYS

Focal Points

- **Language/Lyrics:** English lyrics with witty social commentary.
- **Instruments:** Banjo, guitar, bongo drums, and rumba box (a large lamellophone).
- **Rhythm:** An "upbeat" emphasis, following a steady duple meter at a moderate tempo.
- **Form:** Verse–chorus–instrumental repetition.

TIME	DESCRIPTION
0:00–0:27	Instrumental introduction following a duple meter. Listen for the "upbeat" emphasis and timbre of the different instruments.
0:28–0:39	First verse. (*From ever…*)
0:40–0:52	Chorus: The lead singer is joined by backing vocalists to create harmony. (*Not me…*)
0:53–1:04	Instrumental break, with banjo lead solo.
1:05–1:17	Second verse. (*I was…*)
1:18–3:10	Song continues in the verse–chorus–instrumental form until the closing phrase, when the tempo slows (2:53).

The opening introduces the instruments: banjo (lead), guitar, bongo drums, and rumba box. These instruments are typical of rural mento ensembles and reveal African musical influences, which are common to most Caribbean music. The banjo is derived from West African plucked lutes, such as the *akonting*. The bongo drums, a high- and low-pitched drum pair, are also descended from African instruments, as is the rumba box, which is a large lamellophone with metal keys that sound different pitches. The performer of the latter sits on top of the instrument and can add percussive elements by striking the side of the box. The guitar is considered to be of European origin, primarily associated with the Spanish, the earliest European explorers of the Caribbean and Americas.

The lead vocalist sings the first verse, which gives the audience a preview of his social critique of women. This verse alludes to the Christian creation story of Adam and Eve; the last verse (2:18–2:29) also includes a biblical reference. Christianity is the predominant religion in Jamaica, as it tends to be throughout the Western hemisphere, and this dominance is often reflected in the lyrics of folk and popular music. Also, note that the lyrics are sung in English, a reflection of the British colonial influence on Jamaica's history.

The chorus provides the song's melodic/lyrical hook. The lyrical content continues the theme of critiquing women while cleverly earning their praise by insisting that they are smarter than men. The remaining verses continue to address gender politics in a humorous way. The form follows a consistent verse–chorus–instrumental pattern. This form lends itself well to music with a message since it allows the listener ample time to consider (and react to) the story line of each verse while singing along with the repeated chorus.

Rumba Box.

Throughout the performance, the banjo takes the lead for the instrumental breaks but provides additional harmony during the sung verses and chorus. The use of the banjo is important for later developments in Jamaican popular music, as the "thin" quality of the timbre is imitated in the treble (higher sound-wave partials) quality of the electric guitar found in reggae and other styles from the island.

The rhythm of the banjo during these sections is also important: It emphasizes the upbeat pulses of two and four. This rhythmic emphasis was later described as **skank**, in association with Jamaican ska dancing (see below). The vast majority of Jamaican folk and popular songs follow a four-beat meter, which allows for this syncopation. The lowest pitch of the rumba box, along with a low-pitch articulation on the bongo drums, marks the first pulse of each measure. The contrasting timbre and range between these instruments on the opposing beats (1 and 3 for the low percussion versus 2 and 4 for the upper-range harmonic instruments) is an essential characteristic of mento and its descendants.

Although rural mento remained common to folk song in Jamaica, mento performers in urban areas, including Rupert Lyon (aka "Lord Fly," 1905–1967), performed with dance bands influenced by big-band jazz music typical throughout the Caribbean during this period. The popularity of mento peaked during the 1950s as the music industry took a greater interest in Caribbean music, but the attention was short-lived. For the next decade ska, along with American rock music (see Chapter 2), dominated Jamaica's music scene.

Skank a rhythmic pattern common to Jamaican folk and popular music that emphasizes the upbeat

Ska

By the mid-1960s American popular music, in particular rhythm and blues, commanded the airwaves and dancehalls of urban Jamaica. As mento filtered from rural areas to urban settings, the "country" instruments were replaced by modern equipment commonly found in jazz swing era dance bands, namely saxophones, brass instruments, drum set, piano, electric guitar, and acoustic bass. Although urban mento maintained a focus on the vocalist, the instrumental offspring of rural mento was ska, a faster-tempo dance music that used saxophones and trumpets to carry the main melody.

Ska is a dance-oriented popular style with repetitive themes and improvisational solos that became popular in Jamaica during the 1960s. Our Focus Example, "The Guns of Navarone," was originally recorded by Don Drummond (1932–1969) in 1967 and borrowed its melody from the theme song of the 1961 Hollywood film of the same name, which starred Gregory Peck and Anthony Quinn. The song became popular in Great Britain, breaking the top ten of the UK pop charts.

Drummond was an original member of the Ska-talites, an influential ska band that had a short-lived career from 1963 to 1965. Their influence, however, was far-reaching as many of the members formed their own ska bands that played throughout the decade. The band reformed in 1983, playing songs they had made popular both as a group and as individual performers. The Ska-talites have continued to perform internationally with differing personnel. The "Guns of Navarone" is one of the standards of the ska repertoire and has been recorded many times by the Ska-talites and other bands.

FOCUS EXAMPLE
SKA

"GUNS OF NAVARONE," PERFORMED BY THE SKA-TALITES

Focal Points

HEAR MORE
Download the iTunes playlist link on MyMusicKit

- **Instruments:** Western instruments, including trombones, trumpets, saxophones, percussion, piano, etc.
- **Improvisation:** Extended solos typically provided by trumpet, trombone, and/or saxophone.
- **Rhythm:** Characteristic skank syncopation on every offbeat.

TIME	DESCRIPTION
0:00–0:03	Introduction.
0:04–0:11	Saxophones play melodic riff.
0:12–0:20	Skank syncopated rhythm is highlighted. Note the vocal declarations.
0:21–0:37	Main melody enters with an open ending.
0:38–0:54	Main melody repeated with a closed ending.
0:55–1:15	Second melody enters.
1:16–1:32	Main melody reappears with a closed ending. Note the vocal declarations at 1:27.
1:33–1:58	Trumpet improvised solo. Note the accompanying skank rhythm of the saxophones.
1:59–2:04	Short vamp after solo concludes.
2:05–2:21	Drum cues entrance of main melody (open ending). Note the vocal declaration at 2:18.
2:22–2:29	Main melody repeats as music fades.

The ska versions of "The Guns of Navarone" are all quite similar, using the same melodic theme but differing instrumental solo improvisations on trumpet, trombone, and/or saxophone. The recommended example includes a trumpet solo, as indicated in the listening guide, and represents the fundamental features of the 1960s ska style. The most characteristic element is a steady duple meter, with an emphasized skank (offbeat) syncopation on every beat. The use of this rhythm is inspired by its musical predecessor, mento, which sounds the skank rhythm on every other beat (see previous section). Ska is also characteristically faster than either mento or reggae (see following section) and has a regular "walking" bass line, sounding on every beat. Although vocal parts may be included, they are not featured as soloists; rather, they support the rhythm or provide the main theme.

Ska became a popular trend during the 1960s in the dancehalls of Kingston, Jamaica, as well as in London, England, which continues to have a large Jamaican immigrant population. Skanking, a dance movement characterized by bending forward, raising the knees, and swinging the arms (in alternation) in time with the skank rhythm, followed the music and became widespread as a style among in time with the skank rhythm, followed the music and became widespread as a style among dancers listening to mainstream popular styles as well. After reggae appeared in the 1970s, ska lost its place as Jamaica's primary musical export.

Rock Steady

The exclusion of vocal lines on ska recordings provided an opportunity for dancehall DJs to ad-lib vocal improvisations (i.e., toasts). This practice was common since the early 1950s at dance parties throughout Jamaica. Most of these vocal improvisations focused on physical attraction between the sexes and a party atmosphere. After Jamaica's 1962 independence from Great Britain, however, a growing dissatisfaction with economic conditions and the government prompted some DJs toward more pointed and confrontational social and political commentary. The clever witticisms of the earlier mento and calypso artists did not satisfy the subculture of disaffected youths growing up in the ghettos of Kingston. Their frustrations fueled the next development in Jamaican popular music: rock steady.

The young men who spawned rock steady, the immediate predecessor to reggae, were collectively known as "rude boys." Rude-boy culture grew throughout the 1960s and was the topic of much criticism at all levels of the country's socioeconomic spectrum. Although disdained by officials in government rhetoric, wily politicians recognized the potential influence of the powerful street gangs at election time and began supplying them with weapons and financial support.

Rock steady became the musical outlet for the rude boys to express their civil discontent and rebel image. Sound-system operators, who sometimes hired "rudies" to crash competing parties, and rock steady recording artists, such as Alton Ellis, incorporated lyrics that reflected the rude-boy values: sharp suits and a "rude" (Jamaican slang for "cool" or "hip") attitude. The musical qualities also shifted to emphasize a more relaxed rhythm and streamlined instrumentation, which was considered more "rude," conveying confidence and a calmness under pressure. Like ska, the skank syncopation sounded on every pulse; however, the tempo of rock steady slowed to a walking pace that made it easier to "groove," whether vertically (as in dancing) or horizontally (that is, sex). These musical elements provided the foundation for the emergence of reggae.

Reggae

Ska and rock steady were successful among Jamaicans, but it was only after the success of the 1972 Jamaican cult film *The Harder They Come* that local popular music garnered considerable international appeal. By this time, reggae had emerged as the island's new sound, continuing the musical progression from mento to ska to rock steady. Reggae artists had advanced the ideas initiated with the rock-steady style, such as a slower tempo and soulful singing, inspired by American R&B and soul music, to which they added new instruments, such as the electric organ. They also experimented with studio techniques to give their recordings a more polished sound.

As Jamaica's economy declined during the 1970s, unemployment and poverty made life extremely difficult for the country's lower classes. Referenced in many reggae lyrics, "Trenchtown" became symbolic of the challenges faced by Jamaica's underprivileged. A housing project established in a squatter's camp area of West Kingston that had been wiped out by a hurricane in 1951, Trenchtown had initially been considered desirable. The government buildings provided shelter, communal cooking facilities, and water dispensaries for people with little income. Unfortunately, the project planners had failed to include an adequate sewage system, and Trenchtown came to signify a stench-ridden ghetto for outcasts and "ragpickers," or scavengers, since it was located near a city garbage dump.

Music was a means of alleviating the feelings of social and economic discrimination among the populations of Trenchtown and elsewhere in Kingston, Jamaica's capital. Rock steady/reggae singers started gravitating toward more socially conscious lyrics that expressed their frustrations with the worsening living conditions as well as their aspirations for a better future. The "rude-boy" rebel image of the 1960s became symbolic of these musicians, who felt they were fighting society's ills with music rather than weapons. The film *The Harder They Come* highlighted these problems of the downtrodden in not only Jamaica but the United States and Great Britain, whose urban youths were also in need of new musical means to express their angst.

The movie featured Jimmy Cliff (b. 1948), a popular ska and rock steady/reggae performer, in the lead role as an aspiring musician who falls into a life of crime. Cliff also performed the title track and contributed several songs to the sound track. Other Jamaican artists participated as well, most notably Toots and the Maytals, who are credited with making the first recording to name the emerging style that was to become reggae, "Do the Reggay" (1968). The new sound was featured along with other popular styles, including rock steady, and helped draw attention to Cliff as both a musician and an actor. Although rock steady and reggae had earlier found a limited international audience, the movie's success prompted the music industry to consider the Jamaican styles more seriously.

ISLAND RECORDS AND THE WAILERS   Among the period's music-business entrepreneurs was Jamaican-born Chris Blackwell (b. 1937), founder of Island Records. Blackwell had moved his production company from Jamaica to London in 1962, scoring early hits with Laurel Aitken's "Boogie in My Bones" and the Lord Creator's "Independent Jamaica." Island Records began to reach a wider market with its first international ska success, "My Boy Lollipop," by Millie Small, which reached No. 2 on Billboard's list of top singles in 1964. Blackwell's successes attracted many of Jamaica's top producers, including Leslie Kong (1933–1971) and Clement Dodd (1932–2004).

Among Island Records' artists was Jimmy Cliff, as well as such alternative rock groups as the Spencer Davis Group. After the success of *The Harder They Come*, Blackwell sought out promising reggae musicians to add to his label. He signed a trio of musicians known as the Wailers, who had gained a reputation in the early 1960s with their ska hit "Simmer Down" (1963), accompanied by the Ska-talites. The group had continued popularity with other songs, such as "Rude Boy," but remained largely a local success until being signed to Island Records in 1972.

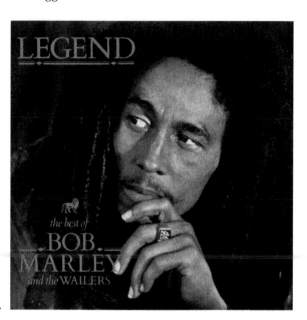

Bob Marley's
Legend album.

The Wailers consisted of reggae icons Robert "Bob" Marley (1945–1981), Peter Tosh (b. Winston McIntosh, 1944–1987), and Bunny Wailer (b. Neville Livingston, b. 1947). "Simmer Down" represents music from the ska era of the 1960s but includes lyrics that anticipate the spirit of the group's later work in the rock steady and reggae styles. The song was written in reaction to the gang violence Marley and his friends witnessed in Trenchtown. Such social commentary stems from the group's life experiences in the ghettos of Kingston and appeals for a resolution to conflict. Like themes would become hallmarks of Marley's burgeoning career. The band's initial records with Island, *Catch a Fire* and *Burnin'*, sold well enough that Blackwell encouraged the group to tour internationally. Based on the success of the songs "Stir It Up" and "Get Up, Stand Up," Blackwell wanted to promote their "rude-boy rebel" image and the rock steady/reggae sound to an international market. Tosh and Wailer did not like the new direction, however, and left the band to pursue solo careers.

Marley continued with Island Records, recording with the female backing vocals of the I-Threes, and the band was renamed Bob Marley and the Wailers. His career received a major boost when legendary rock musician Eric Clapton (b. 1945) released a chart-topping cover of the Wailers' "I Shot the Sheriff," from *Burnin'*. Marley's fame quickly spread, and he produced a steady stream of reggae hits that established him as one of the greatest icons of popular world music. He remained Island Records' biggest-selling artist until the Irish alternative rock band U2 became an international phenomenon with the release of *The Josuha Tree*, in 1987.

BOB MARLEY   Robert Nesta Marley (1945–1981) was born in a small rural village known as Nine Miles, in St. Ann Parish, in northern Jamaica. His father was a former British soldier who was frequently absent and died when Marley was ten years old. After his death, Marley's mother, Cedella (Marley) Booker (1926–2008), moved the family to Kingston in hopes of a better life. By age fourteen, Marley had quit school and began to frequent recording studios and dancehalls with his friend Neville Livingston (aka Bunny Wailer). The two eventually teamed up with Winston McIntosh (aka Peter Tosh) to form the (Wailing) Wailers.

The oppressive conditions in which Marley and his friends found themselves as young adults fueled his music in different ways. When partnered with Peter Tosh, Marley's music had a confrontational tone, as in such songs as "Slave Driver" and "Concrete Jungle." By contrast, much of his solo work reflects his beliefs in Rastafarian spiritualism. The lyrical content of Marley's music, and that of others, during the so-called classic period of reggae (1969–1987) is infused with spiritual ideals, linguistic idiosyncrasies, and social markers, such as the wearing of dreadlocks, identified with the Rastafari religious movement.

Rastafari is a religious movement that emerged in Jamaica in the early 1930s. The central tenent is an acceptance of the former emperor of Ethiopia Ras Tafari Makonnen Haile Selassie I (1892–1975) as the second coming of Jesus Christ, or the "Black Messiah." The movement has a strong Afrocentric orientation, inspired by the writings and speeches of Jamaican native Marcus Mosiah Garvey (1887–1940), who is viewed as a prophet by Rastafari adherents. Garvey was an ardent black nationalist and strongly encouraged African-descended populations in the western hemisphere to "redeem" Africa through repatriation. During a lecture tour in the United States in the 1920s, he is quoted as saying, "Look to Africa, for there a king will be crowned."

When Ras Tafari Makonnen was crowned emperor of Ethiopia in 1930, some of Garvey's followers claimed the event was fulfillment of his prophecy, reinforced by Selassie's honorific title as "King of Kings, Lord of Lords, and conquering Lion of Judah." Although Garvey did not adhere to this belief, nor did Haile Selassie consider himself a reincarnation of Jesus Christ, the Rastafari movement gained a large following throughout Jamaica, particularly in Trenchtown.

In 1966, Haile Selassie visited Jamaica, which did much to encourage the growth and respectability of the religion throughout the country. Among the converts was Alpharita Anderson (b. 1946), better known as Rita Marley, the soon-to-be wife of Jamaica's most famous musical icon, Bob Marley. Her conversion led to Marley's own adherence to the religious movement, which became the cornerstone for his musical and spiritual activities.

Marley's solo work was influenced by American R&B music of the 1970s. His lyrics successfully blend Rastafari religious ideals of peace and unity with rude-boy social criticism of institutions that he viewed as oppressing the common man. References to his spiritual beliefs permeate the majority of his songs, though most listeners have little knowledge of the Rastafari movement and miss the connection. His rebuke of social injustice is equally important as a fundamental theme of his music, and many of his most successful songs, including "Exodus," "No Woman No Cry," and "Redemption Song," convey these intentions. Because his music covers such a varied array of emotional, intellectual, and spiritual content, it speaks to a wide audience.

A song like "One Love," for example, may appeal to the casual listener because of its danceable laid-back rhythm. The spiritually minded listener may focus on the references to "the Lord," considering the song an affirmation of their faith, whereas those knowledgeable of the Rastafari movement may recognize that Marley is slyly criticizing the religious mainstream (i.e., Christians), whom he suggests persecute people of other faiths. The socially conscious may find his reference to "hear the children crying" as a plea from those living in poverty, while the politically motivated may cite the reference to "fight this Holy Armagiddyon [Armageddon]" as a call to arms against the "oppressors" (government authorities). Others will note the "Let's get together" refrain in connection with Marley's historic 1978 "One Love" concert, during which the leaders of Jamaica's two main political parties, Michael Manley (1924–1997) and Edward Seaga (b. 1930), linked arms during the performance of the song "Jammin'" as a gesture of reconciliation. Certainly, the overarching theme of our Focus Example is its expression of peace and unity among all humanity ("One Love/One Heart"), which can be considered a universal ideal.

FOCUS EXAMPLE
REGGAE

HEAR MORE
Download the
iTunes playlist link on
MyMusicKit

"ONE LOVE/PEOPLE GET READY,"
PERFORMED BY BOB MARLEY AND THE WAILERS (1977)

Focal Points

- **Language/Lyrics:** English lyrics, with poignant social commentary.
- **Vocal timbre:** Male vocalist. Bob Marley is among the most recognized voices in popular-music history.
- **Rhythm:** Listen for the skank syncopation and "one-drop" rhythm characteristic of many reggae songs. Also, note the slower tempo of reggae as compared to other Jamaican popular music.

TIME	DESCRIPTION
0:00–0:14	Instrumental introduction using a rock steady-skank pattern and "one-drop" rhythm. Also, note the relatively slow walking tempo of the beat.
0:15–0:46	Chorus. *(One Love…)*
0:47–1:11	First verse. *(Let them…)*
1:12–1:42	Chorus.
1:43–2:07	Second verse. *(Let's get…)*
2:08–2:53	Chorus to end of song.

One of the most distinctive features of Jamaican popular music is the regular use of the syncopated rhythm, known as skank, which emphasizes the upbeats, or offbeats, of a four-beat measure. Although skank rhythm can be played by a variety of instruments, certain ones tend to emphasize it, depending on the genre. For example, in rural mento, considered the root of all Jamaican popular music, this rhythm is most often articulated by a banjo (see above). In ska, low-range instruments, such as baritone or tenor saxophones or trombones, will emphasize the pattern. Rock steady and reggae music feature a muted electric guitar and/or a keyboard instrument, such as an electric organ or piano, playing the skank rhythm.

Tempo is another important indicator of a Jamaican popular-music style. Of the four genres we have reviewed, ska tends to have the fastest tempo; mento and rock steady have moderate tempos; and reggae has the slowest tempo. Certainly, there is some overlap—for example, a fast reggae may equate to the speed of a slower rock steady—but the general tendencies of the differing styles fall into these relative tempos. The challenge is to "feel" where the basic beat is. If we consider the skank rhythm as falling on the "&" of each pulse, then the relative tempos are easier to recognize. Listen to a recommended example of each style to compare the tempo.

The placement of the skank rhythm, however, does not always fall on the "&" of each beat. Although this placement is common to ska and rock steady, mento and reggae typically sound the skank articulation only on the second and fourth pulses, nevertheless giving the music a syncopated feel. In the introduction to our Focus Example, "One Love," there are a total of eight measures, so you will hear the skank articulation sixteen times before the verse begins.

Ska/Rock Steady vs. Mento/Reggae skank articulation

	1	&	2	&	3	&	4	&
Ska/Rock Steady		X		X		X		X
Mento/Reggae			X				X	

((• **HEAR MORE**
On www.musickit.com
Ska vs Mento rhythms

While the skank articulation of ska/rock steady is a syncopated accent on every pulse, mento/reggae accent the second and fourth pulses.

Another rhythmic aspect of reggae music is the practice of the **"one-drop" beat**. Popular-music genres (and other styles as well) typically emphasize the first beat of a measure, which helps the listeners/dancers find the underlying meter. The bass (kick) drum commonly serves this function. Many reggae songs, however, purposefully miss this beat, instead sounding the bass drum on the third beat. This delayed emphasis is reflective of the "rude" attitude and encourages a relaxed mood to the music.

"One-drop" beat a reference in reggae music to a rhythmic de-emphasis of the first beat of a measure

Not all reggae songs utilize the one-drop beat, but our Focus Example does. Listen carefully to the low-range bass drum "kick" on the third pulse of each measure. The first occurrence sounds simultaneously with the entry of the piano. You will hear the kick seven times; the last (eighth) occurrence is overshadowed by a snare drum fill pattern. Listen for the one-drop beat throughout the rest of the recording as well.

The lyrical content begins with the chorus, which is repeated twice more with variation at 1:12 and 2:08. The singers include Bob Marley and his female backing vocalists, the I-Threes. Marley's declamatory shouts ("Hear the children cryin'") single out his voice from the other singers' voices, which can help listeners recognize his unique vocal timbre.

Identifying vocal timbre comes with familiarity. Because of Marley's prominence in the global music industry, many people have heard his songs enough times to recognize his voice within the context of his music. A good way to test whether you are familiar enough with Marley's vocal timbre is to listen to several covers of this song performed by other artists. Although the musical arrangement may assist you, you should eventually be able to distinguish Marley's voice from the others' based on vocal timbre alone. This tool can be useful in helping you identify Marley in unfamiliar songs, allowing you to deduce that the performance is likely a Jamaican popular-music style.

A socially conscious message is an important aspect of reggae music. Many of today's reggae songs have lost this philosophical predilection, but poignant social commentary is an important element of the lyrics from "roots" reggae artists such as Bob Marley. The subject matter can be varied, using themes of love, politics, economic disparity, religion, and so on. Celebrating, partying, and sexual activity are certainly a part of reggae lyricism as well, but often these topics are expressed with the sentiment of promoting peace and unity. Although the tone of many of Marley's songs is more confrontational, his broad cultural appeal is in part due to songs such as "One Love" that encourage nonviolent resolutions to humanity's differences and dilemmas.

The second verse indirectly suggests Marley's association with Rastafarian spiritualism. A frequent focus of Rastafari believers is Judgment Day, or Armageddon, as foreshadowed in the Christian Bible's Book of Revelation. Marley frequently references aspects of such spiritual beliefs in his songs, using terminology particular to the Rastafarian spiritual tradition. Although reggae artists and their fans are not necessarily followers of this belief system, familiarity with so-called Rasta terminology leads to a better understanding of the lyrics and the message the artist is often trying to convey.

Rastafari References

- **Reggae lyrics**—often include Rastafari references. These idioms reflect not only the religion's beliefs but also the anti-oppressor sentiment that is fundamental to the faith.
- **Rasta**—a reference to followers of the Rastafari movement.
- **Dreadlocks**—a hairstyle characterized by long locks of braided hair, commonly worn by Rastafarians and reggae enthusiasts.
- **Jah (Yah)**—a reference to God, shortened from the Hebrew terms *Jehovah* or *Yahweh*.
- **Babylon**—a label applied to governments and institutions that Rastafari adherents consider decadent and oppressive.
- **Ganja**—refers to marijuana, which is often used in Rastafari rituals as a means of heightening spiritual awareness.
- **Zion**—a biblical reference to Ethiopia/Africa as the spiritual home of Rastafari adherents and all African-descended populations.
- **I (I and I)**—Rastafari adherents substitute "I" for "me" and "I and I" for "we" to indicate the belief that all humans are spiritually united and one with Jah (God).
- **Armagiddyon (Armageddon)**—a biblical reference to the end of the world, which Rastafari adherents accept as the current state of the planet, especially since 1974, when Haile Selassie I was deposed as king of Ethiopia.
- **H.I.M. (His Imperial Majesty)**—pronounced "him," refers to Haile Selassie I, whom Rastafari adherents accept as the second incarnation of Jesus Christ, that is, the Messiah.

By the time of the "One Love" concert in 1978, Marley was an international superstar and reggae icon. His touring schedule was extremely demanding, requiring extensive travel throughout Europe and the United States. A concert highlight indicative of his global success was a performance in Zimbabwe in 1980 to celebrate the country's

Bob Marley and the Wailers performing in Jamaica, 1978. On stage with them were Prime Minister Michael Manley (far left) and his political opponent Edward Seaga (third from left).

independence from British colonial rule. Later that year, Marley performed his final concerts at Madison Square Garden in New York City and Pittsburgh, Pennsylvania. Having been diagnosed with cancer as early as 1977, he was too weak to continue the tour and finally succumbed to the disease on May 11, 1981.

Marley was awarded the Jamaican Order of Merit a month before his death, and more than one hundred thousand people attended his funeral. He is regarded as a national hero in Jamaica, and the Bob Marley Museum at his former home in Kingston attracts thousands of tourists each year. He is buried in Nine Miles, the same town in which he was born.

Dub and Dancehall

At the same time that Bob Marley and other reggae artists were bringing Jamaican popular music to the forefront of the global music mainstream, producers and DJs were experimenting with new instruments, **riddims** (percussion rhythm with bass), and studio techniques. During the late 1960s and early 1970s reggae was still primarily a local phenomenon and commonly mixed with other genres on records spun by local DJs at dance parties. Vocals were generally absent on instrumental ska recordings popular during the 1950s and 1960s, so DJs were able to ad-lib vocal improvisations without much trouble. Rock steady and reggae recordings already had substantial vocal elements, making it difficult for the DJs to display their poetic prowess.

Since many of the prominent producer/engineers of the local reggae recordings were also DJs, some began to record alternate versions of the songs, referring to them as "doubles," or "**dubs**." These so-called dub recordings were instrumental versions of the same song, excluding the lead vocals, which allowed DJs the freedom to add their own toasts (i.e., lyrics). The dub versions usually appeared as the B-side of a reggae record.

Soon engineer/producer/DJ/musicians, such as Osbourne "King Tubby" Ruddock (1941–1989) and Lee "Scratch" Perry (b. 1936), began recording new material that included only the reggae rhythm ("riddim") and no vocals. They experimented with sound-processing equipment to add lush reverb and echo effects. The dub recordings became popular among DJs, who would often blast them from sound systems mounted on trucks and ad-lib along to advertise an upcoming event or to promote a product or politician. These dub recordings and toasts led directly to the American hip-hop style that developed during the 1970s, when Jamaican-born DJ Clive "Kool Herc" Campbell introduced the practice by using songs popular in the United States as the backing instrumentals for his toasts (see Chapter 2).

By the 1980s, economic conditions were steadily improving in Jamaica. Technological advances made it easier for DJs to create their own rhythms, laden with heavy bass and kick drum beats, which often diverged from the skank pattern that had until then dominated Jamaican popular music. With the death of Bob Marley, a new generation of DJs was less concerned with making a social statement and more interested in entertaining the audience. The topics of their toasts focused on partying, violence, and casual sex. Sound-system battles became increasingly popular as DJs competed against each other for audience support. DJs often used lyrics that were intentionally crude and included frequent profanity, referred to as **slackness**, to incite the crowd and make a name for themselves. Several DJs, such as Winston Foster (aka "Yellow Man," b. 1959), made recordings with their own vocals already included to increase their exposure locally and overseas.

With digital technology more readily available by the mid-1980s, DJs and producers began creating music that was largely void of melodic instruments, emphasizing

Riddims percussion rhythm and bass melodic pattern in reggae, dub, and Jamaican dancehall music

Dub a mostly instrumental version ("double") of a reggae or rock steady recording

Slackness slang term for profanity and crude commentary during a DJ vocal improvisations

Dutty Rock CD cover, 2002.

instead the creative use of drum machines and digital samplers. They labeled their rid-dims with marketable names, such as *sleng teng*, and promoted the image of a *raggamuf-fin*, a term used to suggest a street-smart attitude (similar to *rude* in the 1960s). *Ragga* became the new label for the music of the dancehall DJs, such as Shabba Ranks (b. 1966), who specialized in slackness and deft dance riddims.

The obscenity used in ragga, however, kept much of the music off the airwaves, and the songs drew heavy criticism from a growing number of Jamaicans who denounced the violent themes that all too often seemed to play out in real life. Later artists, such as Buju Banton (b. 1973), returned to spiritual and social themes, while others scored international hits with rapid-fire toasts that were dancehall directed, but radio friendly. Dancehall DJ Sean Paul, in particular, became an international superstar with his second album, *Dutty Rock* (2002), and its follow-up, *The Trinity* (2005), which produced several hits, including "Get Busy," "We Be Burnin'," and "Temperature." He has performed with such popular American artists as Busta Rhymes (b. 1972) and Beyoncé Knowles (b. 1981), helping to solidify his stature on the international market.

FOCUS EXAMPLE
RAGGA-DANCEHALL

((•● **HEAR MORE**
Download the iTunes playlist link on **http://www.routledgetext books.com/textbooks/9780136 128984/**

"GET BUSY," PERFORMED BY SEAN PAUL

Focal Points

- **Language/Lyrics:** English, with frequent slang and colloquial terminology and grammar.
- **Rhythm:** Heavy dance beat, with minimal melodic/harmonic accompaniment.

TIME	DESCRIPTION
0:00–0:09	Introduction (*Shake that…*)
0:10–0:28	First verse. (*Get busy…*)
0:29–3:31	The steady dance beat continues throughout the song, with varied verses.

Even though the heavy dance riddim does not appear until the first verse, the introductory verse already establishes the beat with Paul's rhythmic vocal delivery. The lyrics signal that the song is intended to motivate the audience to dance, particularly the female participants. The minimal melodic instruments play only a supporting role throughout the song.

The steady bass pulse is established in the first full verse while the lyrics follow their own rhythm, extending through the measures to enhance the rapid-fire feel of Paul's vocal delivery. The use of colloquialisms and slang terminology, such as "jiggy," "crunked up," "percolate," reference the age demographic of his intended audience—young adults and teenagers, who are most likely to understand their meaning. This language also gives the music a historical time reference, since such terms are current at the beginning of the twenty-first century, helping to distance ragga-dancehall from roots reggae and earlier established Jamaican popular music genres. These terms are likely to be dated in the next decade or so, such that scholars will look at this example as reflective of the period of its popularity.

Even with the new trends in popular music, reggae remains a staple of Jamaica's local music scene due to the influx of international tourists, who expect to find reggae clubs for their evening celebrations. Bob Marley's legacy is as prominent today as it ever was, especially in Africa, where he is much revered as a humanitarian icon. Ska-punk bands and reggae-inspired popular groups such as the Clash, the Police, U2, the Red Hot Chili Peppers, Black Uhuru, and No Doubt have achieved worldwide recognition, and many Jamaican artists, including Bob Marley's son Ziggy (b. 1968), perform internationally to enthusiastic audiences. Reggae clubs abound throughout the globe, spawning local stars who keep the music relevant to their circumstances. Jamaica's influence on the world-music scene remains one of the most potent of any locale in the Caribbean, if not the world.

SUMMARY

In this chapter, we explored some of the most prominent popular world-music genres of the Anglophone Caribbean islands. We limited our review to Trinidad and Jamaica, where the oratory skills of calypso and mento singers have underpinned the development of popular music in these countries since the early 1900s. We introduced the modern Trinidadian style of soca (soul-calypso) and presented an overview of Jamaican ska and rock steady, the immediate predecessors to reggae, which produced one of the world's most prominent musical icons, Bob Marley. Finally, we covered more recent popular-music styles from Jamaica, including dub and ragga-dancehall, which incorporate many of today's musical innovations.

LEARN MORE
on www.mymusickit.com
Chapter summary
and exam

Pathways

- **Book:** Manuel, Peter, with Kenneth Bilby and Michael Largey. *Caribbean Currents: Caribbean Music form Rumba to Reggae*. Philadelphia: Temple University Press, 1995.
  - A thorough overview of the history and musical aspects of several Caribbean and Latin American music styles from Cuba, Puerto Rico, the Dominican Republic, Haiti, Jamaica, and Trinidad. Highly recommended.
- **Internet:** *rumandcocacolareader.com/*
  - An introduction to the history and controversy of the popular calypso song "Rum and Coca-Cola."

- **DVD:** *Calypso Music History: One Hand Don't Clap*, Efor Films, directed by Kavery Dutta.
  - A documentary about the history of calypso and some of its legendary artists, such as Lord Kitchener, Calypso Rose, and David Rudder.
  - *www.musicafilm.it/music-dvds/calypso-music-history.html*
- **DVD:** *The Harder They Come*, directed by Perry Henzel, 1972.
  - Classic film starring reggae/rock steady artist and actor Jimmy Cliff that encouraged greater interest in Jamaican popular music, especially reggae.
  - *www.imdb.com/title/tt0070155/*
- **Book:** Barrow, Steve, and Peter Dalton. *The Rough Guide to Reggae* (3rd edition). London: Rough Guides, 2004.
  - A comprehensive review of Jamaican popular music, with detailed information on artists and recordings.
  - *www.roughguides.com/website/shop/products/Reggae.aspx*
- **DVD/Audio CD:** *Legend: The Best of Bob Marley and the Wailers*, Island Def Jam Music Group, 2004.
  - A three-disc collection that includes the original *Legend* audio songs remastered, a CD of remixes, and a DVD with the documentary "Time Will Tell," about the life of Bob Marley.
  - *www.bobmarley.com*
- **Book:** Veal, Michael. *Soundscapes and Shattered Songs in Jamaican Reggae*. Middletown, CT: Wesleyan University Press, 2007.
  - A thoroughly researched and comprehensive review of the evolution of dub music.
  - *www.upne.com/0-8195-6571-7.html*
- **Internet:** Bob Marley, One Love Peace Concert
  - Excerpts of the famous 1978 concert
  - Search: Marley One Love Peace Concert
- **Internet:** Bob Marley Zimbabwe
  - Excerpts of Marley's performance in Zimbabwe
  - Search: Bob Marley Zimbabwe

Keywords for Additional Music Examples

- Steel drum artists
  - Ray Holman
  - Boogsie Sharpe
  - Ellie Manette
- Steel drum standards
  - "Marianne"
  - "Pan in A Minor"
- Early calypso recordings
  - "Ugly Woman"
  - "Fire Brigade"
- Pre-performance to Lord Invader's "Rum & Coca-Cola"
  - **Search by:** Lomax Invader Intro Rum
- "Rum and Coca-Cola," performed by the Andrews Sisters
- *Calypso* album by Harry Belafonte
- American folk musicians influenced by Caribbean music
  - Kingston Trio
  - The Weavers
- Classic calypso artists
  - Mighty Sparrow

- Lord Kitchener
  - Lord Shorty
- "Hot, Hot, Hot," performed by David Johansen
- Chutney soca artists
  - Rikki Jai
  - Bunji Garlin
- Modern calypso artist
  - David Rudder
- Mento artist
  - Lord Fly
- Rock steady/reggae artists
  - Alton Ellis
  - Jimmy Cliff
  - Toots and the Maytalls
- "Do the Reggay"
- Island Records
  - Millie Small: "My Boy Lollipop"
  - Leslie Kong's Connection
  - Spencer Davis Group
  - U2
- Bob Marley and the Wailers
  - "Simmer Down"
  - "Rude Boy"
  - *Catch a Fire*
  - *Burnin'*
  - *Legend*
  - "Slave Driver"
  - "Concrete Jungle"
- "I Shot the Sheriff," by Eric Clapton
- Dub
  - iTunes Essentials List—DUB
  - King Tubby
  - Lee Scratch Perry
- DJs—Dancehall
  - Yellowman
  - Shabba Ranks
  - Buju Banton
  - Sean Paul
- Modern reggae- and ska-and-reggae-inspired mainstream artists
  - Ziggy Marley
  - The Clash
  - The Police
  - The Red Hot Chili Peppers
  - Black Uhuru
  - No Doubt

Latin American Popular Music: Tango and Salsa

INTRODUCTION

Latin American popular music has become much more visible to mainstream popular culture in recent years, achieving an international reputation that has earned many artists critical acclaim, not to mention financial rewards. But the popularity of Latin rhythms is not new—Latin music has enjoyed global success for more than a hundred years. Its relative popularity may waiver, but its core audience persists no matter what the latest musical trend.

The success of Latin American popular music is perhaps due in part to its balanced blend of the musical values stemming from two "old world" cultural arenas, that of Europe and Africa. The European-influenced emphasis on melody and supporting harmony catches the ears, while the African-influenced polyrhythmic undercurrent moves the feet. Tango, mambo, cha-cha-chá, and several other dance-music styles have crossed linguistic and cultural barriers to find substantial audiences in all corners of the globe.

Perhaps no other chapter makes it more evident that our survey of popular world-music traditions is limited in scope. We could easily include a dozen or more well-established popular music styles from Latin America, such as *conjunto, cumbia, mariachi, merengue,* or *zouk*, but instead we focus on only those styles that have achieved the greatest visibility historically, namely, tango and salsa (with its antecedents), as well as some genres with more recent global appeal, including Latin pop, *timba*, and *reggaeton*. Explore More

WHO IS "LATIN"?

The Latin language dates to roughly the ninth century B.C., when it was spoken mainly on the Italian peninsula. It was the formal language of the Roman Empire and, until the early 1960s, served as the liturgical language of the Roman Catholic Church. The Latin spoken by common people in the earliest centuries was known as vulgar Latin, which evolved into several distinct branches that today form the Romance-language family.

The romance languages include Spanish, Portuguese, French, and Italian as well as Romanian. The countries in which these languages predominate make up so-called Latin Europe: Spain, Portugal, France, and Italy. Romania's geographic location in Eastern Europe complicates its status as a part of Latin Europe; instead, it is usually considered part of Slavic Europe since most of its neighboring countries consist of Slavic-language speakers.

Latin America, however, is more challenging to define. Strictly speaking, it should include only those countries of the Americas where Romance languages predominate. Territories where French is predominantly spoken, such as French Guiana or Haiti, should be considered Latin as well but often are not, whereas Anglophone countries, such as Trinidad or Jamaica, are frequently characterized as part of Latin America, but are debatably so.

Such confusion becomes even more difficult when discussing the identity of Latino populations. Some populations of pre-Columbian heritage, such as the Inca or Arawak, find the "Latin American" label disturbing: they believe that it diminishes their indigenous cultural identity in favor of association with populations often still viewed as colonial intruders. Brazilians recognize their linguistic categorization as a Latin American country, but their Portuguese, rather than Spanish, connection to Latin Europe often motivates separate consideration. Certainly, populations of every nation feel strongly about the uniqueness of their cultural heritage, despite being generalized as Latin Americans. To consider an Argentinean, Mexican, Cuban, and Nuyorican (member of the Puerto Rican diasporas in New York City and surrounding areas) as culturally identical is absurd. Yet, these populations frequently find themselves and their music characterized under a single label: Latin.

LATIN POP

Perhaps nowhere is this unified portrayal in music more evident than the recent appearance of the Latin Grammy Awards, which was established in 1997 and first aired on television in the United States in 2000. The Grammy Awards are presented annually to recognize outstanding artistic and technical achievement in the music industry, but the Latin Grammy Awards focus solely on participants who are of Latin ethnicity, including those from the Americas and Europe, or who have participated in the production of Latin music. Even so, the music considered for a Latin Grammy Award can be sung only in either Spanish or Portuguese; French and other languages spoken in Latin Europe or America are excluded from consideration.

Although the television show focuses on pop artists, a brief review of the categories reveals an expansive range of music genres that are considered for the awards. Salsa, merengue, cumbia, samba, tango, and flamenco are several of the individual categories, along with many pop/rock awards. The best album/song awards are generally won by artists from the pop/rock genres, such as Spanish sensation Alejandro Sanz (b. 1968) or Colombian diva Shakira (b. 1977). The award show is not without criticism, but it has done much to promote Latin music to a wider audience.

Latin pop first found success with mainstream American audiences in the burgeoning years of rock and roll, during the late 1950s, with performer Ritchie Valens (1941–1959), most famous for his version of the Mexican folk song "La Bamba" (1958). His career was short-lived: He died in a plane crash, along with American rock music idol Buddy Holly (1936–1959), on February 3, 1959, only five months after "La Bamba" was released as the B-side to his English-language crooner, "Donna." Few other Latin artists found crossover success in the mainstream American music industry until the 1980s, notably Carlos Santana (b.1947), whose group, *Santana*, charted in 1970 with a rock cover version of Tito Puente's "Oye Como Va" (1963) (see below).

In 1984 Julio Iglesias (b. 1943) paired with country music legend Willie Nelson (b. 1933) for the song "To All the Girls I've Loved Before." Though the Spaniard had achieved some success with international audiences, the duet launched Iglesias into the spotlight for English-speaking Americans and brought him worldwide fame. In 1988 his *Un Hombre Solo*

⊙► EXPLORE MORE
on www.mymusickit.com
Interactive Globe

Gloria Estefan.

(A Man Alone) won the Latin Grammy Award for Best Latin Pop Album, and he continues to record and tour internationally. His son Enrique Iglesias (b. 1975) has become a successful crossover artist in his own right, with several platinum albums since the late 1990s, including his self-titled 1995 release as well as *Vivir* (1997), *Escape* (2001), and *Quizás* (2002).

Julio Iglesias may have hinted toward a growing market for Latino artists in the mainstream music industry, but it was the emergence of the Miami Sound Machine and the success of its lead vocalist, Gloria Estefan (b. 1957), that thrust Latin pop onto the global scene. Based in Miami, Gloria and her husband, Emilio Estefan Jr. (b. 1953), have been a force in Latin popular music for more than three decades. With Miami Sound Machine, the Estefans found initial success with the 1980s pop tune "Dr. Beat," which paved the way for the group to play to a greater number of non-Latino audiences.

With the group's next release, *Primitive Love* (1985), Gloria Estefan achieved superstar status with the smash hit "Conga," a song that successfully melded rhythmic elements of salsa with a clearly defined duple-meter dance beat essential to the era's pop music. The follow-up album, *Let It Loose* (1987), was the last to name Miami Sound Machine on the cover art; later releases highlighted Gloria Estefan as a soloist to make the group more marketable. The album continued to draw on the band's Afro-Cuban musical heritage, as heard in "The Rhythm Is Gonna Get You," whose lyrics and polyrhythmic percussion breaks evoke images from the Santería religion. The band found steady crossover success with several albums featuring Estefan as the solo artist, earning her numerous honors, including five Grammy awards. She is often hailed as the "Queen of Latin Pop," recording songs in both English and Spanish.

GLORIA ESTEFAN   Estefan was born Gloria Fajardo in Cuba in 1957 but left the country as a toddler with her family during the upheavals of the Cuban Revolution. She spent most of her childhood and adolescence in Miami, Florida, amid the large Cuban exile population that had settled there. During the late 1970s she attended the University of Miami, which has one of the most recognized music programs in the United States, having been among the first to offer degrees in jazz, studio music, and other areas of the music business, such as merchandising and studio engineering. This environment attracted many excellent music students from around the country and encouraged interest in careers in the music business. Although Estefan did not pursue a degree in music, she performed with the Miami Sound Machine, then a popular local Latin pop group.

The group performed for local events such as weddings and holiday celebrations, playing a mixture of American popular songs, Latin jazz, and Cuban *son* (pronounced "sohn"), and was soon inspired to compose their own music drawing elements from these genres. They released several Spanish-language albums locally until 1984, when they received a recording contract from Epic/Columbia to record their first English-language studio album, *The Eyes of Innocence* (1984), which was a moderate success. Their follow-up album, *Primitive Love* (1986), fueled their future fame with the singles "Bad Boy," "Words Get in the Way," and "Conga," each breaking into the top ten on the U.S. pop charts. Future hits, such as "1, 2, 3" "Anything for You," and "The Rhythm Is Gonna Get You," continued to have crossover appeal as pop ballads and salsa-inspired dance numbers.

Tragedy struck Estefan in 1990, when a speeding semitrailer truck struck her tour bus during her *Cuts Both Ways* tour. She suffered a spinal fracture that required intensive rehabilitative physical therapy but she miraculously returned to international touring within a year. Her memorable performance of "Coming Out of the Dark," from her 1991 album *Into the Light*, at the American Music Awards highlighted her return to the public spotlight. She has released more than twenty albums in her career, singing in both English and Spanish, and remains one of the most prominent figures in the Latin popular music industry.

FOCUS EXAMPLE
LATIN POP

"CONGA," PERFORMED BY GLORIA ESTEFAN AND THE MIAMI SOUND MACHINE

Focal Points

- **Language/Lyrics:** Sung in English (though Spanish and Portuguese languages are also common in Latin pop). Listen for implicit references to Cuba and the emphasis on percussion instruments.
- **Instruments:** A mixture of Latin percussion (e.g., timbales), European melodic instruments (e.g., trumpets), and electronic instruments (e.g., synthesizer).
- **Form:** Includes *montuno* instrumental breaks, the piano *ostinato* patterns in particular, which are inspired by Cuban *son*.
- **Rhythm:** Although a clear duple-meter dance beat presides, the music is rhythmically dense, with added percussion, such as the cowbell and timbales. Note the absence of a *clave* pattern, which is typical of other forms of Latin popular music (e.g., salsa).

TIME	DESCRIPTION
0:00–0:08	Chorus introduction.
0:09–0:15	*Montuno*: piano ostinato pattern.
0:16–0:24	Synthesizer portamento punctuation and dance-beat break.
0:25–0:32	Chorus repeats with dance-beat.
0:33–0:46	Timbales solo break.
0:47–1:03	Melodic instruments return.
1:04–1:33	First verse. (*Everybody…*)
1:34–1:40	Timbales solo break.
1:41–1:56	Chorus and instrumental break.
1:57–2:26	Second verse (*Feel the…*) emphasizes themes of partying and dancing.
2:27–2:43	*Montuno*: piano ostinato pattern returns.
2:44–2:59	Piano solo.
3:00–3:07	Chorus.
3:08–3:23	Brass break with new melodic content.
3:24–4:14	Continued instrumental sections and chorus repetition.

Carnival   a pre-Lent festival common to areas with a prominent Roman Catholic population

The conga is a dance that is believed to have originated in Cuba with **Carnival** celebrations; it became popular in the United States during the early years of jazz, in the 1930s through 1950s. The participants form a long procession and take three shuffle steps followed by a kick step. Variations have occurred in American popular music, notably the Loco-Motion (1962), danced in conjunction with the recording of the same name by Eva Boyd (aka "Little Eva"; 1943–2003).

Loud brass instruments typical of Latin jazz—for example, trumpets and trombones—open to our Focus Example. Next comes the chorus, which makes reference to the conga dance and includes the studio technique of layering Gloria Estefan's voice on multiple tracks. Also, note the cowbell accompaniment (0:05), an instrument commonly heard in Latin American music.

Montuno   (1) instrumental solo breaks common to salsa and Afro-Cuban son; (2) repeated ostinato pattern of the piano during a son or salsa music performance

Chromaticism   using pitches of a chromatic scale (half-step intervals)

The term **montuno** has two meanings in Latin American music. The general term refers to instrumental solo breaks that can be performed by a variety of instruments, such as timbales, trumpets, piano, and so on. Montuno also refers to the repeated ostinato pattern of the piano. The piano style utilized in montuno is a loud and percussive sound that is complex, with rhythmic syncopation and harmonic **chromaticism**. This style of playing is typical of Cuban son and its derivatives, for example, salsa.

Although this song includes several elements of Latin popular-music, the key component that makes it Latin pop is its adherence to popular music conventions, such as the use of electronic instrumental sounds that reflect current trends in mainstream media. For example, the distinctive portamento slide (0:16) and pounding dance beat with electronic drum fills are typical of 1980s popular music in Europe and the United States.

Note the absence of a *clave* rhythm. Although the clave does appear in Latin pop, the rhythmic basis of pop music tends to be on steady duple-meter patterns, rather than syncopated rhythms. "Conga" emphasizes an easily discernable four-beat pattern with the use of a low kick drum and electronic handclap sound. Additional instruments contribute to the music's rhythmic vibrancy, particularly in sections when the kick-drum/handclap combination is subdued for the solo breaks, such as the timbales solo at 0:33.

The lyrics of the first verse refer to Estefan's birthplace, Cuba, with mention of "the island" and "sugar cane," one of the country's major exports. Although this song was an international hit, her home audience in Miami was primarily made up of Cuban exiles. The references to Cuba indicate this connection, but the remaining lyrics are directed to people of non-Cuban descent, encouraging them to learn the dance—the conga—by focusing on the rhythm ("listen to the beat").

As the song moves through the remaining sections, the instrumental solo breaks on timbales (1:34) and piano (2:27 and 2:44) reflect the musicians' Cuban musical heritage, similar to the styles of son and salsa music. The brass break with new melodic material (3:08) also reveals this connection through its frequent syncopation, but, again, the music maintains a steady adherence to the duple-meter dance beat.

Since Miami Sound Machine first broke through to English-speaking audiences, numerous Latin pop stars have found success in the global arena. By the late 1990s, several Latin pop icons had reached international audiences thanks to successful English-language albums, such as Ricky Martin (b. 1971), Marc Anthony (b. 1968), and Enrique Iglesias. Jennifer Lopez (b. 1969), previously known as a film actress, got a taste of pop-music fame while playing the role of Latin Tejano music star Selena Quintanilla-Pérez (1971–1995) in the film *Selena* (1997). Lopez has since become a notable Latin pop star in her own right. The widening market of Latin pop has even enticed English-speaking superstars such as Christina Aguilera (b. 1980) to produce Spanish-language recordings.

Latin pop requires only that a song be sung in Spanish or Portuguese, yet Latin music has long been a part of the global popular-music scene. Often, the mainstream success of a Latin music comes by way of a popular-dance style. Several dance crazes have initiated interest in Latin musical styles that continue to be popular today, such as tango, rumba, merengue, mambo, and salsa. We will now explore a few of these trends from South America and the Caribbean that have become staples of Latin American popular-music styles.

TANGO

In the 1910s, ballroom dance icons Vernon and Irene Castle (see Chapter 2) popularized their version of the Argentinean tango. Soon the dance was a favorite among the social elite but it became an international phenomenon only after Rudolph Valentino (1895–1926) danced it in the silent film *The Four Horsemen of the Apocalypse* (1921). Both the Castles' and Valentino's versions of tango, however, are quite different from the original improvised tango performances born in the brothels of Buenos Aires during the 1880s.

Often described as "the vertical expression of horizontal desire," tango was by no means a well-respected dance in its early history. Created by the *porteños* (people of the

Tango dancers performing on the streets of Argentina in front of a poster of Carlos Gardel.

port) dwelling in slums near the docks of Buenos Aires, tango symbolized the swelling number of disenfranchised immigrants and unemployed citizens, often former soldiers, during the latter half of the nineteenth century. The original tango ensembles included just violin, guitar, and flute, but by the turn of the century a button-box accordion, known as the *bandoneón*, was added. By the 1930s, the standard ensemble included two violins and two bandoneóns, to which were later added a piano and double bass; by the 1940s, the ensembles grew to include larger string sections. A variety of instrumentation has since followed, but the bandoneón has maintained a central role in both small and large ensembles, commonly referred to as **orquesta típica**, though it is often less prominent in larger ensembles.

Orquesta típica an ensemble common to tango music performance

A common distinguishing element of the tango is the inclusion of a distinctive rhythm derived from the *habanera* rhythm that originated in nineteenth-century Cuba. The basic habanera rhythm follows a four-beat unit that skips the second pulse, instead sounding on the second half of the beat.

((• **HEAR MORE**
on www.mymusiclab.com
Habanera and Tango
Rhythms

Habanera	1		2		3		4	
	X	-	-	X	X	-	X	-

This anticipation of the third beat is common in music throughout Latin America and can be heard with variation in many styles, including samba (see Chapter 5) and tango. Perhaps the most widely known use of the habanera rhythm in "classical" music is from the 1875 opera *Carmen*, written by Georges Bizet (1838–1875), in which the main character sings over a continuous repetition of this rhythmic motif in the aria "L'amour est un oiseau rebelle," which is simply known as "Habanera."

Because most tango music follows a four-beat meter, the tango variation of the habanera rhythm can be represented as follows:

Tango	1		2		3		4	
Tango "Habanera" Rhythm	X	x	-	x	**X**	-	(X)	-

The accented pulses are indicated by a capital "X," the lesser-emphasized rhythm by a lowercase "x." The fourth pulse is in parentheses, for much tango music will omit accenting this beat. The most significant beat in the pattern is the anticipated third pulse (shown in boldface). The musical phrasing of much tango music "pushes" toward this beat, even if its volume is the same as the first and fourth beats. Oftentimes, however, there is a subtle swell, change in harmony or instrumentation, or even slight increase in tempo to highlight this focal pulse.

Such musical subtleties do not occur consistently throughout a performance. If dancers are present, the third beat focus is sometimes apparent visually in their choreography. In modern arrangements, the bass line usually articulates the basic tango rhythm, allowing the melody and harmony instruments more freedom to "dance" around the pattern. This feeling of fluidity is essential for tango music to evoke a variety of moods.

Tempo variations, harmonic shifts, dramatic swells contrasting with serene laments, and a recurring feeling of imbalance are characteristic of "pure" tango music. When these features become rigid, the music often sounds stale and loses the sense of passion that attracts tango connoisseurs. The lead violin and/or bandoneón performers typically play the central role in guiding the musicians through these mood changes, being cognizant of the dancers' movements. Minor keys are most often utilized for the harmony in tango music, but occasional glimpses of "happiness" are expressed through the appearance of major key interludes.

Although tango is more commonly thought of today as an instrumental genre, *tango canción* (tango song) is well established in its native Argentina. An important figure in the rise of tango in terms of social status and popularity, was Carlos Gardel (1887–1935), the most famous of tango canción singers. His first recorded tango, "Mi Noche Triste" (My Sorrowful Night) (1917) sold an estimated one hundred thousand copies throughout Latin America and corresponded with the rising popularity of the tango dance throughout Europe and America. Through recordings, radio, and film, as well as numerous concert performances in Europe and the Americas, Gardel and his music set the standard by which all future tango singers are judged. A fatal airplane crash in 1935 abruptly ended his growing popularity, but he remains a revered figure in Argentina.

"Por Una Cabeza" (1935) is one of Gardel's most famous tango compositions, which he recorded several times. Numerous instrumental ensembles, large and small, have recorded the song, and it has appeared on the sound tracks of several films, most notably as accompaniment for a tango-dancing Al Pacino in a scene from *Scent of a Woman* (1992). We will review an instrumental version of the song to better understand the musical elements of tango, and then take a brief listen to a Gardel performance to introduce the lyricism of tango canción.

EXPLORE MORE
on www.mymusickit.com
Interactive Globe

🎵 *FOCUS EXAMPLE*
TANGO

"POR UNA CABEZA" ("BY A HEAD"), PERFORMED BY THE TANGO PROJECT, COMPOSED BY CARLOS GARDEL AND ALFREDO LE PERA

HEAR MORE
Download the
iTunes playlist link on
MyMusicKit

Focal Points

- **Instruments:** Two violins, accordion, piano, acoustic bass.
- **Melody/Improvisation:** The lead violin takes liberties with the main melodic material, especially in the second appearance of the main theme (1:36).
- **Harmony:** Shifting emphasis from major to minor keys during the verse and title theme.
- **Rhythm:** The habanera rhythm appears most prominently in the piano accompaniment.
- **Dynamics:** Note the volume variations between the verse sections and chorus.

TIME	DESCRIPTION
0:00–0:33	First verse with the violin pair playing lead and supporting harmony. Note the habanera rhythm has yet to appear.
0:34–1:04	Volume increases as the piano leads into the main theme ("Por Una Cabeza"). Note the appearance of the habanera rhythm, which continues throughout the remainder of the performance.
1:05–1:35	Second verse with habanera rhythm. Note the change in background accompaniment compared to the first verse.
1:36–2:15	Main theme returns, played by the accordion. The tempo slows in the final phrase.

Because of the absent vocalist, a violin, with a second violin providing a contrasting melodic line, provides the main melody. The piano and bass work together to articulate the meter. The bass enters on beat 4 and follows on beat 1, with the piano sounding on beat 2. Both instruments are silent on the third pulse.

((•● **HEAR MORE**
on www.mymusickit.com
Opening Rhythm

Meter	1	2	3	4
Bass	X	-	-	X (begins here)
Piano	-	X	-	-

By beginning the piece with this "empty" third pulse, the contrast of mood is enhanced between the lyrical, seemingly pleasant opening melodic material and the darker, more melodramatic tone of the main theme ("Por Una Cabeza"), which initiates the habanera rhythm.

The habanera rhythm is introduced by the piano, which pounds out the rhythm at the end of the first verse (0:34), beginning on the anticipation before the third beat to fill in the space that had previously been silent on this pulse and finishing strongly on the first beat of the next measure. Note that, in this particular performance, the after-beat of pulse one is missing from the tango-habanera pattern (compare with p. 64).

((•● **HEAR MORE**
on www.mymusickit.com
Piano "Habanera"
Rhythm

	1		2	3		4	
Piano "Habanera" Rhythm	X	-	-	x	X	-	X	-

The harmony also changes during the "Por Una Cabeza" theme to emphasize minor chords, giving the section a sadder sentiment compared to the verses, which have a major key tonality and thus a seemingly happier mood. All the instruments play with a louder, more aggressive sound through the title theme. The accordion, in particular, uses full harmony, rather than just subtle single-pitch background tones, to emphasize the contrast in emotion.

The lead violin continues the main melody with additional improvisation, while the second violin plays **pizzicato** accompaniment to offer a new sound quality. The accordion continues to play with full, predominantly major chords and contrasting melodic lines to complement the violin lead. The piano maintains the habanera rhythm, with the bass sounding on the 4 and 1 beats.

Pizzicato plucking the strings of a violin or other bowed instrument with the finger

The piano break (1:36) again signals the return to the title theme, which is now carried by the accordion. The lead violinist improvises new melodic material in response, and the second violin provides complementary ascending runs. The music's tonality has again shifted to minor until the performance draws to a close, with a slowing tempo and final major chord.

FOCUS EXAMPLE
TANGO CANCIÓN

"POR UNA CABEZA" ("BY A HEAD"), PERFORMED BY CARLOS GARDEL

Focal Points

- **Lyrics/Language:** Spanish language. Listen for the recurrent "Por una cabeza" reference.
- **Instruments:** A larger orquesta típica; note the absence of the accordion (bandoneón).
- **Melody:** Compare the melodic interpretation of the instrumental version of this song (in the previous Focus Example,) with the sung version here.

- **Rhythm:** Listen for the extended durations of the melodic pitches in the title theme section, as compared with the verse sections.

TIME	DESCRIPTION
0:00–0:14	Instrumental introduction.
0:15–0:47	First verse.

SPANISH	ENGLISH TRANSLATION
Por una cabeza de un noble potrillo	Losing by a head of a noble horse
Que justo en la raya afloja al llegar	who slackens just down the stretch
Y que al regresar parece decir:	and when it comes back it seems to say:
No olvides, hermano,	Don't forget, brother,
Vos sabes, no hay que jugar …	You know, you shouldn't bet
Por una cabeza, metejon de un dia,	Losing by a head, instant violent love
De aquella coqueta y risueña mujer	of that flirtatious and cheerful woman
Que al jurar sonriendo,	who, swearing with a smile
El amor que esta mintiendo	a love she's lying about,
Quema en una hoguera todo mi querer.	burns in a blaze all my love

0:48–1:18	Title theme with backing vocals.
Por una cabeza	Losing by a head
Todas las locuras	there was all that madness;
Su boca que besa	her mouth in a kiss
Borra la tristeza,	wipes out the sadness
Calma la amargura	it soothes the bitterness
Por una cabeza	Losing by a head
Si ella me olvida	if she forgets me,
Que importa perderme,	no matter to lose
Mil veces la vida	my life a thousand times;
Para que vivir …	what to live for?

1:19–1:51	Second verse.
Cuantos desengaños, por una cabeza,	Many deceptions, losing by a head …
Yo jure mil veces no vuelvo a insistir	I swore a thousand times not to insist again
Pero si un mirar me hiere al pasar	but if a look sways me on passing by
Su boca de fuego, otra vez, quiero besar	her lips of fire, I want to kiss once more
Basta de carreras, se acabo la timba	Enough of race tracks, no more gambling
Un final reñido yo no vuelvo a ver,	a photo-finish I'm not watching again,
Pero si algun pingo llega a ser fija	but if a pony looks like a sure thing on
el domingo,	Sunday,
yo me juego entero, que le voy a hacer	I'll bet everything again, what can I do?

1:52–2:34	Title theme and lyrics are repeated.

This ensemble is larger than the previous example. Discerning the number of instruments is often difficult when the ensemble includes more than three or four musicians, unless, of course, you can see the performers or they are specified on the recording notes. This is especially true when some of the performers play the same type of instrument, as with the violins in this example.

Another important aspect of recognizing the timbre of instruments is to notice when they are absent from a performance. In tango music today, the use of an accordion, preferably a bandoneón, is commonplace, but in the 1930s the practice had yet to become standard. As such, our recognition of this example as tango must rely on other musical aspects, such as vocal style, lyrical content, or rhythm.

Gardel sings in Spanish, the official language of Argentina. His vocal timbre is very "full," with precise diction and a controlled use of vibrato, similar to an opera singer. This is typical of tango cancíon singers, who model their style on Gardel.

The lyrics compare the addiction of a horse-racing gambler with that of a lover obsessing over a woman who pretends to return his affections. Such lyrics are typical of tango cancíon, which often have sentimental and nostalgic themes that usually deal with the heartbreak of a man consumed by sorrow, jealousy, and/or lust. Many evoke "underworld" imagery (e.g., murder, prostitution, gambling) stereotypically associated with the bar-brothel context of tango's origins.

Today, the tango is commonly performed as a couples dance, but the original dance involved at least three performers: a single woman and multiple male dancers vying for her affections. Since the setting for the original dance was in a brothel, the woman was generally a harlot, who played the men off each other to earn a higher price for her services. In "Por Una Cabeza," Gardel likens this to the man bidding on a horse and then losing again and again as he succumbs to his addiction.

Although the words *Por una cabeza* begin each of the four opening stanzas, the title theme is distinguished by Gardel's change in melody. Although the pitches are different, the main distinction between the opening verse and this section is the extended duration of the pitches. The first two lines of the stanza include melisma on the last word (*cabeza* and *locuras*), allowing Gardel to express his passion more effectively. His voice swells at the title phrase and then seems to sigh as the lover resigns himself to sadness.

The second verse continues the story of the lover's obsession with women being likened to a race-track gambling addiction. Gardel's passion becomes even more dramatic through the end of the performance. The orchestra drops out before the final word to highlight his voice and its expression of hopelessness.

Although Rudolph Valentino's depiction of an Argentinean *gaucho* ("cowboy") dancing the tango is sometimes mocked, the scene does suggest the original context that inspired this music style. Carlos Gardel's tango cancíon lyrics, usually written by a partner, such as Alfredo Le Pera (1900–1935), present similar story lines and affections to which his listeners could relate, given the challenges of their everyday lives. Modern tango depicts a similar sentiment, though the story line of a conflicted lover is often unrealized by the audience. Nevertheless, tango continues to be one of the most passionate popular-music genres from Latin America.

With the advent of rock music in the United States in the 1950s, the popularity of tango declined globally. As icons of this new popular style, such as Elvis Presley and the Beatles, entranced the planet's youth, tango receded from the international limelight back to Buenos Aires, where a new tango sound would emerge. The progenitor of this resurgence was Ástor Piazzolla (1921–1992).

Ástor Piazzolla playing the bandoneón, ca. 1969.

ÁSTOR PIAZZOLLA   Born in Argentina, Piazzolla spent much of his childhood in New York City, where he was exposed to myriad musical styles, especially jazz and classical. His father encouraged him to learn the bandoneón, which he mastered quickly. While he was still a teenager, his prodigious abilities earned him an invitation to tour with Carlos Gardel. Fortunately, his father did not grant his permission, for it was during this tour that a plane crash ended the famous tango singer's life.

In 1937, Piazzolla returned to Argentina and earned a living by performing in cabarets where tango music was featured. His skill was well regarded throughout Buenos Aires, where he began to study the compositions of such art music masters as Bach, Bartók, and Stravinsky. In 1953, he traveled to Paris to study with Nadia Boulanger (1887–1979), one of the twentieth century's most influential composition instructors. With her guidance, Piazzolla dispatched his earlier efforts and created his own sound by composing jazz and classically influenced tango music, which he dubbed *nuevo tango* (new tango). His objective was to establish tango as concert music in and of itself.

Initially, this new vision for tango was ill-favored by many of his fellow Argentineans. Scorned, ostracized, and even threatened with death, Piazzolla traveled frequently to New York, Paris, and elsewhere to perform his music, receiving much critical acclaim throughout the 1970s and 1980s. Eventually, his work was accepted in his homeland and paved the way for other tango artists, such as those collaborating on the Gotan Project recordings, to experiment with new elements from jazz, classical, rock, and electronic music, fusing them with traditional tango. Today, Piazzolla's success is held in high esteem with Argentineans, to whom he is known as "*El Gran Ástor*" ("The Great Astor").

THE SPIRIT OF SALSA

In a nonmusical context, *salsa* is Spanish for "sauce." But not just any sauce; in the United States and abroad, salsa is most commonly thought of as a tomato-based blend of varying spices and ingredients. Even so, a trip to your local grocery makes it evident that there are dozens of salsa flavors. This is how it is with salsa music: Certain ingredients are essential, but the end result is tastefully varied.

In reference to music, the term *salsa* is hotly contested. Most scholars and musicians consider salsa to be derived from Afro-Cuban music, but many others regard it as an innovation of Puerto Ricans. Some disregard the term altogether, asserting that salsa is just a new name for Latin music that has been popular throughout the Americas since the early decades of the twentieth century. For example, Tito Puente (1923–2000), known as "The King of Latin Music," did not consider himself a salsa musician.

> Salsa is a mish-mash. It's not a musical terminology. It's a wonderful marketing word.... . Next year, maybe they'll call it something else. But I keep playing the same music.
>
> —Tito Puente

Beyond its musical reference is the use of the term *salsa* to describe a "spirit" or "feeling" in Latin music. In some ways, the ambiguity of this usage is the most perceptive, for the numerous styles embodied by the "salsa spirit," such as *son, charanga, guaracha, rumba, mambo, cha-cha-chá, bomba, plena,* and even *timba,* are often performed by the same "salsa band." Whatever the mix of styles, the music of the moment inspires an enthusiasm shared by performers and onlookers alike, from the mildest and sweetest-sounding *bolero* to the spiciest hip-shaking *comparsa*; this inspirational spirit is the essence of salsa.

As with much music of the Americas, we can trace the musical roots of salsa to both Europe and Africa. Its musical heritage draws primarily from the melody, harmony, and vocal forms of the Iberian Peninsula (Portugal and Spain), with an undercurrent of polyrhythmic percussion transplanted mainly from West Africa. Many instruments found in the "New World," such as the guitar or *agogo* (double-bell), come from Europe or Africa; others, such as the conga drums, are heritage-inspired innovations demanded of new musical and cultural circumstances in the Americas. Respecting the "Old World" ancestry of Latin music, salsa results from the cross-fertilization of these musical predecessors and has evolved into an entirely new sound that is unique from anything found earlier in either Europe or Africa. The "New World" gardens that cultivate this hybrid creation are threefold: Cuba, Puerto Rico, and New York City.

Cuba

Cuba was visited by Christopher Columbus on his first exploration of the Western hemisphere, in 1492. He claimed the island for Spain, and it became an important focus for Spanish colonialists. Over the course of its colonial history, it became home to a diverse ethnic population. The indigenous peoples, mostly Taíno, were forced by the Spaniards to work as miners and farmers; by the seventeenth century, they had been replaced first by enslaved labor of African-descended peoples born in Spain (known as *Ladinos*) and then, by the late eighteenth century, by those from the African continent itself. After the

Haitian Revolution (1791–1804), many French immigrants took refuge in Cuba, and the middle of the nineteenth century saw the arrival of a significant minority of Chinese workers. Cuba remained one of the last vestiges of Spain's political dominance in the Americas: Spanish colonial powers ceded control of the island only in 1898, after the Spanish-American War, in which the U.S. military forced their withdrawal.

● EXPLORE MORE
on www.mymusickit.com
Interactive Globe

American influence there has always been controversial. After Cuba's formal independence in 1902, local politicians frequently found themselves in puppet-like positions, with the American government or powerful business leaders pulling the strings. During the years of Prohibition (1920-1933) in the United States, Cuba became a major hub for the production and trafficking of alcohol, and by the 1950s it had gained a reputation as a playground for Mafioso and America's social elite.

American excesses and the Mafia's influence on Cuban politics, coupled with an increasing disparity between the rich and the poor, prompted the emergence of Cuba's most prominent political figure, Fidel Castro (b. 1926). By 1959, Castro had successfully ousted the dubiously elected president, Fugencio Batista (1901–1973), and shifted the country's alliance from the United States to the Soviet Union. In 1961, Castro declared Cuba a socialist republic, which led to economic sanctions by the United States and its allies. With the fall of the Soviet Union in 1991, Cuba lost its major trading partner and continues to struggle economically, though foreign investment has recently helped to improve the situation.

This brief historical review reveals the changing circumstances that have influenced the development of music throughout Cuba's history. Classical and folk music are abundant throughout the country, providing the popular music and dance with continual inspiration. Musicians still actively compose and perform in a great variety of these styles, such as *danzón*, *bolero*, *charanga*, *changui*, and *guajira*, but the most important genre to inform salsa is known as *son*.

For Cubans, son *is* salsa, only noncommercialized and uncorrupted by American media influence. Though such feelings reflect a strong sense of nationalism, it is true that son is uniquely Cuban and provided the foundation for the later development of salsa. In the 1930s, Americans first became familiar with son, referring to it as *rumba*, which, strictly speaking, in the Cuban context is a purely percussion-based style, with accompanying vocals. By the 1940s, the style had evolved into *son montuno*, an innovation of Arsenio Rodríguez (1911–1970).

In America, the genre later became known by the more generic term *Latin jazz* and was popularized by recognized jazz icons, such as Dizzy Gillespie (1917–1993), as well as Latin music artists, including Tito Puente (1923–2000) and Francisco Raúl Gutiérrez Grillo (1909–1984), better known as "Machito." Cuban popular music reached a peak in the United States during the 1950s as mambo and cha-cha-chá dance crazes swept the globe, as exemplified by the music of singer-bandleader Beny Moré (1919–1963). The success of the "I Love Lucy" television show, which co-starred and was produced by Cuban bandleader Desi Arnaz (1917–1986), brought the sounds of Latin jazz into American homes during this period.

The presence of Cuban popular music declined significantly with the advent of rock music in the mid-1950s, as did the changing political circumstances of Cuba's relationship with the United States. The Cuban Revolution of 1959 was divisive: Many musicians left the island to maintain their personal and musical freedoms while those who remained found themselves largely isolated from international audiences. As Cuba's political situation during the 1960s presented new challenges for its population, the government recognized the contribution of its musical heritage to the national identity. Folk and classical traditions were supported in state-sponsored conservatories, and musical instruments were mass-produced to encourage musical activity as a part of daily activities. Most significant in this period was the development of Cuban revolution *nueva trova*, a guitar-accompanied vocal genre with politically oriented lyrics, akin to American folk music of the era made popular by such artists as Bob Dylan (b. 1941). However, nueva trova artists, such as Silvio Rodríguez (b. 1946), were generally supportive of the Castro government and rarely established themselves outside Cuba.

By the 1970s, the propagation of Cuban-derived music was left to exiled musicians, such as "The Queen of Salsa"—Celia Cruz (1925–2003)—or Latin musicians hailing from other countries, such as Rubén Blades (b. 1948) from Panama. While New York City and Miami became the major centers for the evolution of salsa, Cuban musicians maintained the son and other native genres with lesser outside influence. Some performers, such as jazz trumpeter Arturo Sandoval (b. 1949), fled the country to escape political pressure and to find new audiences; others, such as guitarist Compay Segundo (1907–2003), accepted their situation and continued to play and record in Cuba in relative obscurity.

The late 1990s, however, brought new life to Cuban music, thanks to the success of *Buena Vista Social Club* (1997), one of the highest-selling world-music albums of all-time. A project spearheaded by American guitarist Ry Cooder (b. 1947) and bandleader Juan de Marcos González (b. 1954), the album brought attention to some of Cuba's "old guard" musicians, in particular, the aforementioned Segundo, vocalists Ibrahim Ferrer (1927–2005) and Omara Portuondo (b. 1930), and pianist Rubén González (1919–2003), among others.

Though the album is controversial among Cuban music scholars and musicians, its success, and that of the subsequent documentary film of the same name (directed by Wim Wenders), reacquainted the world with son and other music genres that persist in Cuba. The island's tourist industry has benefited from the increased exposure, and many musicians have found their services in greater demand, both in Cuba and abroad. Several of the Buena Vista Social Club members recorded solo albums afterward, and others continue to tour abroad. Whether based in nostalgia or artistry, the group's acclaim has helped to re-establish Cuba's primary role in the success of Latin American music worldwide.

Buena Vista Social Club, 1997.

FOCUS EXAMPLE
CUBAN SON MONTUNO

"EL CUARTO DE TULA" ("TULA'S BEDROOM"),
PERFORMED BY THE BUENA VISTA SOCIAL CLUB

((•● **HEAR MORE**
Download the
iTunes playlist link on
MyMusicKit

Focal Points

- **Instruments:** guitar, trumpet, bass, cowbell, maracas, bongos, conga, timbales, *dumbek*, *laoud*.
- **Rhythm:** Polyrhythmic percussion referencing the "reverse" *clave* rhythm.
- **Form:** The opening narrative section (*largo*) is followed by a vamp section (*montuno*) with improvisational solos.

TIME	DESCRIPTION
0:00–0:18	Instrumental introduction.
0:19–0:47	Sung narrative.
0:48–1:32	Composed section (*largo*) repeats.
1:33–7:25	Vamp section (*montuno*) with sung response and improvised solos.

The opening introduces the ensemble, which consists of a mix of European-derived melodic instruments and African-inspired percussion. A variety of timbres is one of the distinctive aspects of Cuban son and other Latin jazz styles. Melody and harmony balance with a vibrant percussion section. Most of the instruments heard in this example are essential instruments typical of salsa music as well. Others, such as the trombone, saxophone, *guiro* (scraped gourd), or *pandereta* (frame drum with cymbals), may also be included.

With regard to the percussion, each instrument contributes to the polyrhythmic foundation of *son montuno* by playing a unique pattern that interweaves with its percussion partners. The central, or reference, rhythm is known as the *clave rhythm*. (*Clave* means "key" [as to open a lock] in Spanish.) This rhythm is often played on the *claves* (wood sticks) or substituted by a similarly bright sound, such as striking the rim of a snare drum. The clave rhythm extends through two four-beat measures and is of two types, either 3+2 or 2+3. Our Focus Example utilizes the latter pattern, sometimes called a *reverse clave*.

	1	-	2	-	3	-	4	-	5	-	6	-	7	-	8	-
Clave (3+2)	X "1"	-	-	X "2"	-	-	X "3"	-	-	-	X "1"	-	X "2"	-	-	-
"Reverse" (2+3)	-	-	X "1"	-	X "2"	-	-	-	X "1"	-	X "2"	-	-	-	X "3"	-

((•● **HEAR MORE**
on www.mymusickit.com
Clave and Reverse Clave
Rhythms

These standard clave patterns are known as *son clave* due to their prevalence in Cuban son music. A common variation is the *rumba clave*, which delays the "3" pulse by a half-beat in both the 3+2 and 2+3 rhythms.

	1	-	2	-	3	-	4	-	5	-	6	-	7	-	8	-
Rumba Clave (3+2)	X "1"	-	-	X "2"	-	-	-	X "3"	-	-	X "1"	-	X "2"	-	-	-
"Reverse" (2+3)	-	-	X "1"	-	X "2"	-	-	-	X "1"	-	X "2"	-	-	-	-	X "3"

((•● **HEAR MORE**
on www.mymusickit.com
Rumba Clave Rhythms

Although one of these clave rhythms is typically present in salsa music, it is often implicitly articulated through the interplay of rhythm and melody instruments. The musicians (and audience) "feel" the clave rhythm, even if no single instrument explicitly sounds the pattern.

Son montuno has two basic sections in its overall form: ***largo*** and *montuno*. The *largo* refers to the opening section that includes composed melody and an extended harmonic progression. The *largo* starts when the piece begins. This example opens with the ensemble and trumpet lead, followed by a sung narrative. The entire section repeats with the same lyrical content.

Latin jazz lyrics often refer to "hot" things, making a multitude of innuendos in the process. These can be about sex, dancing, a musician's technical skill, a woman's scorn, and so on. In this case, it is literally about fire: "Tula" forgot to blow out a candle before falling asleep causing a fire in her bedroom. Note the background vocal imitating the sound of a fire engine siren (0:33 and 1:20). The *largo* narrative sets the scene and asks a question, which will be answered at the start of the montuno (1:33).

We have encountered the term *montuno* in reference to the ostinato pattern played on a piano (see "Latin Pop," above). That is essentially what the montuno section is in a broader sense: a repetition of a relatively short length of musical material (i.e., vamp). The sung "answer" to the opening narrative provides a refrain heard periodically throughout the performance. Between each repetition is an instrumental or vocal improvisation, which is the essence of son montuno, as well as of salsa music in general. The musicians "jam" for the remainder of the performance, until the rehearsed conclusion. Such ***descarga*** (extended improvisational vamps) generally have no set length: The performers continue to play until the music seems to "cool down" or someone signals the ending material, as likely occurred with this recording.

Largo opening composed section of a *son montuno* performance

Descarga extended improvisation during performance of son montuno

Puerto Rico

Puerto Rico's role in the development of salsa is less conspicuous than that of Cuba. The two most influential styles are that of *bomba* and *plena*. The former is as much a dance genre as an instrumental style. A performance consists of dancers challenging the lead drummer, who improvises on a high-pitched bomba drum, while a low-pitched bomba drum sounds a consistent repeating rhythm along with other instruments, such as the *guiro* (scraped idiophone), maraca (shaken idiophone), and often a cowbell, to create an underlying polyrhythmic structure. The dancer improvises movements to which the lead drummer is meant to synchronize rhythms. A vocalist often accompanies, and onlookers are expected to sing a group response to the singer's calls. These characteristics draw a clear connection to Africa, though the music's roots are not isolated to a single tradition. Modern bomba performances frequently mix elements of other styles, such as salsa, as evidenced by the frequent inclusion of brass instruments, notably trumpets and trombones.

Plena is probably the most popular "folk" music of Puerto Rico. Originally, it was a subdued couple's dance. Spanish influence was apparent in the use of melodic instruments, such as guitar or concertina (small accordion), and the primary role of the *pandereta* (a hand-held frame-drum) over other percussion. By the early 1900s, a lead vocalist was included, adding lyrics that were topical and laden with astute social

((⊙ HEAR MORE on www.mymusickit.com Interactive Globe

commentary, as with other Caribbean vocal genres, such as calypso from Trinidad (see Chapter 3). The narrative soon became the focus of a plena performance, alternating with a short choral refrain.

As Cuban popular music gained prominence throughout Puerto Rico during the 1930s, plena gradually declined in its traditional form as it incorporated many jazz elements brought with the imported style. Though a few artists, such as César Concepción (1909–1974), Mon Rivera (1899–1978), and Rafael Cortijo (1928–1982), were able to find some commercial success with the new features, plena in its original form became a mostly local phenomenon. Though still important to Puerto Ricans and ethnically related communities in the United States, both bomba and plena are infrequently recognized by international audiences.

New York City

Cuba and Puerto Rico may be the parent countries, but New York City is where salsa was born. One of the most populous metropolitan areas in the world (with a population of more than 18 million), New York City is internationally recognized as a powerhouse of cultural, economic, and political activity. Home to many of the world's most famous landmarks, such as the Statue of Liberty, the Empire State Building, and Ellis Island, millions of immigrants and tourists from around the globe have been initiated into the American experience by the sights and sounds of the country's largest city. Few other cities around the globe, perhaps only Paris, conjure as many romantic images. Certainly, the city has all the ailments of any major urban center (poverty, crime), but it remains a beacon of hope for many who view the United States as a symbol of freedom and prosperity.

Throughout its history, millions of immigrants have settled within and around the city's limits. It is perhaps the most ethnically diverse center in the world. It comprises five boroughs—the Bronx, Brooklyn, Manhattan, Queens, and Staten Island—each home to ethnic communities that have tended to settle together. In northeast Manhattan is the neighborhood of Harlem, perhaps best known as an African American cultural and economic center. Yet, since the 1950s East Harlem, often referred to as "Spanish Harlem," has been home to a growing number of Puerto Rican immigrants.

Puerto Rico is an unincorporated territory of the United States; Puerto Ricans are therefore American citizens, though they lack political representation in Congress. After World War II, many Puerto Ricans took advantage of advances in air travel to immigrate to New York City, where they faced discrimination by local residents, many of whom were of European descent. The 1957 Broadway musical *West Side Story* (made into a film in 1961) depicted this animosity, pitting street gangs representing Polish American and Puerto Rican communities against each other.

Shortly after this production, the Puerto Rican community began to develop a distinctive cultural identity that reflected both its native island roots and the tension of the new urban environment. By the mid-1960s, many Puerto Rican intellectuals, artists, musicians, poets, and actors had laid the groundwork for a New York–Puerto Rican identity, today known as "Nuyorican." Although the term refers specifically to those of Puerto Rican descent, many other Latin communities have become inspired by the growing confidence and achievements of the Nuyorican population. The Fania All-Stars, a powerhouse ensemble of the Fania record label's various musicians—including Willie Colón (b. 1950 in New York City), Johnny Pacheco (b. 1935 in the Dominican Republic), Hector Lavoe (1946–1993, from Puerto Rico), Ray Barretto (1929–2006, from Puerto Rico), Larry Harlow (b. 1939 in Brooklyn), Celia Cruz (1925–2003, from Cuba), and Jorge

Santana (b. 1951 in Mexico)—perhaps best represents this eclectic mix of cultural backgrounds working together to create a cohesive cultural identity through music. Thus, it is from New York that salsa became a unifying voice for those with a variety of Latin ethnic heritages.

SUDDENLY SALSA

Sorting out the process of salsa's creation and evolution is a perplexing, often maddening proposition. The more you listen to salsa, the more you realize that the term is rather loosely applied to a great many musical styles. Furthermore, the term itself is used to describe not only a musical style but also a specific dance that can be performed to a variety of different music types, not exclusively salsa. Indeed, the term *salsa* can be considered similarly to the terms *jazz* or *classical*. They suggest a certain recognizable sound but encompass a variety of specific subtypes. With regard to salsa, many of these subtypes are the predecessors that led to the sound today considered to be salsa.

A simplified historical evolution of salsa might look something like this:

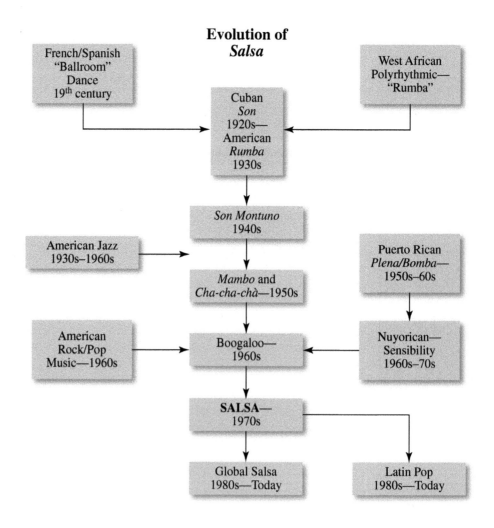

This chart highlights only the major historical predecessors until the regular use of the term *salsa* in the early 1970s. The center path represents the core stages in salsa's development, with several important outside influences noted along the sides, such as American jazz. Considering all the styles encompassed by the term *salsa* would be a book in itself (and is; see "Pathways," at the close of this chapter). Some of the earlier styles that embody the "salsa spirit" include rumba, charanga, son, son montuno, mambo, cha-cha-chá, pachanga, plena, bomba, and boogaloo, among others created after the establishment of the salsa label, such as salsa romántica and salsa-erótica. Even nonrelated genres are sometimes characterized as salsa, such as bolero, merengue, cumbia, and even samba. Modern versions of salsa are influenced by other popular genres, such as American hip-hop music, creating new styles, such as *salsatón* and *timba*.

Salsa, comprises a great variety of musical subgenres. Many performers consider the label a marketing tool and prefer other descriptive titles.

TITO PUENTE   Tito Puente was one such prominent figure who never described himself as a *salsa* performer, instead considering his music by the equally all-encompassing term *Latin jazz*. Puente's career spanned more than five decades. He got his start playing with many great rumba ensembles, such as the Noro Morales Orchestra, during the late 1930s and early 1940s before being drafted into the U.S. Navy during World War II, when he played saxophone in a jazz swing band.

After the war, Puente studied orchestration and conducting at the Julliard School of Music in New York City and soon formed his own band, which helped build his reputation as a gifted musician and conductor. He was invited to be a regular performer at the Palladium Ballroom, which quickly became the hotspot for the country's Latin jazz scene. Along with many Latin jazz greats, such as Tito Rodríguez (1923–1973) and Francisco Grillo (aka "Machito"), Puente helped the Palladium Ballroom spawn the 1950s "Mambo Craze" that swept the country. Professional dancers such as Augie and Margo

Celia Cruz and Tito Puente performing at the Grammy Award's Latin Celebration, 1999.

Rodriguez (n.d.), Hollywood celebrities Bob Hope (1903–2003) and Marlon Brando (1924–2004), and jazz greats the likes of Dizzy Gillespie and Duke Ellington (1899–1974) would visit the club to hear the world's top mambo bands perform, dancing to their intoxicating rhythms.

Puente also initiated his solo recording career during this period, producing more than one hundred albums in his lifetime, including *Mambo Beat* (1957), *Dance Mania* (1958), and *Cha cha chá—Live at Grossingers* (1959). During the 1960s, while rock music was quickly gaining an audience among teenagers throughout the country, Puente's success remained steady. His association with Cuban diva Celia Cruz (1925–2003), known as "The Queen of Salsa," produced numerous recordings that are among the most prized in salsa music's history. His song "Oye Como Va" was first released on his 1963 album *El Rey Bravo*, making reference to his popular moniker as the King (*el Rey*) of Mambo. (Note that the term *salsa* to describe the music had not yet been coined.) By this time, Puente had already released more than forty albums. The song soon became his signature piece, and he recorded several versions of it, including the live version we will examine in our Focus Example.

FOCUS EXAMPLE
SALSA

(((• **HEAR MORE**
Download the
iTunes playlist link on
MyMusicKit

"OYE COMO VA" ("HEAR HOW IT GOES"),
PERFORMED BY TITO PUENTE

Focal Points

- **Instruments:** Piano, flute, saxophones, trumpets, trombones, bass, congas, timbales, guiro
- **Improvisation:** The flute improvises throughout the performance.
- **Melody:** Sophisticated orchestration of composed melodic phrases that highlight each instrument section.
- **Rhythm:** The clave rhythm is intuitive and "un" articulated by the piano and other instruments.

TIME	DESCRIPTION
0:00–0:13	Piano establishes ("un") clave rhythm. Flute (and bass) improvises as background handclaps indicate the beat.
0:14–0:29	Remaining instruments enter with the ("un") clave rhythm. Flute continues improvisation.
0:30–0:44	Band plays first melodic theme as flute provides contrasting "answer" improvisations.
0:45–0:51	Unison "punch" signature phrase.
0:52–1:22	Sung refrain. (*Oye...*)
1:23–1:37	First "mambo" melody played by the saxophones and trombones, with flute improvisations.
1:38–1:52	Trumpets add a contrasting melodic line.
1:53–2:22	Second entrance of the sung refrain.
2:23–2:38	Second "mambo" melody played by the saxophones and trombones, with flute improvisations.
2:39–2:53	Trumpets enter with the same melody to help build intensity to the extended solo section.

2:54–3:23	Flute improvised solo. Note the piano drops the ("un") clave rhythm.
3:24–3:39	Saxophones and trombones enter with third "mambo" melody.
3:40–3:54	Trumpets enter with the same melody, leading into the sung refrain.
3:55–4:25	Third entrance of the sung refrain.
4:26– 4:33	Dramatic crescendo achieved through layering of instruments and ascension from low to high pitches.
4:34–4:48	Third "mambo" melody played by the saxophones and trumpets.
4:49–5:03	Two-note syncopated pattern played by the trombones and low saxophones. A trumpet joins at 4:57. Also, listen for the timbales break at 5:01.
5:04–5:18	Full band closing melodic material, emphasizing high-register trumpets.
5:19–5:36	Unison "punch" signature phrase closes the performance.

The piano initiates this performance with an interesting twist on the clave pattern. Rather than articulating the rhythm explicitly by sounding out the 3+2 pattern, the piano syncopates around this rhythm, leaving silence where the clave rhythm would appear, except for the first beat of the pattern. For the sake of our example, we will call this the ("un") clave rhythm.

	1	-	2	-	3	-	4	-	5	-	6	-	7	-	8	-
Clave 3+2	X	-	-	X	-	-	X	-	-	-	X	-	X	-	-	-
Piano	X	-	X	-	-	X	-	X	-	-	-	X	-	X	-	-

((•● **HEAR MORE**
on www.mymusickit.com
Clave Rhythm

("Un") clave rhythm entrance of the piano in "Oye Como Va."

The handclaps become louder at the second appearance of the pattern (0:03), articulating the basic beat. The piano's use of syncopation to "surround" beats 4 and seven gives the clearest indication of the expected clave pattern (3+2). This implication of the pattern, rather than explicit performance of it, is indicative of the rhythmic sophistication of most salsa music. Try clapping the clave rhythm at 0:14, when the rest of the band enters with the same ("un") clave rhythm as the piano.

The melodic instruments play the first melodic theme while the flute "answers" with short improvisations at the end of each phrase. (In the original recording, the flute alone presented this theme.) The piano continues with the ("un") clave rhythm while the percussion instruments provide a steady beat. The latter instruments provide an interesting array of timbre, such as the scraping sound of the guiro and the metallic pulse of the cowbell, which are characteristic of salsa music.

Another important feature of this example is that it represents a style known as cha-cha-chá. This label describes a couples dance choreography that uses a shuffle-step pattern that corresponds with the "4 & 1." Below is the basic step:

1	2	3	4 &	1	2	3	4 &	1, etc.
R (Right)	L (Left)	R	L R	L	R	L	R L	R

Cha-cha-chá dance steps.

The cha-cha-chá is a standard Latin dance taught in ballroom classes around the world. Amateur dancers frequently misplace the cha-cha-chá step on the 3 & 4, rather than the 4 & 1 beats, particularly in this song, "Oye Como Va," which is probably the best known of all cha-cha-chá music. Many consider this variation of step placement an interpretive freedom afforded to the dancers, though musicians consider the 4 & 1 placement correct. The original recording includes the handclaps and *claves* (wooden sticks) articulating the 4 & 1 rhythm, but many people do the shuffle-step choreography on the 3 & 4, where the flute "answers" the main melody. The cha-cha-chá dance was very popular during the 1950s and 1960s and is today performed to a variety of musical styles, even group line-dances without a partner.

The unison "punches" (loud, short bursts of sound) at 0:45 anticipate the entrance of the vocal refrain. The lyrics address the rhythmic aspect of the music, enticing its listeners to dance and sing along. The vocalists are the band members themselves, a common occurrence in salsa music. Note that most of the melodic instruments drop out during the singing, whereas the percussion, bass, and piano play throughout the four repetitions of the sung refrain.

Cha-cha-chá is a slower tempo subgenre of mambo, a musical style descended from the son montuno. The music is essentially a melding of Afro-Cuban rhythms with big-band jazz melodic and harmonic elements. Mambo differs from son montuno primarily in its instrumental emphasis. The opening *largo* section, which features the vocalist and main composition, is regularly absent from mambo, which is intended primarily to be dance music.

Mambo, however, is more than just a montuno vamp, for it incorporates composed arrangements that highlight the different sections of the band. These instrumental sections are referred to as *mambo*. In our example, the saxophones and trombones play the main melody of the opening mambo. The trumpets make their own melodic statement at 1:38 while the flute continues its solo improvisations.

After the sung refrain, a new "mambo" theme appears that is more rhythmic in its use of syncopation and shorter durations than the earlier section. Whereas the earlier melody seemed "connected," this one is "choppier," presenting a melodic contrast. The trumpets join the saxophones and trombones to lead into the extended flute solo. To highlight this section, the piano stops playing the ("un") clave rhythm and changes to a basic vamp (2:54).

((•● **HEAR MORE**
on www.mymusickit.com
Vamp Rhythm

	1	-	2	-	3	-	4	-	1	-	2	-	3	-	4	-
Piano	X	-	-	-	X	-	-	-	X	-	-	-	X	-	X	-

After the third sung refrain, the orchestration of the ensemble plays a more prominent role, beginning with the "buildup" crescendo at 4:26. The flute continues its improvisations while the piano returns to the ("un") clave rhythm. The saxophones and trumpets move into a third mambo melody, emphasizing the higher saxophones and trumpets, in contrast to the earlier mambo melodies that focused on the low-range instruments. The two-note syncopations of the trombones at 4:49 provide a unique contrast, before the timbales signal the band to play the closing melodic material (5:04). The unison signature "punches" that appeared near the beginning of the song round out the performance (5:19).

"Oye Como Va" remains one of the most recognizable songs in popular world music and has been recorded by numerous artists, most notably Carlos Santana, whose 1970 rock version catapulted him to superstardom and attracted new worldwide audiences to Latin popular music. Modern versions sometimes incorporate heavy dance beats and hip-hop elements to appeal to younger audiences. With Puente's death, in 2000, and that of Celia Cruz, in 2003, a new generation of salsa musicians, such as Linda Caballero (aka "La India"; b. 1970) and Tito's son, Tito Puente Jr. (b. 1971), carry the torch that will keep salsa burning hot into the next millennium.

While Cubans, Puerto Ricans, and Nuyoricans debate over who should be credited with originating the genre, salsa music today represents a great many Latin populations from throughout the Americas and the Caribbean. Latin pop frequently draws on the salsa sound, and the music is particularly popular in Colombia and Venezuela, where such local traditions as *cumbia* have been adapted to create distinctive cultural versions. Many West African musicians, such as Papa Wemba (b. 1949) or the salsa-dedicated group Africando, have found commercial success including this distinctive musical style in their repertory. Indeed, salsa is now a global phenomenon, heard from Japan to India to the mountains of Peru, but its heritage is still strongly linked to the Cuban–Puerto Rican–Nuyorican tripartite that sustains it today.

TIMBA AND REGGAETON

While popular music from Latin America has continued to thrive in both mainstream Latin culture and local folk contexts, two genres with increasing visibility on the global music scene are *timba* and *reggaeton*. These genres maintain strong Latin musical roots but also draw on an eclectic variety of more recent urban influences to create new sounds that appeal to contemporary audiences. Both styles first appeared in the 1980s but required at least a decade of development before flourishing in the late 1990s until today.

Timba is often referred to as Cuban salsa. Rooted in the son tradition, timba musicians incorporate many of the recognized features of mainstream "American" salsa and Latin pop but also add a variety of folk, classical, and popular traditions found on the island. American rock influences often appear in the form of the electric guitar or synthesizer, usually used to add an orchestral "string" sound, and a drum set with a prominent kick drum. The lyrical content of timba songs often expresses Cuban nationalism and is critical of U.S. politics and social indulgences. Timba also tends to utilize the "reverse" clave rhythm (2+3) and may exclude any clave rhythm altogether, opting for a straight, less syncopated, duple dance beat. Many members of the early timba groups, such as Los Van Van and NG La Banda, have recently established new groups, including Klimax, Bamboleo, and Pupy Pedroso y Que Son Son, that utilize the traditional son sound but generously incorporate modern musical idioms with soulful backing vocals or electronic sound effects, all in hopes of reaching audiences outside Cuba.

Reggaeton, in contrast, has already established itself on the global popular music scene. Appearing in the mid-1990s, the genre draws heavily from Jamaican reggae and dancehall, African American and Latin hip-hop, as well as techno and other electronic music subgenres. Sampling, synthesizers, drum machines, and rapping vocal delivery, most often in Spanish, are some of its recognizable features. The use of a specific rhythm, known as **dem bow**, is the key marker distinguishing reggaeton from other types of Latin urban popular music.

Reggaeton musicians and enthusiasts consider the dem bow "riddim" (a rhythm articulated by percussion and a melodic bass) as a recent innovation; in fact, its basic pattern is inspired by the habanera rhythm, which has been common to Latin American music for well over a century (see above). The basic pattern is the same, repeating before the end of each melodic phrase (8 beats). The pattern is usually split between the bass and a snare drum. The bass falls on beats 1 and 3, and the snare drum interlocks by sounding on the offbeat of 2 and on 4 (see below). A keyboard, guitar, or other instrument will usually sound on each beat to articulate the regular meter.

EXPLORE MORE
on www.mymusickit.com
Interactive Globe

Dem bow the basic rhythm used in reggaeton music

HEAR MORE
on www.mymusickit.com
Dem Bow "Riddim"

	1	-	2	-	3	-	4	-	1	-	2	-	3	-	4	-
Dem Bow "Riddim"	X	-	-	x	X	-	x	-	X	-	-	x	X	-	x	-
Habanera	X	-	-	X	X	-	X	-	X	-	-	X	X	-	X	-

The uppercase boldface **X** in the table equals the bass pattern; the lowercase "x" marks the interlocking snare drum rhythm.

FOCUS EXAMPLE
REGGAETON

Focal Points

- **Instruments:** Electronic drum machine, bass, synthesizers, sound effects.
- **Voice:** Male lead with rapid syllabic vocal delivery. Female responses on refrain and male group shouts.
- **Language/Lyrics:** Spanish. Lyrics use slang and references to partying, sex, and dancing.
- **Rhythm:** Dem bow rhythm indicates the reggaeton style.

TIME	DESCRIPTION
0:00–0:09	Introduction with male vocal shouts (Ho!) and reference to lead vocalist, "Who's this? Daddy Yankee!" (0:06).
0:10–0:19	Lead vocalist sings with a processed distortion of vocal timbre.
0:20–0:29	First verse.

SPANISH	ENGLISH
Mamita… (Duro!)	Honey… (Hard!)

0:30–0:49	"Gasolina" refrain (repeats).
0:50–1:09	Second verse continues with the partying theme.
1:10–1:29	Refrain (repeats). Dem bow rhythm drops out and returns at 1:20.
1:30–1:49	Third verse shifts focus to singer as a "killer" on the dance floor.
1:50–1:53	Sound effect of engine starting and revving.
1:54–2:11	Dem bow rhythm drops out again until 2:02 as vocalist shifts to a higher range.
2:12–2:21	Opening lyrics and processed distortion of vocal timbre return. The dem bow rhythm is absent.
2:22–2:31	First verse lyrics repeated. Dem bow rhythm returns.
2:32–2:51	Refrain (repeats).
2:52–3:12	Vocals drop out as dem bow rhythm continues to end the piece.

Reggaeton is often infused with Spanish slang terms derived from the vocalists' cultural background, in this case, Puerto Rican. The use of slang leaves the innuendos open to interpretation. The literal translations are often "radio-friendly," and the accompanying videos have the ubiquitous "booty dancer" women, who wear sexy clothes and gyrate to the beat. The imagery may be suggestive but usually falls short of the "R-rated" interpretation of the lyrics.

The opening to our Focus Example gets the party started with hollers to the crowd and a shout out to the lead vocalist, "Who's this? Daddy Yankee!" (0:06). Daddy Yankee's voice is processed to give it a distorted timbre. His lyrics reference the *"gatas"* (slang for "sexy women," his dancers) needing everyone to "mambo" in order to get started ("turn on the engines"), suggestive of the song's theme, (i.e., cars). Fast cars and sexy women are stereotypical images associated with reggaeton artists and are frequently referenced in lyrics and accompanying videos.

The dem bow riddim begins with the first verse (0:20), taking a short break before the "Gasolina" refrain. The lyrics continue to address the theme of partying and "gasoline," meaning "fast cars." However, the gasoline reference can be interpreted several ways. Fast cars is the most apparent reference, but the singer may also be referring to the female subject of the story line being full of "fuel," or energy. The reference to her going out every weekend to have fun suggests a celebratory context, such as a nightclub or dance hall. This, too, is a relatively tame interpretation of the lyrics.

Other interpretations rely more heavily on the slang innuendos of youth culture. The term *gasolina* is sometimes used in Puerto Rican slang to mean alcohol, specifically rum, and more generally to drugs. Thus, the female subject likes to "go out to have fun," with the implication that she is addicted to the lifestyle of drinking, dancing, and having fun. The R-rated version of the lyrics is understood by the listener to mean that the female subject is addicted to oral sex, since *gasolina* is also slang for ejaculation.

The lyrics for the remainder of the song continue with the themes of partying and fast cars. Any alcohol or sex references are never explicitly stated, ensuring that the song receives radio airplay. Indeed, the song reached the top ten on popular-music charts around the world, though it peaked at only No. 32 on the U.S. Billboard charts. Nonetheless, the song is credited as one of the early successes that helped reggaeton break through to the American mainstream popular-music industry.

The 1991 recording "Dem Bow," by Jamaican dancehall artist Shabba Ranks (b. 1966), is credited with introducing the reggaeton signature beat to the world. A Spanish-language cover, "Son Bow," by Panamanian artist Edgardo Franco (aka "El General"; n.d.), made the "new" beat popular among Latin audiences. Puerto Rican youth coupled the new sound with a "grinding" dance style, known as **perreo**, which was sexually suggestive enough to motivate the Puerto Rican government to ban the dance. That, of course, had the opposite effect, making the dance and associated music more popular among young adults throughout the country and elsewhere in Latin America and the United States. The music and dance thus went underground and thrived at house parties and in a cassette culture where new mixes were distributed from garages and hand to hand. As the music gained prominence, the reggaeton label was adopted by Puerto Rican youth to acknowledge its Jamaican roots, and it suggested a "walking" tempo similar to that found in Jamaican reggae. The label also helped distinguish the style from Spanish hip-hop and other underground music genres.

Perreo a "grinding" dance associated with reggaeton music

As reggaeton spread to Spanish-speaking youth in other countries, artists continued to draw from the reggae and hip-hop culture, adopting similar fashions, performance gestures, and lyrical themes, this last focusing on teenage angst interests, such as love/sex, dancing/fun, cars, and the like. Artists such as Tego "El Abayarde" Calderón (b. 1972), Ramón "Daddy Yankee" Rodríguez (b. 1977), and Don Omar (b. 1978) found growing audiences within the United States, in particular, and have since become popular with non-Latino audiences. As artists have become more established, the lyrical content often includes more socially perceptive topics, notably, Latino identity or current political or economic issues. By the mid-2000s, reggaeton artists had begun to collaborate with American hip-hop producers and musicians, such as Snoop Dogg, to expand the genre's audience. The music has fused with other popular world-music styles to create related subgenres, such as *bhangraton*.

Daddy Yankee performing, ca. 2005.

SUMMARY

LEARN MORE
on www.mymusickit.com
Chapter summary
and exam

In this chapter, we addressed the issue of defining what populations are Latin American. The broad cultural backgrounds of the many peoples considered to be Latin American make for a diverse array of vibrant musical traditions throughout the Caribbean and the Americas. We began our exploration of musical styles with an overview of features characterizing Latin pop from the 1980s to today. Though this genre is popular now, we discovered that the first wave of Latin popular music began much earlier, with the global interest in Argentinean tango, a style that is still common today.

After familiarizing ourselves with the importance of rhythm in Latin music, we delved into the history of salsa music and its many styles, focusing on cha-cha-chá, which reached its peak of popularity in the 1960s. Salsa has inspired people of all ages to dance to the rhythms of Latin America, such as timba music, and we concluded with a brief review of reggaeton, which targets youth culture today and has established itself as one of the rising popular world-music genres.

Pathways

- **DVD:** *Roots of Rhythm*, directed by Eugene Rosow and Howard Dratch. Docurama, 1994.
  - A documentary hosted by Harry Belafonte about the history of Latin American music in the New World. Highly recommended.
  - *www.docurama.com/productdetail.html?productid=NV-NVG-9435-NVG-9476*
- **DVD:** *Salsa: Latin Pop Music in the Cities*, directed by Jeremy Marre, Shanachie, 2000.
  - A documentary about the history and pivotal artists of salsa music.
  - *www.shanachie.com/*
- **DVD:** *Latin Music U.S.A.*, various directors, PBS, 2009.
  - A documentary about the history and styles of Latin American music in the United States.
  - *www.pbs.org/wgbh/latinmusicusa/#/en*
- **DVD:** *The Mambo Kings*, directed by Arne Glimcher, Warner Brothers, 2005.
  - A fictional story about two brothers who are musicians, played by Armand Assante and Antonio Banderas. The film includes cameo appearances by Celia Cruz and Tito Puente.
  - *www.warnerbros.com/?page=movies/#/page=movies&pid=f-29562702/THE_MAMBO_KINGS&asset=058357/Mambo_Kings_The_-_Trailer_1&type=video/*
- **DVD:** *Buena Vista Social Club*, directed by Wim Wenders, Road Movies Production, 1997.
  - A documentary about the making of the *Buena Vista Social Club* album produced by Ry Cooder in Cuba.
  - *www.worldcircuit.co.uk/#Buena_Vista_Social_Club*
- **Book:** Fernandez, Raul A. *From Afro-Cuban Rhythms to Latin Jazz*. Berkeley: University of California Press, 2006.
  - A personable account of the history and experience of playing Latin jazz.
  - *www.ucpress.edu/books/pages/10358.php*
- **Book:** Lise Waxer, ed. *Situating Salsa: Global Markets and Local Meaning in Latin Popular Music.* New York: Routledge, 2002.
  - A collection of essays regarding the cultural and musical aspects of salsa music.
  - *www.routledge.com/books/Situating-Salsa-isbn9780815340201*
- **Book:** Flores, Juan. *From Bomba to Hip-Hop: Puerto Rican Culture and Latino Identity*. New York: Columbia University Press, 2000.
  - A thorough review of the Puerto Rican culture and musical activity in New York City.
  - *http://cup.columbia.edu/book/978-0-231-11076-1/from-bomba-to-hiphop*
- **Internet:** *www.grammy.com/latin/*
  - The Grammy Awards—Latin music Web site.
- **Internet:** *www.music.miami.edu/*
  - Web site of the Frost School of Music at the University of Miami.
- **Internet:** *www.gloriaestefan.com/cms/*
  - Gloria Estefan's official Web site.
- **Internet:** *www.salsa.com/*
  - An online resource to everything salsa.
- **Internet:** Gloria Estefan: Coming Out of the Dark
  - Gloria Estefan's 1991 performance at the American Music Awards.
- **Internet:** Tango Dancing: Rudolph Valentino
  - Excerpt of Rudolph Valentino dancing the tango in *The Four Horsemen of the Apocalypse* (1921).
- **Internet:** Salsa, Palladium Era
  - An excerpt from a documentary about Latin Music, highlighting the Palladium Ballroom era of the 1950s.

Keywords for Additional Music Examples

- Latin Pop Artists
  - Alejandro Sanz
  - Shakira
  - Ritchie Valens
  - Julio Iglesias
  - Enrique Iglesias
  - Selena
  - Jennifer Lopez
- Gloria Estefan and the Miami Sound Machine
- "The Loco-Motion," performed by Little Eva
- Christina Aguilera Spanish album
- Bandoneón tango music
- "Habanera," from the opera *Carmen*
- "Mi Noche Triste," performed by Carlos Gardel
- Nuevo tango artists
  - Ástor Piazzolla
  - Gotan Project
- Latin jazz artists
  - Tito Puente
  - Arsenio Rodríguez
  - Dizzy Gillespie (Keyword: Dizzy Latin)
  - Beny Moré
  - Desi Arnaz
- Nueva trova
  - Nueva Trova Silvio
- Salsa artists
  - Celia Cruz
  - Ruben Blades
- Cuban artists
  - Arturo Sandoval
  - Compay Segundo
  - Buena Vista Social Club
- Salsa styles and related genres
  - Plena Artists
    - César Concepción
    - Mon Rivera
    - Rafael Cortijo
  - Rumba
  - Charanga
  - Son
  - Son montuno
  - Mambo
  - Cha-cha-chá
  - Pachanga
  - Bomba
  - Salsa romántica
  - Salsa-erótica

- Bolero
- Merengue
- Cumbia
- Samba
- Boogaloo
- Salsatón
- Timba
- Tito Puente associations and collaborations
  - Noro Morales Orchestra
  - Celia Cruz
- Studio recording and cover versions of "Oye Como Va"
  - Studio version with "cha-cha-chá" handclaps.
    - Keywords: Oye Como Va Salsa Titres
  - Carlos Santana's rock version
    - Keywords: Oye Como Va Santana
  - Various styles
    - Keywords: Oye Como Va remixes
- African Salsa music
  - Papa Wemba (Jeancy)
  - Africando
- Timba
- Reggaeton
  - Origin of dem bow riddim
    - Dem Bow Shabba
  - Tego Calderón
  - Daddy Yankee
  - Don Omar
  - Bhangraton

Samba: The Sound of Brazil

INTRODUCTION

Brazil is the largest country in South America. Its interior is dominated by rainforests and the second longest river in the world, the Amazon, which has a greater volume of water flow than the Nile (Egypt), Mississippi (United States), Yangtze (China), and several other great rivers combined. Indigenous culture persists in the Amazon rainforests, while descendants of European (Portuguese) and African populations dominate the coastal cities.

Musical life in Brazil is vibrant and varied. Indigenous traditions continue to be the subject of much intrigue among anthropologists and linguists as well as ethnomusicologists. Such music, however, has minimal influence on the popular-music traditions emanating from within the country relative to its primary musical force: samba. Samba and its related genres represent Brazil's musical culture to the outside world and remain integral to the cultural identity of its population. We will explore the roots of this music and learn about some of its permutations that are now among the most recognized in popular world music.

MAXIXE AND CHORO

The predecessors of samba appeared in Rio de Janeiro during the 1800s. These were primarily art-music traditions associated with the Portuguese court. Among the era's most popular music was the polka (see Chapter 6), which fused with African-based dance styles to become known as *maxixe* (pronounced "mah-shish") and is regarded as an early form of samba.

The maxixe was popular in Brazil during the 1870s and eventually appeared as a ballroom dance in the United States during the early 1900s, promoted by Vernon and Irene Castle (see Chapter 2); it was sometimes referred to as the Brazilian tango. The dance is a walking two-step that includes a "studder" step before the second pulse, essentially a "polka" step. Maxixe was among the first Brazilian music-dance genres to find an international audience. A variety of maxixe styles emerged, which can be heard on early recordings in mediums as varied as acoustic guitar solos, string bands, marching bands, and even big-band jazz ensembles during the 1930s.

Paralleling the popularity of maxixe was *choro*, a small instrumental ensemble comprised of guitarlike instruments and a lead wind instrument, usually a flute or clarinet. At the turn of the century, choro was popular among street musicians and in Rio's bohemian cafés. The lead musician was considered to "cry" or "lament," hence the name of the genre (*choro* means "to cry" in Portuguese). By the turn of the century, the music was popular among local musicians, such as Alfredo da Rocha Vianna Filho (aka "Pixinguinha"; 1898–1973), an early choro composer and performer. The choro style at that time was quiet and intimate, with an improvisatory feel that highlighted the lead instrument's fluid melodic runs. Saxophones and other jazz instruments were gradually introduced, but vocalists and prominent percussion, common to choro today, were not featured in the early style. While choro was meant mainly for listening, it utilized a similar rhythmic syncopation found in the maxixe dance, that is, the "stutter" step, which is often linked to early samba music. The maxixe and choro styles, along with other traditional and popular dances at the turn of the century, became common music activities associated with the Carnival celebrations of Rio de Janeiro, which provided the original setting for samba.

EXPLORE MORE
on www.mymusickit.com
Interactive Globe

CARNIVAL (OR CARNAVAL)

Carnival festivals occur the world over but are particularly celebrated in the Caribbean and South America. (See Chapter 3 for the origins of Carnival.) The parallel to Carnival in the United States is Mardi Gras (French for "Fat Tuesday"), which is celebrated primarily in New Orleans, Louisiana. Although the festival is of European origin, two of the biggest celebrations today are found in Port of Spain, Trinidad, and Rio de Janeiro, Brazil. The event itself, and the music that permeates the celebration's activities, has become an integral part of the cultural identity of the peoples of both nations.

ESCOLAS DE SAMBA (SAMBA SCHOOLS)

The term *samba* derives from *semba*, a word that refers to the "belly bump" of the *batuque*, an African ritual dance from Angola transplanted to Brazil. Samba today describes a variety of musical styles, in much the same way that the term *jazz* identifies an array of music forms. Some of these include *samba rural* (rural samba), *samba de morro* (hill samba), *samba corrido* (verse samba), *samba choro* (choro samba), *samba da cidade* (city samba), and *samba canção* (song samba). We will focus on *samba enredo* (theme samba), which is one of the most important styles in Carnival celebrations.

At the turn of the nineteenth century, samba was not yet a solidified form. Earlier traditions, such as maxixe and choro, along with other folk styles were found together in the Carnival celebrations in Rio. The street parades were improvisatory and consisted primarily of participants with lower incomes dancing to loud percussion instruments and singing in a call-and-response manner.

Though musicologists continue to debate samba's specific origin, it is commonly recognized as spawning from the Rio *bairro* (neighborhood) known as "Little Africa." Dominated by former slaves and black business owners, this area thrived during the Carnival celebrations at the turn of the century. During the festivities, poorer participants, who normally resided on the hillside *favelas* (shanty towns) overlooking Rio proper, reinforced the number of revelers in this neighborhood to several times its normal population.

The predominantly European-descended establishment was disturbed by what they perceived as lewd dance activity emanating from "Little Africa," as well as the

Brazil's Sambadrome.

African-based polyrhythmic music performance, which they regarded as chaotic and loud. The result was frequent police raids to arrest *sambistas*, as the revelers were known. These circumstances are perhaps the impetus for the development of more organized neighborhood dance processions and the creation of the samba sound, which utilizes African polyrhythm but features a prominent two-beat pulse as its fundamental rhythm. The "orderly" music and dance attracted less criticism from the urban elite.

As samba came to dominate the musical activity of Carnival revelry in "Little Africa," a corresponding "shuffle step" dance evolved that today often includes extremely fast hip shaking, most often seen in female performance. The new samba rhythm and dance encouraged an organized group activity that led to the establishment of *escolas de samba* (samba schools). Over the years, these schools have evolved into the spectacular display of revelry, costumes, floats, and music that epitomizes Rio's Carnival celebrations.

Samba schools generally consist of members from the same community. Each school has a distinctive "theme" expressed through the costumes, dance, and lyrics of original music, known as *samba enredo* (theme samba), that plays during their Carnival procession. The subject of these themes is varied, ranging from historical events to Brazilian Indian mythology to modern politics and current social issues. Huge floats accompany the modern samba school processionals, the most famous venue being Rio's Sambadrome, a 65,000-seat arena built specifically to feature the Carnival samba schools. We will focus on the *bateria* that provides the rhythmic foundation for samba enredo, before exploring the melodic/harmonic elements that characterize the overall sound.

FOCUS EXAMPLE
ESCOLAS DE SAMBA

"A TODO VAPOR," PERFORMED BY *ESCOLA DE SAMBA NOCIDADE INDEPENDANTE DE PADRE MIGUEL*

((• HEAR MORE
Download the
iTunes playlist link on
MyMusicKit

Focal Points

- **Instruments:** A variety of percussion (see list that follows), most notably the *surdos* (bass drum) and *cuíca* (friction drum).
- **Timbre:** The cuíca drum "squeaks" throughout the performance.
- **Rhythm:** Listen for the incessant two-beat samba rhythm, complemented by a variety of polyrhythmic percussion.

TIME	DESCRIPTION
0:00–0:08	Performance begins with surdos (low drums), *chocalho* (cymbal-rattle), and two cuíca (friction drum).
0:09–0:20	*Repinique* (high-pitched drums) play improvised fills.
0:21–0:48	*Caixa* (snare drums) and *agogo* (double-bell) enter.
0:49–1:01	Cymbal crash and hi-hat heard, suggesting standard drum set is included.
1:02–1:37	Repinique return and join with caixa rhythm.
1:38–1:51	Tom-tom (pitched drums) fills from drum set.
1:52–3:32	*Bateria* performance continues. Cuíca become more active.

Samba schools consist of a variety of percussion instruments, collectively known as the **bateria**. These can include *surdos* (bass drum), *repinique* (high-pitched drum), *caixa* (snare drum), *tamborin* (frame drum), *pandiero* (tambourine), *agogo* (double-bell), *chocalho* (cymbal-rattle), *rêco-rêco* (scraped gourd), and *cuíca* (friction drum).

Bateria percussion
ensemble typical of a
samba school

Surdos and snare
drummers.

The samba rhythm follows a quick two-pulse pattern, derived from the habanera rhythm (see Chapter 4). In the street-parade samba, (*samba carnavalesca*), the surdos, a large drum, typically articulates this fundamental rhythm. A basic samba rhythm emphasizes each beat, but with a quick anticipation before the second pulse. If, for example, each beat is divided into four subbeats (sixteenth notes), the two-pulse pattern can be said as "One-ee-&-ah, Two-ee-&-ah." This consistent rhythm is played by the chocalho (cymbal-rattle) at the opening of the performance and articulated by other instruments, the caixa (snare drum) in particular. The rhythmically dense pattern provides a grounded subdivision of the beats, but with varying accents to add a syncopated feel.

The surdos plays a two-pulse pattern that anticipates the second beat by playing on the "ah" of the first beat: "One - - ah, Two - - -." This anticipation reinforces the second pulse, which has a higher tone than the low downbeat sounded on the first beat and anticipation. In performance, a surdos performer will use both a hand and a stick, or often two different sticks, to provide contrasting timbres. The first pulse is usually played with the heavier stick striking the center of the drum while the hand or lighter stick may play varied patterns anticipating the second pulse, generally by striking the rim of the drum.

((•● **HEAR MORE**
on www.mymusickit.com
Samba Rhythm

Chocalho/caixa	1	ee	&	ah	2	ee	&	ah	1	ee	&	ah	2	ee	&	ah
Agogo	x		X		X			x	x				X	X		
Surdos	x			x	X				x			x	X			

The surdos provides the fundamental samba rhythm as the chocalho and caixa provide a steady, rhythmically dense pulsation. The agogo (double-bell) contributes a middle density pattern, using various high/low patterns.

Surdos are found in different sizes and may vary the basic rhythm to make the music more interesting. As is typical of African-rooted polyrhythmic music, numerous other percussion instruments can be added. In our example, the agogo plays a prominent role, adding a rhythmic layer that has a middle degree of density. The high and low pattern is varied at different points in the performance, but the basic rhythm is outlined in the table above. Other percussion, as mentioned, may also contribute to the overall polyrhythmic structure.

While these instruments lay down the rhythmic foundation, the cuíca plays with a seemingly conversational improvisation. In this example, two such instruments play throughout the performance. The cuíca is a one-headed drum about 10 inches in diameter, with a frame of roughly 18 to 20 inches in depth. A stick made of bamboo or wood pierces the center of the drum face. This stick is then "rubbed" back and forth to create friction against the membrane, which produces sound. The performer's free hand presses on the drum face to change the membrane's tension and, consequently, the frequencies of sounds produced. The result is an easily identified "squeaky" timbre, often changing pitch as if to "speak." The cuíca is not heard in all samba styles. However, because it is infrequently heard in other genres of popular world music, its presence is one of the key markers for recognizing a performance as being Brazilian samba.

As samba schools came to dominate the Carnival activities, the middle and upper classes of Brazilian society became increasingly interested in the music for their own interests. Brazil became a republic in 1889, with slavery having been abolished only a year earlier. For the next forty years, the country prospered due to increasing immigration, industrialization, and exploration of natural resources.

Gold, cattle, and coffee were major exports, and the United States became Brazil's primary trading partner. In 1929, when the American stock market crashed, so too did the economy of Brazil. A political climate of distrust ensued as an increasingly influential middle class voiced their discontent with political corruption and the fledgling state of the economy.

SAMBA ENREDO (THEME SAMBA)

Backed by the population and militaries of several Brazilian states, in 1930 Getúlio Vargas (1882–1954) deposed the allegedly fraudulently elected presidential candidate, Washington Luiz, initiating a new era of government influence on civilian life. Officially elected as president in 1934, Vargas took advantage of growing fears of Nazi and Communist expansion to support his establishment of an authoritarian government by declaring an *Estado Novo* ("New State") in 1937.

Fundamental to the Estado Novo was the perception that, in the eyes of the new government, all Brazilians were equal: A Brazilian patriot could be from any racial, social, or economic background. The Carnival celebrations were an ideal setting to promote this new image since the festivities were traditionally considered a time when people of all classes and races set aside their differences to enjoy the revelry before **Lent**. Already a common feature of Carnival, samba became the "national music" of Brazil thanks to its appeal to the widest population. The samba street processions were a primary vehicle for promoting Vargas's new ideology. The government subsidized samba schools to pay for costumes and instruments, provided they incorporate themes that promoted the nationalist agenda.

> **Lent**   period preceding Easter in the Christian calendar

FOCUS EXAMPLE
SAMBA ENREDO (THEME SAMBA)

"AQUARELA BRASILEIRA," COMPOSED BY ARY BARROSO
AND PERFORMED BY DOMINGUINHOS DO ESTÁCIO,
NEGUINHO DA BEIJA-FLOR, PIRES, AND RIXXA

Focal Points

- **Language/Lyrics:** Portuguese. Lyrics tend toward nationalist themes.
- **Vocals:** Lead male vocalist and group sung melody.
- **Instruments:** Bateria and melodic chordophones from the guitar family, such as the *cavaquinho* (a small four-stringed guitar).
- **Melody/Harmony:** Extended melody with harmonic accompaniment.
- **Rhythm:** Samba rhythm provided by a bateria.

TIME	DESCRIPTION
0:00–0:21	Introduction and "La, la, la, ai" choral opening.
0:22–2:05	Two male vocalists exchange lead. Note the *cavaquinho* accompaniment.
2:06–2:20	Reveler chorus joins lead vocalists on the last stanza.
2:21–2:34	"La, la, la, ai" choral opening returns.
2:35–4:31	Samba school sings as a group on the final stanza.
4:32–5:00	"La, la, la, ai" choral opening repeated until the end. Note that the bateria drops the samba rhythm until 4:46.

Samba enredo (theme samba) utilizes the bateria of samba carnavalesca but also includes sung text with harmonic accompaniment. Each samba school has its own theme music that has been selected by the school's leaders after weeks of deliberation. This theme song plays an important role in the judging of the samba-school contests during Carnival. Having a "hit" song for the year's festivities encourages favorable reviews for the entire school and can bring fame and fortune to the song's composer and/or the **puxador** (lead singer).

Puxador   lead vocalist of the samba school processions at Carnival in Rio de Janeiro

Samba enredo includes the bateria percussionists as well as vocalists and melody/harmony instruments. The majority of the latter instruments are usually from the guitar family, such as the *viola* (a guitar with five single or double courses of strings), the *violão* (Portuguese for the common six-stringed guitar), *cavaquinho* (a small four-stringed guitar), and *bandolim* (a small high-ranged mandolin with four double courses of strings). Though infrequent today, brass band instruments, such as cornets and tubas, known as *bombardinos*, are sometimes heard in samba enredo, revealing the early influence that marching band music played on the samba street parades.

Important to the samba enredo is the narrative text, which is often organized in call-and-response form. The lead vocalist (*puxador*) "tells the story," and the group response can include hundreds of revelers singing in harmony or with a unison melody. In our Focus Example, two male vocalists exchange the lead melody to the accompaniment of a cavaquinho and the bateria. The chorus of revelers joins in on the final stanza (2:06) before repeating the entire song in unison.

Lyrical content varies in subject matter, but many samba enredo focus on nationalist themes that promote Brazilian identity or relate to Carnival activities. Our Focus Example, "Aquarela Brasileira," was written by Ary Barroso (1903–1964), one of Brazil's most famous composers. The lyrics evoke romantic images of Brazil's most

Cavaquinho

famous locales and everyday scenes, mentioning Carnival, beautiful islands and beaches, magical nights of music, grand cities, luscious rainforests, and an eclectic racial mix of people. The intent is to encourage listeners to take pride in being Brazilian and to celebrate the country's many wondrous attributes. While other samba styles are often critical of the government and other social institutions, the context for samba enredo generally avoids such social commentary in concession to the celebratory atmosphere of the festival. This is especially true of Barroso's songs, such as "Aquarela do Brasil," (a different song from our Focus Example) his most famous piece and the unofficial anthem of Brazil, which was composed during the promotion of Vargas's Estado Novo policies.

Samba enredo is performed primarily during Carnival, but the advent of radio prompted a new style of samba that could be heard year-round and without the specific festival association. Since its primary means of dissemination was the radio, the music was aimed at a listening audience, rather than a dancing one. The lyrical content and melodic features took precedence over the percussive sound of the street sambas.

Samba canção (song samba), as this new style was known, often features a slower tempo, with the cavaquinho and other melodic instruments playing a more obvious role. The samba canção emerged during the Vargas era of the 1930s and 1940s as many performers were contracted to perform on national radio, with the expectation that they would promoted the Estado Novo initiatives.

CARMEN MIRANDA

Among the stars to encourage the nationalist spirit promoted by the new government was Carmen Miranda (1909–1955), likely the most internationally recognized Brazilian performer of the twentieth century. Born in Portugal, she spent her youth in Rio de Janeiro, Brazil, attending school and singing for parties and festivals. At one time, she operated a successful hat shop, an interest that undoubtedly spawned the iconic fruit and flower hats that she donned for her many movies and concert performances.

By her early twenties, Miranda had achieved a modicum of fame as a radio star in Brazil, and by 1930 she had earned a recording contract with RCA/Victor Records. Throughout the 1930s, she appeared in several Brazilian films, among them *Alô Alô Brasil!* (1935) and *Banana da Terra* (1939). By the end of the decade, she traveled to the United States with her band, Bando da Lua, to perform on Broadway, where she met with immediate success. The following year she began her American film career, starring in *Down Argentine Way* (1940), which initiated a string of films throughout the decade. She was soon the highest-paid female entertainer in the United States, a distinction she held for several years, earning more than $200,000 in 1945 alone.

Amid her successful film career, Miranda performed nonstop around the globe and was known as the "Bombshell of Brazil." Her extensive touring and the weight of success ultimately took its toll, and she battled against depression with drugs, alcohol, and even electroshock therapy. She suffered a heart attack on August 5, 1955, after filming a television episode for *The Jimmy Durante Show*, and died later that night.

Miranda's legacy is fraught with controversy. During her lifetime, fellow Brazilians often criticized her as being a sellout to the American music and movie industry. Her Hollywood image was considered outlandish, and her music was disparaged as being ambiguously Latin, drawing from too many styles to represent a distinctive Brazilian sound. Although her American film debut was well received in the United States, the movie flopped in Brazil and was banned in Argentina for its "ridiculous" portrayal of the country.

Carmen Miranda, ca. 1940.

Miranda was well aware of such controversies, addressing her image in songs such as "Disseram Que Eu Voltei Americanizada" ("They Say I've Come Back Americanized") and "Bananas Is My Business." The tensions (and likely her busy work schedule) kept her away from Brazil for more than a decade after leaving for the United States in 1940. Her detractors, however, could not argue with her popularity, even in Brazil. Nearly half a million people attended her funeral procession through Rio de Janeiro, and the Brazilian government declared a period of national mourning. A museum dedicated to her opened in Rio in 1976, and in 1998 Hollywood honored her with "Carmen Miranda Square," along with a star on the Hollywood "Walk of Fame."

BOSSA NOVA

By the late 1950s, samba canção had acquired a softer sound that reflected the interests of a growing middle class. No longer wanting to be labeled a "developing" nation, many Brazilians sought a new cultural image portraying sophistication, affluence, and romance. Musicians were also looking for a new way to express their creativity without abandoning their musical heritage. Bossa nova fulfilled this desire, with its whispering vocals, stuttering guitar, and melancholy atmosphere, conjuring images of firelight and friends stargazing on the beaches of Ipanema (a neighborhood in south Rio de Janeiro), where the music was born.

In a few short years, *bossa nova*, meaning "the new trend," found audiences throughout Brazil, South America, the Caribbean, and the United States. Its originators, Antônio Carlos Jobim (1927–1994), Vinicius de Moraes (1913–1980), and João Gilberto (b. 1931), set out to create a music rooted in the samba tradition, but with an intimate feel better suited for the area's rising number of nightclubs than the large big-band halls typical of samba canção and other music of previous decades. Their first recording, *Chega de Saudade* (1958), often translated as "No More Blues," remains one of the most popular bossa nova recordings.

After the album's release, bossa nova musicians and recordings quickly became popular throughout Rio de Janeiro and, within a few short years, rivaled the success of the samba-canção artists and other recordings from within Brazil and imported from the United States. Vital to its international success was the 1963 album *Jazz Samba*, a collaborative recording by guitarist Charlie Byrd (1925–1999) and saxophonist Stan Getz (1927–1991). Byrd had earlier traveled to Brazil on a state department tour of South America, where he first heard the bossa nova sound.

Jazz Samba (1963) introduced bossa nova to American audiences and is one of the best-selling jazz albums of all time. Its success brought attention to several Brazilian artists, João Gilberto and his wife, Astrud Gilberto (b. 1940), in particular. The Gilbertos, along with Antônio Carlos Jobim, collaborated with Getz on the album *Getz/Gilberto* (1964), which represents the "peak" of the bossa nova craze in the United States. This album includes the international hit song "Garota de Ipanema (Girl from Ipanema)," which is one of the most covered jazz recordings in history.

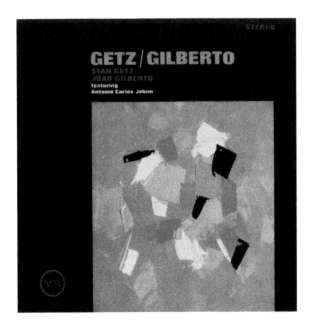

Cover of the famous *Getz/Gilberto* album.

FOCUS EXAMPLE
BOSSA NOVA

"GIRL FROM IPANEMA," PERFORMED BY JOÃO GILBERTO, ASTRUD GILBERTO, AND STAN GETZ. MUSIC BY ANTÔNIO CARLOS JOBIM. LYRICS BY VINICIUS DE MORAES

Focal Points

- **Voice:** Single male then female voice with intimate vocal delivery.
- **Instruments:** Saxophone, guitar, piano, acoustic bass, drum set with "brush" sticks.
- **Language/Lyrics:** Portuguese and English lyrics with romantic themes.
- **Melody/Harmony:** Lyrical, but often dissonant, melody over complex jazz harmonies.
- **Rhythm:** Bossa nova rhythm characterized by interlocking bass line and guitar/piano chords.
- **Form:** (AABA) The piece uses two sections of melodic material.

TIME	DESCRIPTION
0:00–0:06	Introduction, with guitar playing bossa nova rhythm.
0:07–0:21	First verse: Male voice sings in Portuguese (Form: A section).
0:22–0:36	Remaining instruments enter. Note the "samba rhythm" bass line and steady hi-hat pattern.
0:37–1:06	Harmony shifts to emphasize minor chords (B section).
1:07–1:21	Return to opening melodic material emphasizing major chords (A section).
1:22–2:34	Female vocalist sings with English lyrics.
2:35–3:47	Saxophone improvised solo.
3:48–4:16	Piano improvised solo.
4:17–5:00	Female vocalist returns with saxophone improvisations.
5:01–5:23	Vamp to end.

The hallmark of bossa nova is the consistent "stutter" of the guitar, which subtly interplays with the melodic line and subdued samba rhythm of the acoustic bass. The guitar chords sound on the first, second, and last half of the third beat, supplying the "new trend" rhythm, while the traditional samba rhythm is grounded by a bass line on the first and third beats of a four-beat measure. A subtle kick drum sometimes sounds this latter rhythm as well (though not in this example), reminding the listener that the surdos plays this pattern in the more vibrant styles of Carnival samba. The quiet hi-hat cymbals substitute for the chocalho and caixa instruments playing the steady subdivisions of the beat, while the piano adds subtle melodic responses to the voice.

Bossa Nova Rhythm

	1		2		3		4	
"Bossa Nova" Guitar	X		X			X		
"Samba Rhythm" (Bass)	X			(X)	X			
Hi-Hat cymbals	x	x	x	x	x	x	x	X

((•● **HEAR MORE**
on www.mymusickit.com
Bossa Nova Rhythm

The overall tempo of bossa nova is slower than that of other samba styles. Percussion instruments are minimized, if present at all, and soft brushes, rather than sticks, are commonly used to play the drum set.

The vocal melodies for bossa nova are usually quite lyrical, moving to different pitches, rather than continually repeating the same pitch in a rhythmic fashion. These melodies often move through the pitches utilized in the complex harmonies provided by the guitar or piano. These harmonies are often chromatic or employ chords common to jazz music, such as major sevenths, flatted ninths, or diminished/augmented harmonies.

Bossa nova ensembles tend to be small to reflect the music's intimate character. If a vocalist is not present, a "soft" instrument, such as a flute or saxophone, typically plays the melody. Certainly, there are arrangements of bossa nova compositions for larger ensembles, especially classical Muzak covers of famous songs such as this one, but the idea of a loud, bombastic bossa nova is contrary to the musical spirit of the genre.

Although the harmony is complex, a definite shift in tone can be heard between the opening melodic material (Form: A) and the middle passage (Form: B), which shifts to emphasizing minor chords. The melody, as well as the lyrics, reflects this change in mood by using a sustained pitch at the beginning of each phrase in the middle section, where the male subject broods over the indifference of the woman he admires. Even without understanding Portuguese, the listener can feel the transition from the appreciation of the woman's beauty (0:07) to the sorrow of the male protagonist (0:37) and back again to the girl walking along the beach (1:07).

The Portuguese lyrics, sung by João Gilberto, shift from first to third person when sung by his wife, Astrud, due to the story line of a man watching a young girl stroll down Ipanema beach. The 45-rpm version omits the Portuguese verses and shortens the saxophone solo to make the song more radio-friendly for American audiences. This version became a huge hit in the United States, reaching #5 on the popular-music charts, and was successful in other overseas markets as well.

The saxophone solo begins by stating the main vocal line but then embellishes the melody. The ornamentations are subtle throughout the solo, keeping the mood intimate through a complete runthrough of the verse. The shorter piano solo also adheres closely to the main theme but uses chords, rather than a single-pitched melody. The vocalist returns along with the saxophone at the "sadder" middle section (B) before the piece moves into the closing material.

The "Girl from Ipanema" remains the signature song of the bossa nova catalog. Numerous artists have recorded covers, often changing the lyrics to "Boy from Ipanema" when sung by a female performer. For anyone who has strolled the beaches of Brazil, changing the gender roles loses the cultural flavor of the country, which holds great admiration for the female form. Americans may perceive this idea as chauvinistic, but Brazilians generally accept machismo as an expected personality trait of men, certainly in a seaside setting where slender women regularly wear thong bikinis and men of all shapes and sizes sport Speedo-style swimsuits.

TROPICÁLIA

The year 1964 marked an important turning point in Brazil's musical as well as political history. While bossa nova retained a following throughout the decade, the "British Invasion," initiated by the Beatles in 1964, captured most of the general public's musical interest on a global scale. Brazil's economy had faltered since the start of the 1960s, and growing fears of leftist radical revolution prompted the military to seize power. From 1964 to 1985, the military's influence over government affairs amounted to an authoritarian state.

By the late 1960s, growing discontent with the government encouraged many artists to voice their criticisms through music and art. This movement became known as *tropicália* (or *tropicalismo*) and was inspired by ideas originating from the writings of Oswald de Andrade (1890–1954), a Brazilian author and poet. Andrade considered Brazil's greatest cultural assets to be its "cannibalistic" creations, which drew from various sources to form uniquely Brazilian art and ideology in the postcolonial period.

Music of the tropicália trend drew from an eclectic variety of sources, combining contemporary music genres, including bossa nova, rock, and even psychedelic influences, with folk music rooted in indigenous, Portuguese, and African traditions. Politically defiant and socially conscious lyricism was also a feature. By the late 1960s, criticism of the government was rarely tolerated by military leaders, forcing many outspoken artists to seek exile. Among these were the leaders of the tropicália movement—Caetano Veloso (b. 1942) and Gilberto Gil (b. 1942), who were briefly jailed in 1969 and then fled to London. Their departure marked the end of the tropicália period. They returned to Brazil in 1972, when amnesty was granted to all musicians. Ironically, Gil became Brazil's Minister of Culture in 2003, and today both he and Veloso are considered international cultural and musical icons.

MPB (MÚSICA POPULAR BRASILEIRA) AND BEYOND

Though tropicália was short-lived, upon their return to Brazil Veloso and Gil found themselves at the forefront of MPB (Música Popular Brasileira). This "new" label for Brazilian popular music had its roots in the Vargas era of the 1930s, when national radio was used to promote regional music styles of diverse populations and cultural backgrounds into a single unified Brazilian national identity. The acronym resurfaced in the mid-1960s as regional music and artists were again highlighted on national radio and television broadcasts.

From the 1970s to 1990s, MPB came to represent the great variety of popular music-making by artists throughout Brazil, though primarily those from its major urban centers in the states of Rio de Janeiro, São Paulo, Minas Gerais, and Bahia. Salvador, the capital of Bahia, and its surrounding areas spawned the largest number of successful artists, including Gil and Veloso and João and Astrud Gilberto. Later artists, such as Margareth Menezes (b. 1962), Daniela Mercury (b. 1965), and the heavy percussion-based group Olodum, had their roots in Bahia and continue to be successful performers today.

By the late 1980s, American rock, funk, and jazz music had influenced much of the evolving Brazilian popular sound, resulting in an array of artistic styles categorized generically as MPB. Basic to most of these was the continued use of the samba rhythm and multilayered percussion, either subdued or in the forefront. The compilation albums *Brazilian Classics: Volumes 1 & 2*, produced by Luaka Bop, an independent label founded by rock artist David Byrne of the Talking Heads, were released in 1989 and 1990, respectively. These albums proved enormously successful internationally, and they reacquainted American and European audiences with the sumptuous sounds of Brazilian popular musicians, such as Clara Nunes ("The Queen of Samba"; 1943–1983) and Chico Buarque (b. 1944). The series has continued through seven volumes, highlighting many Brazilian artists from the 1980s and into the twenty-first century.

The music of Bahia has continued to play a prominent role in Brazil's popular-music scene. Afro-Brazilian styles, such as *axé* and *lambada* (which is more of a dance style than a specific music genre), have found some success internationally. Female vocalists such as Ivete Sangalo (b. 1972), Virginia Rodrigues (b. 1964), and Marisa Monte (b. 1967) have achieved the widest appeal, though several seasoned male veterans, such as Gilberto Gil and Caetano Veloso, continue to create and perform with

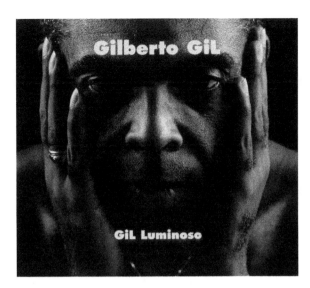

Gilberto Gil, one of the founders of MPB (Música Popular Brasileira).

great success. Regional music is vibrant, and established traditions, such as *forró* (an accordion-based music), find audiences along with many folk genres that frequently adapt to modern music aesthetics, such as *bumba-meu-boi, capoeira,* and *candomblé.* Reggae, rap, and hip-hop have their Brazilian counterparts, but samba continues to infiltrate and inspire the newest artists and styles emanating from Rio de Janeiro and elsewhere throughout the country.

SUMMARY

In this chapter, we familiarized ourselves with some of the most prominent popular music emanating from Brazil. After a brief introduction to maxixe and choro, we focused on the musical activity associated with one of the world's biggest celebrations, Carnival. We listened to the music of the escolas de samba that take center stage during the festival, the samba enredo (theme samba) in particular, before moving to more radio-friendly music styles, including samba canção and bossa nova. We also became acquainted with many of Brazil's most prominent performers, especially Carmen Miranda, and wrapped up our overview with musical trends since the 1970s, namely tropicália and MPB (Música Popular Brasileira).

LEARN MORE
on www.mymusickit.com
Chapter summary
and exam

Pathways

- **Book:** Perrone, Charles A., and Christopher Dunn, eds. *Brazilian Popular Music and Globalization.* New York: Routledge, 2002.
  - A collection of essays by scholars and musicians about popular-music styles in Brazil.
- **DVD:** *Carmen Miranda: Bananas Is My Business,* directed by Helena Solberg, 1994. (Also available on iTunes.)
  - A documentary about the life of Brazilian actress/singer Carmen Miranda. Highly recommended.
- **DVD:** *The Spirit of Samba.* From the *Beats of the Heart* series, produced by Shanchie, 2001.
  - A documentary film from the 1980s about samba music and culture.
- **DVD:** *Carnaval,* produced by Televista, 2006.
  - A documentary from the 1980s about the Carnaval experience in Rio.

- **Book:** Veloso, Caetano. *Tropical Truth: A Story of Music and Revolution in Brazil.* Da Capo Press, 2003.
  - An autobiography written by one of the legends of tropicália and MPB music.
- **Internet:** *www.brazilianbeats.info/*
  - Fan Web site for the Brazilian Beats series, dedicated to the traditional and popular music of Brazil.
- **Internet:** *www.justbrazil.org/*
  - A tourist-oriented Web site that includes extensive information about a variety of Brazilian-related topics.

Keywords for Additional Musical Examples

- Maxixe
- Choro
  - Pixinguinha
- Samba-carnavalesca
- Samba enredo
  - "Aquarela do brasil"
- Bossa nova
  - Chega de Saudade
  - "Boy from Ipanema"
- Tropicália
- MPB (Música Popular Brasileira) artists
  - Margareth Menezes
  - Daniela Mercury
  - Olodum
  - Clara Nunes
  - Chico Buarque
  - Ivete Sangalo
  - Virginia Rodrigues
  - Marisa Monte
- Forró [Ruiz]
- Brazilian folk music
  - Bumba-meu-boi
  - Capoeira
  - Candomblé

CHAPTER 6

Euro-Pop and Folk Fusions

INTRODUCTION

Popular "world music" in Europe falls into two basic categories: Euro-pop or folk fusions. The former is today primarily a dance-oriented genre that is variously defined to include popular music from Continental Europe only, Continental Europe and the United Kingdom, and sometimes popular music from non-European countries that have historically been governed by a European power, such as Australia. The Euro-pop style rarely draws from the ethnic roots of the performers or its primary audience, instead opting for predictable instrumentation of electronic keyboards, guitars, and drums, with a formulaic melody and repetitive refrains.

Folk fusions may also include such instrumentation but purposefully draw from local traditions, using instruments, melodies, forms, or other recognizable features considered traditional, such as associated dance choreography or costume. Extracting the folk elements of a fusion tradition is sometimes difficult because the sound may bear little resemblance to the nonpopularized predecessors. In other cases, the new sound of a folk music can be viewed as an evolution in the development of the tradition itself.

In this chapter, we explore both Euro-pop and folk fusions. We begin with the Eurovision Song Contest, a popular musical competition that includes a great variety of both popular and folk music. We will look briefly at two performance groups that directly benefited from Eurovision to achieve international fame: ABBA and Riverdance. ABBA represents the Euro-pop sound and was hugely successful at crossing over to the mainstream music industry during the 1970s. In contrast, the Riverdance phenomenon of the early 1990s is a folk fusion that fits more clearly into the notion of a popular world music, although some would argue that it merely represents an evolving folk music that has been popularized. We then turn to music artists and genres that have a clear folk connection. Though many such styles exist, we will concentrate on a few familiar types, namely, Celtic music, flamenco, polka, and klezmer, all of which are well known throughout the world. We will also take a brief look at *fado*, a song style from Portugal that fits less comfortably in either the folk fusion or Euro-pop category.

⊙➤ **EXPLORE MORE**
on www.mymusickit.com
Interactive Globe

EUROVISION AND EURO-POP

In 1956, the European Broadcasting Union (EBU), based in Switzerland, aired a live transnational television program called *The Eurovision Grand Prix*. An ambitious project for the early days of television, the program sought to encourage a spirit of (Western) European unity in a post–World War II period, when Cold War tensions were mounting due to the Warsaw Pact of 1955. The participating countries were from among those in which the EBU broadcast, including Switzerland (the host country), France, Germany, Italy, the Netherlands, Belgium, and Luxembourg.

Each country, represented by an EBU affiliate broadcaster, entered two songs to be performed live during the competition. Initially, the idea was that the song entries would be sung twice by different interpreters, so that the focus would be on the song itself, rather than on the musicians performing it. This stipulation was eliminated, however, and in succeeding years each country has been limited to just one song and a single performance. Although the initial Eurovision contest was primarily heard over the radio, the program was aired to an estimated four million televisions across the European continent and the United Kingdom. The first victory went to the host country (Switzerland) for the song "Refrain," performed by Lys Assia (b. 1926). The judging was done secretly, and modern enthusiasts of the contest sometimes speculate about the fairness of the voting since the judges from Luxembourg were unable to attend and were replaced by Swiss nationals.

Eurovision, as the contest is known today, expanded its participant roster over the next several years and has continued to grow as the EBU has spread throughout Europe and into countries bordering the Mediterranean Sea. It draws an international viewing audience estimated between 100 and 600 million people. In addition, it has been broadcast via the Internet since 2000, with a growing audience of nearly 74,000 in 2006. Many of the songs from throughout the contest's history can easily be downloaded from the official Eurovision Web site or other sites, including iTunes.

A hallmark of the contest is the annual relocation of the broadcast venue to the previous year's winning country. Though the invitation to host is not always accepted, the increased international exposure, especially for smaller nations, spurs a strong sense of national pride and a favorable economic boon. In anticipation of the broadcast, many countries air preliminary song contests in order to choose their final Eurovision entry. Though the winning songwriters receive no monetary award, a trophy is customarily presented and the nation gets "bragging rights" until the next year's contest.

The contest's submission rules have changed over the years. Initially, only solo performers, backed by a house orchestra, were allowed to enter. For the first Eurovision broadcast, rock music was in its infancy and the pan-European appeal of an orchestral sound, in contrast to regional folk-music traditions, supported the transnational aims of the contest's creators. A significant stipulation also limited performers to only a soloist or a duet. Perhaps an effort to keep the focus on the song, this rule excluded music written and/or performed by groups, which was commonplace in mainstream popular music during the 1960s (e.g., the Beatles). Furthermore, rock music was still considered an American import by the European mainstream establishment, whereas classical traditions reflected the pan-European heritage of the contest's participants.

Swedish superstars ABBA.

Nevertheless, rock music influences became apparent by the mid-1960s as the use of electronic instruments increased and backing percussion played a more prominent role in a growing number of entries. The restriction on group performances was lifted in 1970, but the majority of entrants still followed the traditional model of a single artist with backing orchestral sound, either live or with electronic synthesizers. When the Swedish quartet ABBA won the 1974 contest with "Waterloo," songwriters and musicians began to rethink the possibilities of a group performance succeeding in the Eurovision competition. Solo performances are still most common, but group entries are now popular as well.

Songs performed for Eurovision have varied widely, from romantic ballads to peppy dance tunes, with the former style being the predominant winner in the current era. As mentioned, early contests focused heavily on the "song" aspect, rather than on music that was danceable; after all, the contest was initially intended as a songwriting competition. By the 1970s, however, rock-music influences had become integral to the entries. Before winning in 1974, ABBA had found success the year before, when they finished third with their entry, "Ring Ring." By claiming the top spot a year later, the group was able to turn their Eurovision victory into a global phenomenon.

The popularity of ABBA's "Waterloo" spread throughout Europe as more than just a Eurovision entry, topping the British pop music charts and rising to No. 6 on Billboard's Hot 100 list in the United States. Few predicted that ABBA would have lasting popularity, but a string of hits throughout the 1970s propelled them to international superstardom: "Dancing Queen" (No. 1, U.K. and U.S.), "Mamma Mia" (No. 1 U.K., No. 32 U.S.), "Fernando" (No. 1 U.K., No. 13 U.S.), "Knowing Me, Knowing You" (No. 1 U.K., No. 14 U.S.), "The Name of the Game" (No. 1 U.K., No. 12 U.S.), and "Take a Chance on Me" (No. 1 U.K., No. 3 U.S.).

FOCUS EXAMPLE
EURO-POP

((• **HEAR MORE**
Download the
iTunes playlist link on
MyMusicKit

"WATERLOO," PERFORMED BY ABBA

Focal Points

- **Language:** Though English is most common in Euro-pop, any European language may be found.
- **Lyrics:** Emphasis on romantic love themes and dancing.
- **Instruments:** Various rock-band instruments (synthesizers, electric guitars, electric bass, drum set or drum machine, saxophones, trumpets, etc.). A "string" effect created by live musicians or synthesizer is common. Other electronic sounds are a common feature of Euro-pop since the 1980s, as are electronically processed vocals.
- **Melody:** A memorable hook melody that corresponds to the repeated refrain.
- **Harmony:** Simple harmony, usually emphasizing major keys.
- **Rhythm:** Steady dance beat.

TIME	DESCRIPTION
0:00–0:05	Introduction.
0:06–0:28	First Verse.
0:29–1:04	"Waterloo" refrain.
1:05–1:27	Second verse.
1:28–2:43	"Waterloo" refrain to end.

The instrumental introduction establishes the song's tempo and tonal center. The lyrics refer to the military defeat of Napoleon Bonaparte (1769–1821) at the Battle of Waterloo in 1815, suggesting that the song's main character was similarly destined to "surrender" to her lover. Such romantic relationships are typical themes of Euro-pop songs, which avoid weighty social commentary on topics such as religion, politics, poverty, and the like.

The accompanying instruments are common to rock bands, including electric bass, electric guitar, piano, and drum set. The harmony throughout uses primarily major chords, except the third line, "The history book … " (0:20), which uses a minor harmony emphasized by the descending piano fills. Major keys predominate in Euro-pop dance songs, which are usually intended to encourage a celebratory atmosphere, though ballads about unrequited love will often use minor keys.

The addition of the saxophone fills and hand claps (0:29) to reinforce the beat give the refrain contrast compared to the verse sections. A strong melodic hook that repeats the title several times helps to embed the song into the listener's memory. This is typical of popular songs in general, but is a particularly emphasized compositional tool in the music business, where a song must have immediate appeal in order to sell to a mass audience. This hook technique is common to mainstream pop songs performed by American-industry icons, such as current pop diva Britney Spears (b. 1981), as well as Euro-pop stars, such as the 1990s Swedish sensation Ace of Base. Oftentimes, the average listener does not know the lyrics of the verse, but regularly sings along with the vocal refrain, which is repeated often, especially toward the end of the song.

Though ABBA disbanded in 1982, their music continues to sell well around the globe, totaling more than 200 million copies sold since their first release, making them second only to the Beatles and a handful of solo artists. Their songs, along with those of the Bee Gees and a few other late 1970s super-groups, provided the soundtrack for the disco era, which, although much derided, continues to reflect the music industry's mainstream objectives of providing enjoyable, danceable music to a mass audience. Disco's cultural impact has resonated with modern audiences, too, who often make light of the fashions and frivolity associated with this period in popular music history.

In 1999, two of ABBA's members, Benny Andersson and Björn Ulvaeus, created the hit musical *Mamma Mia!*, modifying several ABBA songs for the soundtrack, which has encouraged a new generation of audiences to discover the group's music. The 2008 film version, starring Meryl Streep (b. 1949) and Pierce Brosnan (b. 1953), was the highest-grossing movie musical in history. An ABBA museum is currently under construction in Stockholm, Sweden, and will no doubt become a pilgrimage site for the group's die-hard fans worldwide.

Aside from ABBA, few Eurovision winners have achieved much fame beyond the contest itself. Most notable is Céline Dion (b. 1968), who in 1988 sang the winning song, "Ne Partez Pas Sans Moi," for Switzerland, even though she is a Canadian citizen. (Contest rules allow non-nationals to represent a country's song entry.) In 2006 the Finnish power metal band Lordi broke new ground by winning with "Hard Rock Hallelujah." One group that has achieved international acclaim due to Eurovision is Riverdance.

CELTIC POPULAR MUSIC

For the 1994 Eurovision song contest, Riverdance was not a competing group but a troupe of dancers that performed during the interval between the song performances and the presentation of the voting results. The Riverdance troupe capitalized on the acclaim they received after the Eurovision broadcast and, a year later, presented a full-length musical production in Dublin, Ireland. They performed to sold-out crowds for five weeks straight, and the show had successful runs in other cities throughout Europe and in the United States. Due to the popularity of the onstage production, the Irish step-dancing featured throughout has since become known colloquially as "Riverdancing" in the United States and elsewhere.

EXPLORE MORE
on www.mymusickit.com
Interactive Globe

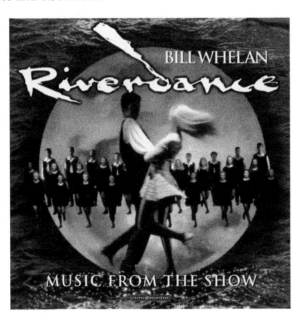

Poster for the popular production, *Riverdance*.

Although the Eurovision entries can infrequently be labeled "traditional" music, the Riverdancing phenomenon is a reflection of the wider interest in Celtic folk music and culture that peaked internationally during the 1980s and 1990s. Irish performers won Eurovision five times from 1987 to 1997, including a record three years in a row from 1992 to 1994. Meanwhile, in mainstream popular culture many Irish music groups became internationally known, in particular the rock band U2, and several successful movies focused on topics relevant to Irish and/or Scottish life, past and present, such as *The Commitments* (1991), *Braveheart* (1995), and *The Devil's Own* (1997).

The 1992 Ron Howard film *Far and Away*, starring Tom Cruise and Nicole Kidman, featured an English version of the song "Book of Days," by the Irish singer/songwriter Eithne Bhraonáin (Brennan) (b. 1961), better known as Enya, who had achieved widespread popularity through her modern renderings of Irish folk music, along with newly composed works, on the multiplatinum-selling albums *Watermark* (1988) and *Shepherd Moon* (1991). The latter received a Grammy award in 1993 for "Best New Age Album," an honor she won again in 1997 for *The Memory of Trees* (1995), in 2002 for *A Day Without Rain* (2000), and most recently in 2007 for *Amarantine* (2005). Although Enya's music is labeled "New Age" rather than "world music" by the industry, she is a good example of the progression many popular world-music artists pursue in their quest to reach a wider audience.

Born into a musical family, Enya spent much of her childhood performing Irish folk music together with her eight siblings, parents, and extended family. Her mother taught music at an Irish-speaking elementary school, and her father was leader of a successful band before opening a family pub in 1968 in a small village in northwestern Ireland. The pub provided a regular venue for the children to develop their performance skills while playing traditional music and pop-song covers.

Three of Enya's older siblings and two of their uncles initiated the Brennan family's success in the record industry by winning a local folk festival competition and receiving a contract to record an album, which was released in 1973. Calling themselves Clannad, an abbreviation of the Gaelic *An Clann As Dobhar* (The Family from Dore), the group was strongly rooted in folk performance and recorded songs in both English and Irish Gaelic. Succeeding albums during the 1970s strengthened their commitment to Irish traditional music and earned them a growing reputation throughout the British Isles that extended to the European continent as well.

Irish folk-fusion group Clannad.

In 1982, the group was invited to compose the theme for a British-produced television program called *Harry's Game.* The song marked a transition in Clannad's musical development, for they took advantage of recording-studio layering techniques and synthesizers to create an ethereal sound that sparked a more successful international career. Sung entirely in Irish Gaelic, the song reached No. 5 on the British charts and received an Ivar Novello award (England's equivalent to the American Grammy award).

FOCUS EXAMPLE
CELTIC-POP

"THEME FROM HARRY'S GAME," PERFORMED BY CLANNAD

Focal Points

- **Language/Lyrics:** Poetic form sung in Irish Gaelic.
- **Instruments:** Synthesizers. Voices are processed to add reverberation.

TIME	DESCRIPTION
0:00–0:03	Low-pitch synthesizer starts the song.
0:04–0:16	First verse.
IRISH GAELIC	**ENGLISH**
Imtheochaidh soir is siar	I will go east and go west
A dtainig ariamh	(To the places) from whence came
An ghealach is an ghrian	The moon and the sun
0:17–0:34	Refrain using vocables.
IRISH GAELIC	
Fol lol the doh fol the day	Nonlexical vocables
Fol the day fol the day	
0:35–0:49	Second verse.
IRISH GAELIC	**ENGLISH**
Imtheochaidh an ghealach's an ghrian	The moon and the sun will go
An Daoine og is a chail 'na dhiadh	And the young man, with his reputation behind him
0:50–1:32	Vocables refrain.
1:33–1:50	Instrumental "swells" in volume and lush harmonies.
1:51–2:05	Third verse.
IRISH GAELIC	**ENGLISH**
Imtheochaidh a dtainig ariamh	I will go wherever he came from
An duine og is a chail ne dhiadh	The young man with his reputation behind him
2:06–2:27	Vocables refrain repeated until end.

Goidelic languages, often referred to as Gaelic, are indigenous to the British Isles and mainly associated with populations in Ireland and Scotland. There are three main types: Irish, Scottish, and Manx (from the Isle of Man). Although English is predominantly spoken throughout the British Isles, the people of Ireland, Scotland, and Wales (whose native language is Welsh, a Brythonic language) take great pride in their cultural heritage as distinct from that of England. Many cultural aspects, including food, dress, and religious practices, are important to maintaining the unique ethnic identities of these populations. The maintenance of the Gaelic languages is a special source of pride and is frequently used in traditional as well as popular-music performance.

A distinctive vocal practice in Ireland and Scotland is the use of **puirt a beul**, or "jigs of the mouth." Generally, this "mouth music," as it is colloquially known, is a creative way to render instrumental melodies into vocal performance, similar to the practice of "scat" singing in jazz. The text incorporates **vocables** (i.e., nonlexical, or "meaningless," syllables) that often follow rhythmic and rhyming patterns. These patterns may render the instrumental melody as a vocal line or, more typically, relate to associated dance choreography.

Some puirt a beul are original compositions relating to neither an instrumental nor a dance tune. Although many such performances use only **vocables**, others are translatable. "Mouth music" contests are frequently found at both social gatherings and formal competitions, where performers sing with a rapid-fire delivery of tongue-twisting text. Though the refrain in our Focus Example is not considered "mouth music," its use of nonlexical syllables does reflect this tradition.

Gaelic poetry often utilizes themes related to nature or daily life. Connecting with nature's elements is a central feature of neopagan spiritualism in the region and often appears in various artistic forms, such as painting, sculpture, needlework, music, and poetry. Astrology and astronomy figure prominently in these endeavors. Such imagery resonates with proponents of New Age spirituality, which flourished in mainstream society during the 1980s and '90s.

The New Age movement has its roots in nineteenth-century metaphysics, but mainstream awareness of this term began only in the late 1960s, most notably associated with the 1967 Broadway musical *Hair*, which reflected the values of the era's hippie counterculture. Throughout the 1970s, New Age interests gravitated toward environmental spiritualism, particularly as it related to Native American beliefs and culture. By the end of the decade, Celtic culture was also a focus for many followers of this emerging spiritual movement.

With advances in studio technology, musicians began to experiment with sound effects to evoke images of nature and to suggest tranquil settings. Rhythm became much more fluid, and reverberation effects enhanced the serenity of sustained melodic lines and lush harmonies. Although Clannad did not consider themselves part of the New Age movement, their music did express its interests in meditation, environmentalism, and maintaining bonds with a cultural past.

Clannad found international success throughout the 1980s and '90s and was at the forefront of global interest in Celtic music due to their combination of traditional music skills and modernized sound. From 1973 to 1997, they recorded fifteen albums that featured many of their family members, including Enya, who were not part of the official group. Several Brennan family members have since pursued successful solo careers. Their legacy is well established among Irish music, New Age, and world-music enthusiasts internationally.

Clannad and Enya may have brought the sounds of modern Celtic music into many homes across the globe, but the group most renowned for promoting the musical heritage of Ireland are The Chieftans, a group founded in 1963. The majority of The Chieftans' music features traditional instruments, such as the tin whistle, fiddle, Irish harp, *bodhran* (frame drum), *uilleann* bagpipes, and concertina (button-box accordion), and their repertoire emphasizes music typical of traditional *céilí* bands found in the

Puirt a beul   vocal practice that uses vocables to substitute for instrumental melody

Vocables   a nonlexical word or syllable

The Chieftains, ca. 1990.

pubs of Ireland. Whereas Clannad's early recordings of traditional Irish music included much vocal performance, The Chieftans have emphasized instrumental performances throughout their career. Collaborative works, however, typically feature a vocalist and often branch out into styles of music that are not considered Celtic, such as classical, mainstream pop, and even reggae.

WHAT IS CELTIC MUSIC?

Introducing these well-known music artists leads us to ask: What is Celtic music? Answering this question can be complex since it involves delving into European history, issues of emigration and cross-cultural contact, modern politics, and endless debates on the authenticity of traditional music and culture around the globe. To indicate a possible Celtic connection, we might rely on the instruments used, such as the traditional tin whistle or uilleann pipes, or the language in a vocal performance, which is usually Gaelic. Still other markers could be the performers' heritage (typically either Irish or Scottish) or the song genre performed (for example, a jig or reel).

But music labeled "Celtic" today often does not easily fit into these suggested recognizable traits. New Age Celtic artists, such as Enya, may use no folk instruments, and other languages (usually English) can be heard in so-called Celtic music. Certainly, people of non-Celtic descent play Celtic music, and there are plenty of Celts who play music not considered Celtic as well. And though the folk-song genres are clear markers of a Celtic connection, playing one of these styles is not a requirement for a music to be considered Celtic.

Acknowledging the dilemma of labeling any popular world music, Celtic artists follow in one of three stylistic veins. Many groups, such as Banshees in the Kitchen or Altan, and individual artists, such as Natalie MacMaster, follow a folk format,

opting for primarily traditional instrumental ensembles and coupling new compositions with many tunes that have been passed down through generations of Irish, Scottish, or Welsh musicians. Some practitioners are offended by the description of their
folk traditions as being "Celtic," which they feel is a music-industry label better left to
artists of the "modern" styles.

The most successful modern style follows in the footsteps of Clannad and Enya.
The artists themselves may consider their music to be Celtic, but the music industry frequently labels the recordings "New Age," primarily to reach a wider audience. This style
incorporates many electronic instruments, varied percussion, and studio techniques to
give the music a more contemporary sound. Often this music does have folk roots, utilizing melodies or lyrical content borrowed from traditional music or poetry (such as our
Focus Example). Recognizing the connection can be difficult for the uninitiated, but the
presence of a traditional instrument or the use of the Gaelic language are generally the
clearest audible markers.

These are also the easiest ways to recognize a Celtic connection in the harder-edged
sound of musicians like Ashley MacIsaac or the Prodigals. Electric guitars and heavy
drums are heard side by side with fiddles and bagpipes, creating a Celtic rock market
niche that is sometimes difficult to label. Kilts and other Celtic iconography become part
of the onstage image, with the inevitable bagpipe solo or extended fiddle improvisation.
Though a far cry from its New Age counterpart, which tends toward the nature- and love-
oriented themes of traditional song, the Celtic rock genre expresses the militant side of
Irish and Scottish folk music that is also a steadfast part of Celtic musical heritage.

FLAMENCO

As with Celtic music, where local pub céilí bands thrive alongside auditorium-packing
New Age artists, flamenco music has maintained a core constituency devoted to traditional styles that complement the slick studio recordings and concert performances of
their modern counterparts. These private and public contexts for flamenco have persisted in tandem for well over a century.

Juergas an informal
gathering of flamenco
enthusiasts

Informal musical gatherings, known as **juergas**, provide the setting perhaps most
adored by flamenco enthusiasts. They occur in private homes or small venues, such as
a tapas restaurant, and the participants number between one and two dozen, including
singers, dancers, musicians, and onlookers. Although some "staged" juergas for tourists and the uninitiated are found today, the most intimate settings for flamenco performance are not advertised for public viewing; most everyone knows one another and
are often considered family. Youngsters are encouraged to model their adult mentors to
learn the tradition and develop their promising talents. Performances in such contexts
have a greater tendency toward improvisation. The intimate setting allows for experi-
mentation and revitalization of older flamenco styles that have more limited appeal
than those performed on the concert stage.

◉▸ EXPLORE MORE
on www.mymusickit.com
Interactive Globe

Concert performances have been common for flamenco artists since the middle of
the nineteenth century. *Cafés cantantes*, essentially nightclubs, appeared in the late 1860s as
popular venues where paying patrons could watch professional flamenco performances.
As audiences grew, the performances quickly acquired a more formal atmosphere than the
private contexts that had earlier characterized the music. Outside influences also affected
the tradition as artists incorporated new elements, typically coming from Latin America, to
keep the music fresh and to attract larger audiences. By the 1920s, flamenco artists, such as
Pepe Marchena (1903–1976), could sell out opera houses and even bullring arenas.

Flamenco Proper

Flamenco consists of many different styles, but the three primary elements are *cante* (song, i.e., vocal), *toque* (instrumental, e.g., guitar), and *baile* (dance). Each element has several subcategories, giving rise to more than fifty different types of flamenco music, known as *palos*. The cante, for example, is typically divided into three basic categories that suggest the level of performance difficulty: *cante jondo* (deep song), *cante intermedio* (intermediate song), and *cante chico* (light song). While the singers of cante jondo are the most respected, these performances highlight the vocalist over the guitar and associated dance, which are often absent.

A flamenco singer, known as a *cantaora*, requires a strong and passionate voice, no matter which style of cante is performed. A performance is characterized by variations of timbre, often strained, and the frequent use of a strongly melismatic melodic line that reveals its roots in Arabic/Indian vocal performance. Flamenco is more a "heart" music than a "head" music, meaning that the emotional expressiveness of a performance takes precedence over the objective of singing every note perfectly. Certainly, it is best to have both, but no one faults performers for missing a pitch as long as they are singing with abandon. In contrast, European art music is much more focused on technical accuracy, and emotional expression tends to be secondary. Such artists are taught to "learn the notes" first and then worry about sentiment, whereas flamenco artists, assuming a traditional rather than conservatory training, are urged to sing with passion, knowing that the ability to sing "correctly" will come eventually.

While passion is the attitude of the vocalist, suffering is the emotion that he or she is most often trying to express. Even the lighthearted styles tend toward tragic humor and sarcasm. Flamenco was born of oppression: It is believed to have originated in the fifteenth century among persecuted populations of the Spanish Inquisition. Cantaoras expressed their sadness through song. Although the early years of flamenco were not associated with any one specific ethnic or religious group, by the mid-eighteenth century the Gitano populations (also known as Romani or "Gypsies") that had migrated to Spain had adopted the tradition as a hallmark of their musical activity, adding guitar and dancing to the already present *palmas* (interlocking hand claps) technique that accompanies performances.

The guitar is the ubiquitous instrument of flamenco music. Similar to an acoustic classical guitar, the instrument used for flamenco is somewhat smaller and typically played with a **capo**, which allows the musician to transpose the pitches to suit the vocalist. Both qualities encourage it to produce a brighter timbre. The flamenco guitar's most noticeable feature is the large pickguard, called a *golpeador*, which protects the guitar face from the musician's strumming and helps to accentuate the frequent tapping and slapping on the instrument that occurs throughout a performance.

The strumming technique frequently incorporates a rapid "outward" flourish that utilizes the fingernail of each finger individually and a "rolling" rhythm, known as *rasgueado*. This parallels the rhythmically dense accents of the *castanets* (see below) and the footwork of the accompanying dancers. Although some scholars debate whether or not this technique originated with classical or flamenco guitar, it is an uncommon practice in lute traditions around the world. The vibrant strumming contrasts with the delicate melodic fingerwork that draws from both European classical guitar and Arabic 'Oud plucking techniques. This difference in technique between percussive strumming and intricate melody often signals a mood shift during a performance, which may also be indicated by a change in rhythm and/or meter, known as *compás*.

FLAMENCO ELEMENTS

• *Cante* (Song)
• *Toque* (Instrumental)
• *Baile* (Dance)

Capo   a clamp used by guitarists to change an instrument's pitch range

Flamenco dancer in Spain.

In traditional flamenco, there are few percussion instruments, primarily the castanets, an instrument of Middle Eastern origin that dates to roughly 1000 b.c. Played by accompanying dancers, castanets are a pair of handheld wooden clappers that resemble miniature clamshells. The dancer holds a pair in each hand and "claps" them together by closing the fingers toward the palm, frequently alternating between the two hands and/or rolling the fingers on the castanet to produce a rapid clicking sound.

A flamenco dancer's primary percussion instruments, however, are the feet and hands. Performers study a variety of choreography that includes foot-stomping techniques (*zapateado*) and hand claps (*palmas*) that add to the rhythmic vibrancy of the music. They wear heavy shoes that sometimes have nails driven into the heel to accentuate the sound, much like the metal plates on the toes and heels of tap-dancing shoes. The movements are often aggressive and interplay keenly with the guitarist. Both men (*bailaores*) and women (*bailaoras*) dance, but the female persona, with her long ruffled dresses, laced shawls, and occasional folding fan, is most associated with flamenco performances today.

The Gipsy Kings created a hybrid music based on Spanish traditions.

Flamenco Fusions

Although dance has become the major focus of flamenco for international audiences, aficionados recognize that the tradition's truest forms highlight the vocalist. Finding a middle ground has been the presence of the flamenco guitarist, who has come to the forefront of the world-music scene in the past few decades. Classic artists, such as Paco de Lucia (b. 1947) and Tomatito (b. 1958), remain mainstays of *nuevo flamenco* (new flamenco), alongside more recent guitarists, such as Vicente Amigo (b. 1967) or Niño Josele (b. 1974).

One of the early pioneers of the "new sound" was Camarón de la Isla (1950–1992), a "Gypsy" singer who in the 1970s introduced instruments atypical of traditional flamenco into his performance. Purists derided his innovations, but the addition of modern instruments, such as the electric bass and synthesizer, and varied percussion, such as *conga* and *cajón*, widened the appeal of flamenco music. Paired with guitarist Paco de Lucia, the two artists were previously acclaimed for their skills as traditional flamenco performers. Thus, these were not young musicians merely imitating the flamenco sound, but highly regarded prodigies who saw new possibilities in adapting the music for international audiences.

Other musicians, such as the duo Lole y Manuel, followed their lead, especially after the death of Francisco Franco (1892–1975), who had controlled Spain's political destiny as head of state since the 1930s. Fusing elements from African, Arabic, and American music traditions, particularly jazz, an increasing number of Spanish artists felt they could remain true to their flamenco heritage while attracting new audiences unfamiliar with the complexities of the traditional styles. Most successful of these fusion artists has been the Gipsy Kings, who have been world-music superstars for nearly two decades.

Hailing from two well-known Gitano musical families, Reyes and Baliardo, the Gipsy Kings first achieved international acclaim in 1988 with a self-titled album and the hit song "Bamboleo." Numerous hits have followed, including adaptations of such popular songs as "My Way" (*A Mi Manera*) (1988) and "Hotel California" (1999). Flamenco traditionalists often dismiss their music, and the Gipsy Kings themselves acknowledge that the majority of their recordings, described alternatively as *rumba flamenco* or *rumba catalana*, are not "pure" flamenco. Rather, their style follows in the musical sense of many generations of gypsy musicians before them, adapting their skills to the local tastes of their audience.

FOCUS EXAMPLE
FLAMENCO FUSION

((• **HEAR MORE**
Download the
iTunes playlist link on
MyMusicKit

"VOLARE" PERFORMED BY THE GIPSY KINGS, WRITTEN
BY DOMENICO MODUGNO

Focal Points

- **Language/Lyrics:** Spanish (and Italian), with romantic imagery.
- **Voice:** Strained vocal timbre with occasional use of melisma.
- **Instruments:** Acoustic guitars, acoustic/electric bass, drum set, synthesizer, as well as palmas (hand claps).
- **Harmony:** Typically follows chord progressions associated with traditional flamenco.
- **Rhythm:** Inspired by Afro-Cuban rumba rhythms.

TIME	DESCRIPTION
0:00–0:27	Opening with only melismatic vocal and acoustic guitar.
0:28–0:43	"Volare" refrain. Ensemble enters with rumba rhythm.
0:44–0:56	Second verse.
0:57–1:13	"Volare" refrain.
1:14–1:19	Guitar improvised solo.
1:20–1:36	Opening verse repeated.
1:37–1:53	"Volare" refrain.
1:54–2:06	Guitar improvised solo.
2:07–2:22	"Volare" refrain.
2:23–2:29	Guitar break.
2:30–2:46	Opening verse repeated.
2:47–3:41	"Volare refrain until end. Palmas appear. Guitar improvised solo in background.

The opening verse and accompanying guitar best reveal the flamenco roots of the Gipsy Kings. The vocal timbre is strained and passionate, with a prominent use of melismatic text setting. These are qualities derived from the cante performance practices of traditional artists. The dexterous finger work of the guitarist similarly shows a roots connection to the artistry of flamenco performance, punctuated by the rolling outward finger flourishes that appear at the end of the verse (0:23).

Domenico Modugno (1928–1994) originally wrote this song in Italian as a popular ballad; its true title is "Nel blu dipinto di blu," but it is better known as "Volare." The song represented Italy in the 1958 Eurovision song contest, earning third place, and the following year won two Grammy awards for Song of the Year and Record of the Year. Modugno's performance topped the popular-music charts, selling more than one million copies, and remains the only Italian-language song to reach No. 1. The success prompted many English-language cover versions performed by pop balladeers, such as Dean Martin (1917–1995), Frank Sinatra (1915–1998), and Bobby Rydell (b. 1942).

The Gipsy King's version, entitled "Volare," was released in 1989 on their second album, *Mosaique*. The song and the success of the album encouraged their rising popularity among world-music enthusiasts, particularly in France, where the group makes its home. The majority of the lyrics were translated into Spanish, though the refrain remains in Italian. Where the original recording and subsequent covers of the 1950s and

'60s had a jazzy pop sound, the Gipsy King's faster-tempo rendering is in a modern style of flamenco performance, known as flamenco rumba.

Flamenco rumba is a style of dance music that fuses rhythmic elements of Afro-Cuban rumba (see Chapter 4) with harmonic progressions and melodic tendencies common to flamenco music. The use of the acoustic guitar and fingering techniques typical of flamenco is the most obvious connection between the popular style and the traditional genre. Percussion instruments are sometimes heard but are used in a subdued manner. The primary percussive element in flamenco rumba is produced by slapping the body of the guitar as part of the strumming technique. Traditional flamenco guitarists do this as well, most typically as part of an improvisation, but the popular style incorporates the guitar strike as part of the stroke pattern. The result is a steady articulation of the beat.

Traditional flamenco, by contrast, frequently changes tempo and meter during a performance, often in conjunction with the movements of a dancer or a cue from a vocalist. The vocal component is more demanding and melodies are not based on popular songs from other genres, as is "Volare." Triple meters are common, and the dancers themselves often articulate the rhythmic component in flamenco proper. Flamenco rumba, however, is meant for mass audience participation, not specialized choreography. The music generally follows a duple meter and remains consistent throughout the performance. A syncopated rhythm, based on either the habanera or a clave pattern (see Chapter 4), is typically present. Our example includes a subtle percussive articulation implying a 3+2 clave pattern, beginning with the entrance of the ensemble (0:28).

Flamenco rumba is often criticized by connoisseurs of flamenco proper for its lack of seriousness and technical difficulty. Certainly, this music is not as demanding for either the vocalists or the musicians, and the lyrical content is lighter, avoiding the darker themes of suffering and discrimination that frequently appear in the older styles. In part, the animosity toward this music may stem from the frequent assumption of uninformed listeners that this style is typical of all flamenco music. It is not; flamenco rumba is inspired by the more serious art form, borrowing elements such as instrumentation, harmony, and performance techniques, but it is not flamenco in the traditional sense. The inclusion of palmas (2:47), the interlocking hand claps characteristic of flamenco proper, is a good example of such inspiration. The Gipsy Kings' style, however, is by far representative of one of the most popular world-music genres today, which, as some traditional artists will admit, does help to broaden their own appeal.

For today's global audience, incorporating elements from varied music traditions has become accepted practice among many of the latest generation of nuevo flamenco artists. Groups such as Ojos de Brujo add elements of hip-hop, rock, reggae, salsa, bhangra, and other popular genres to their versions of this continually evolving world-music tradition. As with most popular world music, flamenco rumba is meant to entertain and, as has been true of Gitano musicians for centuries, the most successful artists, such as the Gipsy Kings, adapt their public performances to appeal to the interests of their audiences.

FADO

Although flamenco is the most prominent music of the Iberian peninsula, Portugal's best-known musical export, *fado*, has also been a mainstay of the region's popular music styles. Like flamenco music, fado has a mournful mood but expresses its sentiment as a soulful reminiscence, rather than a cathartic wail. Its eclectic musical roots can be traced to Brazilian, central African, and Arabic influences, but fado is distinctly European with its use of harmony, a simple meter, and minimal percussion, if any is present at all.

Two types of fado are commonly heard in Portugal: *Coimbra fado* and *Lisboa fado*, named for the cities that are considered to have spawned these traditions. The former is likely the

⊙→ EXPLORE MORE
on www.mymusickit.com
Interactive Globe

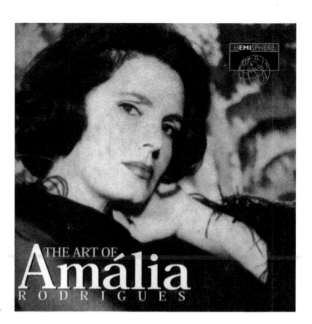

Amália Rodrigues,
the Queen of Fado.

older of the two traditions, while the latter is more popular with international audiences. Although the historical development of fado remains unclear until the nineteenth century, the earliest fado artists are believed to have descended from the troubadour tradition of the eleventh to thirteenth century. These wandering minstrels were common in the countryside of France, Italy, Spain, and Portugal, performing self-accompanied music, usually with a plucked lute, and addressing a variety of subjects, such as love, politics, death, and war. The establishment of the University of Coimbra in 1290 provided a setting in which these musicians found a more receptive and regular audience.

As Europe moved into the Renaissance (fourteenth–seventeenth century) and pursued colonial exploration, the Portuguese established colonies in central Africa (mainly in Angola and Mozambique) and South America (Brazil). By the mid-1700s, the ballad tradition initiated by the troubadours found its way to these areas as well, as did the "salon" art song tradition that was popular among the middle class and social elites throughout Europe. Musical elements from Africa fused with these European styles, resulting in the creation of many new traditions, such as samba, that are important to the musical and cultural identity of modern-day Portuguese descendants.

By the early nineteenth century, Brazilian musical influences were returning to Portugal with the court liaisons, merchants, and sailors who traveled between the two regions. Most influential for the development of fado was the art song tradition of *modinha*, which acquired a nostalgic air in Brazil as performers and composers yearned for their homeland of Portugal. This longing feeling, described as **saudade**, strengthened as working-class seamen and street musicians of the poor neighborhoods in the port city of Lisbon adopted the accompanied song format as a medium for expressing their struggles with everyday life.

Saudade a sorrowful sentiment associated with Portuguese fado.

By the 1830s, this musical style was known as *fado*, meaning "destiny" or "fate." At this time, a young Gypsy **fadista** (vocalist) named Maria Severa (1820–1846) began to attract audiences from Lisbon's social elite. Fueling her success was a scandalous love affair with the Count of Vimioso, who was from a municipality in northeastern Portugal. As Severa lamented her heartache from the short-lived forbidden romance, she established an image for fado performers that persists to this day. Her black shawl became a ubiquitous adornment for female fadistas, and her accompanying instrument, the *guitarra portuguesa*, continues to be standard for fado performance. Her legend was

Fadista a vocalist who sings Portuguese fado.

brought to life in the first Portuguese sound film, *A Severa* (1931), and she is frequently referenced in fado songs today.

A century after Maria Severa's death, fado's second legendary figure, Amália Rodrigues (1920–1999), popularized the genre to its greatest extent, such that fado audiences cut across social classes and international borders. Supported by classically trained composer Frederico Valério (n.d.), Rodrigues's performances redefined the genre, adding an expanded orchestral accompaniment to highlight her vocal talents. Her local success in Lisbon broadened during the 1940s and '50s through recordings and various acting roles in Portuguese and international films, in which she frequently delivered onscreen performances. Christened the "Rainha do Fado" (Queen of Fado), Rodrigues enjoyed a career that spanned more than fifty years and remains the watermark to which current fado artists are compared.

FOCUS EXAMPLE
FADO

"COIMBRA," PERFORMED BY AMÁLIA RODRIGUES,
MUSIC BY RAUL FERRÃO, LYRICS BY JOSÉ GALHARDO

Focal Points

((•● **HEAR MORE**
Download the
iTunes playlist link on
MyMusicKit

- **Language/Lyrics:** Sung in Portuguese, with a nostalgic theme about the city of Coimbra.
- **Voice:** Female vocalist (Amália Rodrigues). Lilting voice, with occasional ornamentation of melody.
- **Instruments:** *Guitarra portuguesa* (Portuguese guitar) and *viola de fado* (classical guitar).
- **Melody/Harmony:** The opening and ending emphasize major chords, while the middle section is in a minor key. (The melody for "Coimbra" was used for the English-language song "April in Portugal.")
- **Form:** ABBAA

TIME	DESCRIPTION
0:07–0:12	Instrumental introduction with Guitarra portuguesa and viola de fado.
0:13–0:38	First verse (Form: A). Guitars play full unbroken major chords.

PORTUGUESE	ENGLISH
Coimbra e uma lição de sonho e tradição	Coimbra is a lesson of dreams and tradition
O lente e uma canção e a lua a faculdade	The lens is a song and the moon is the faculty.
O livro é uma mulher só passa quem souber	The book is a lady. Whoever just passes knows
E aprende-se a dizer saudade.	And learns to say "longing."

0:39–1:03	Second verse (Form: B). Guitars shift to minor chords and play arpeggios (broken chords).

PORTUGUESE	ENGLISH
Coimbra do Choupal	Coimbra of the Choupal (a recreational sanctuary in Coimbra)
Ainda és capital	You are still capital.
De amor em Portugal,	Of love in Portugal,
Ainda	You are still capital.
Coimbra, onde uma vez	Coimbra, where once upon a time
Com lágrimas se fez	With tears took place
A história dessa Inês tão linda	The story of that Inês* so lovely.

*Inês was a virgin saint, elsewhere known as Saint Agnes.

(continues on next page)

1:04–1:28	Third verse (Form: B). Guitars continue as in second verse.

PORTUGUESE	ENGLISH
Coimbra das canções	Coimbra of the songs
Tão meigas que nos pões	So tender that you turn
Os nossos coraçoes à luz.	Our hearts to the light.
Coimbra dos doctores,	Coimbra of the professors,
Pra nós os seus cantors	For us, your singers,
A fonte de amor és tu.	You are the wellspring of love.

1:29–1:55	Return to opening material. (Form: A)
1:56–2:08	Guitar solo improvising on main theme. (Form: A)
2:09–2:20	Vocalist returns to sing final two lines and close the performance.

The harmony for the second and third verses (Form: B) shifts to a minor key to give the music a sadder sentiment. The descending melodic line also conveys a melancholy mood, which is typical of most fado songs. These contrast with the more spritely melody of the opening and closing sections (Form: A), which use major keys. The guitars shift to playing **arpeggios** (broken chords), rather than strummed full chords, which again gives a different feeling to this section. These changes are important to notice, for they add to the subtle beauty of fado.

Arpeggio a "broken" chord in which each note of the harmony is played in succession

The instrumental accompaniment of fado is often varied. The *guitarra portuguesa* (Portuguese guitar), a twelve-stringed pear-shaped lute, is most common, but other instruments, such as the *viola de fado* (classical guitar) and *viola baixo* (bass guitar) make up a typical ensemble. Violin, cello, flute, accordion, and minimal percussion, such as maracas, are also sometimes included. For the most successful fado artists the accompaniment may even include a modern orchestra, but the trio of guitars is the most intimate.

Performers playing the *guitarra portuguesa*.

The themes of fado are varied but usually express a romantic notion. This song conveys a nostalgic reminiscence for the city of Coimbra, the birthplace of fado. The references to the "faculty" and the "book is a lady" remind the listener of the important role the university has played in the city's history since the thirteenth century. Later verses continue the sentimental recollections, reminding the listener that Coimbra was once the capital of Portugal and home to the "tender songs" (i.e., fado).

The closing material repeats the opening verse and instrumental content. The lead guitar adds only minimal embellishments to the main theme during its solo break (1:56). This is also true of the vocalist throughout the performance; subtle fluctuations of pitch, short melismas, and noticeable vibrato are sprinkled throughout her singing. This attention to small details is a determining factor in assessing the abilities of a fadista and in recognizing individual style. Adding too many improvisations destroys the character of the melody, but adding too few suggests an unskilled performer. More important than technical aspects is the emotion, *saudade*, present in the vocal quality. Amália Rodrigues's success was largely due to her heartfelt expression of the lyrical content.

While Rodrigues became the public face of fado, the music maintained a private audience in taverns and cafés throughout Portugal during much of the twentieth century. The authoritarian rule of António Salazar (1889–1970), from 1932 to 1968, created an oppressive political climate in which fado artists were a voice of discontent and dissent against the government. With the establishment of Salazar's *Estado Novo* (New State) in 1933, political dissidents were often jailed and many were sent to a prison in the Cape Verde islands, then a colony of Portugal. Strict censorship laws required fado songwriters to submit their lyrics for approval before public performances in order to curtail political subversives. While these restrictions were largely successful, many fadistas maintained alternative versions of their approved songs that were critical of the government's activities.

After Salazar's death and the end of the Estado Novo in 1974, fado artists were again free to perform as they liked in public venues. Rodrigues's international success attracted many music-minded foreigners to travel to Portugal in search of the roots of her music. Several tourist-oriented clubs appeared and have continued to provide steady work for aspiring fado artists. By largely adhering to the style established by Rodrigues, many such artists have achieved international recognition, including Marisa dos Reis Nunes (aka "Mariza"; b. 1973), who was born in the former Portuguese colony of Mozambique.

Morna

The end of the Portuguese Estado Novo also initiated a new era in the history of the Cape Verde islands, which established its independence in 1975 after more than five hundred years as a Portuguese colony. *Morna*, regarded as the national music of the islands, is strongly linked with Portuguese fado. Evolving from similar roots, namely the Angolan *lundun* and Brazilian-Portuguese *modinha*, the morna repertoire flowered at the turn of the nineteenth century with the poems of Eugénio Tavares (1867–1930), the most revered of morna composers.

Although Tavares was inspired by the music and lyricism of fado, the circumstances of his life as a Cape Verdean and those of his compatriots were very different than those of the Portuguese. As a colony of Portugal, the islands were used primarily as a shipping hub during the transatlantic slave trade period (sixteenth–nineteenth century), resulting in a significant African Diaspora. The African influence permeates Cape Verdean culture, including its national language, Cape Verdean Creole, which is

⊙→ **EXPLORE MORE**
on www.mymusickit.com
Interactive Globe

Morna artist
Cesaria Évora.

based on Portuguese and a mixture of West African languages. Though the sentiment of morna parallels that of fado, the subject matter of the poetry often reflects a disdain for the persecution of its people during slavery and under colonial rule.

Aside from the language and thematic elements, morna differs from fado in its frequent inclusion of percussion instruments used to articulate a more complex rhythmic component that reflects the African heritage of the islands' populace. A solo vocalist is still the central figure of the ensemble, with the most common harmonic accompaniment being the *viola* (classical guitar) and *cavaquinho* (a small, mandolin-like guitar with four-courses of strings; see Chapter 5). Piano, violin, and accordion, as well as electric or acoustic bass, are typical of today's ensembles, along with featured instruments including saxophone, trombone, and traditional African instruments, such as the *kora* (a chordophone from West Africa).

Most prominent of morna singers is Cesária Évora (b. 1941), nicknamed the "barefoot diva" for her preference for performing onstage without shoes. She began performing as a teenager and was encouraged by her uncle, B. Leza, a prolific composer of mornas and a well-known musician on the islands. Though she was a local celebrity in Cape Verde, her international career did not begin until 1988, after minor tours in Portugal and France. Her first recording, *La Diva aux Pieds Nus* (The Barefoot Diva; 1988), was recorded in Paris and became successful enough to encourage further recordings and increasing international celebrity. Although mornas are the staple of her repertoire, Évora performs other sentimental styles, such as *samba-canção*, jazz, and fado. Other Cape Verdean artists, such as Tito Paris (b. 1963), have benefited from Évora's international recognition.

POLKA

EXPLORE MORE
on www.mymusickit.com
Interactive Globe

Polka music is less obviously "popular," in the modern sense, because the performers do not typically find themselves the main attraction of an event. While concertgoers to a flamenco or fado performance observe the musicians that take center stage, a polka band finds itself on the sideline in the role of enabler, merely facilitating the audience's dance participation. A good example is "The Chicken Dance," a circle dance commonly played by polka bands and frequently heard at wedding receptions and Oktoberfests in

Europe and the United States. The focus is entirely on the audience as they "flap" their elbows like a chicken while the band plays a supporting role, providing the music and perhaps including an announcer who calls out dance movements and encouragement. Certainly, polka bands often perform in a concertlike setting, as did the Lawrence Welk Orchestra, but in typical contexts they become the focus of attention primarily as an interlude between dance numbers.

Polka originated in Bohemia, which is today part of the Czech Republic. Its characteristic quick "half-step" choreography (*pulka* is Czech for "half") became popular during the mid-1830s in couples dances among the region's peasant communities. By the early 1840s, the signature step had found its way into ballroom dance venues in Prague and, soon after, Paris. Dance instructors adapted the polka for upper-class contexts, and classical composers began writing new music for the dance. By the end of the decade, the polka's popularity rivaled that of other ballroom dances, such as the quadrille and cotillion, performed at social events for Europe's cultural elites.

The spread of polka was rapid enough that it was found in the United States during the presidency of James K. Polk (r. 1845–49), and the obvious name similarity encouraged the use of polka music and dance as a tool for political aims. It was particularly popular in Chicago among German, Polish, and Czech communities that migrated to the Midwest throughout the remainder of the century. Texas also saw an influx of these populations, who brought the dance and its associated music with them.

Despite the social stigma often given to the music by teenagers and twenty-somethings, polka is still a hugely popular tradition throughout Europe and the United States, particularly among Eastern European communities. The music is strongly influential on many types of popular world music, such as *zydeco* and *conjunto*. The most prominent musical features of polka-influenced traditions are the use of an accordion as the primary, and sometimes the only, instrument and a strong duple-meter rhythm. Polka bands, sometimes referred to as "oom-pah" bands because of this rhythmic emphasis, include several brass and wind instruments, usually a tuba, trumpets, trombones, saxophones, and clarinet, along with a standard drum set. Smaller bands often reduce the ensemble to just an electric bass, drum set, and accordion.

By the 1930s, polka was being played on the radio and distributed on 78-rpm records, which found their way into jukeboxes across America. In 1939 the "Beer Barrel Polka," also known as "Roll Out the Barrel," became a huge hit and was further promoted through subsequent versions popularized by the Andrews Sisters and popular swing bands of the era, such as the Glenn Miller Orchestra and the Benny Goodman Orchestra. In subsequent decades, artists such as Liberace and Lawrence Welk regularly performed it during their television variety programs. The version by Frankie Yankovic (known as "America's Polka King") has been the "seventh-inning stretch" song for the Milwaukee Brewers baseball team since the 1970s. The song is a ubiquitous performance for any polka band playing today.

Since 1985, the Grammy Awards have had an individual polka category. Since the category's inception, Jimmy Sturr and his orchestra have won the Best Polka Album award seventeen times and are the best known of current polka bands. They have performed to sold-out audiences in such prestigious venues as Carnegie Hall and Lincoln Center in New York City and attract enthusiastic audiences internationally as well.

Musicians attempting to expand the genre to attract younger audiences are mostly found in Eastern Europe. The Slovenian groups Atomik Harmonik and Turbo Angels rely on the sex appeal of their female lead singers, typically dressed in tight-fitting dirndl dresses, and perform polka melodies with accordion accompaniment over a heavy dance beat. Such groups have found moderate success in Europe, but youth in the United States probably most associate popular polka with "Weird Al" Yankovic (b. 1959; no relation to Frankie Yankovic), who is famous for his parodies of popular music and culture, which often include accordion performance and a polka-style "oom-pah" rhythm.

⊙▸ EXPLORE MORE
on www.mymusickit.com
Interactive Globe

Polka star
Jimmy Sturr.

KLEZMER

Klezmer bands, a music ensemble commonly heard at Jewish celebrations in Europe
and the United States, incorporate polka music along with other musical styles in their
repertoire. Their function is similar to that of a polka band: facilitating dance and active
audience participation. Although secular, klezmer bands are strongly associated with
Jewish religious events, such as wedding receptions and **bar** or **bat mitzvahs** (coming-
of-age ceremonies).

**bar mitzvah/bat
mitzvah** a coming-of-
age-ceremony in Judaism

Klezmer literally means "musical instrument" and has only come to designate a distinct musical style in the latter half of the twentieth century. It was formerly described
as "Yiddish music" because of the use of the Yiddish language in song, though most
klezmer music is instrumental. The ensemble is referred to as *klezmorim* (the plural of
klezmer) and has traditionally included a variety of instruments from Western Asia
and Eastern Europe. In a typical klezmer ensemble, the clarinet or violin usually plays
the primary melodic role. Also common are other European instruments, such as the
accordion, trumpet, trombone, saxophone, flute, and bass, along with a standard drum
set. Some instruments of Middle Eastern origin include the *tsimbl* (also known as *cimbalom*), a hammered zither, and occasional percussion, such as a tambourine (frame drum)
or even a *darabukka* (goblet-shaped hand drum).

Although klezmer is music played in secular contexts, it is influenced by the sacred
liturgy of the synagogue in its use of melodic scales based on the cantillation modes performed by the cantor during religious services. The cantillation practice utilizes specific
melodic motifs to emphasize key points in the text, and some of these melodies inspired
musical performances in secular contexts related to Jewish celebrations. Other melodies
were influenced by secular traditions in local contexts, particularly those from Romani
("Gypsy") populations, since Jewish and Romani musicians often interacted and performed together.

Klezmer music prospered during the nineteenth century with the rise of Hasidic
Judaism, which encouraged joyful celebration of the religion through song and dance
as a way of developing inner spirituality. Given the Eastern European context in which

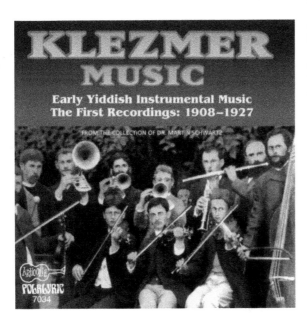

A Klezmer CD showing an Eastern European ensemble from the turn of the 20th century.

Hasidic Judaism originated, the folk-music activity in the modern countries of Poland, Russia, Lithuania, Belarus, Ukraine, and particularly Romania greatly influenced the music performed by klezmer ensembles. As Jewish communities spread throughout Europe, the klezmer musicians found new musical influences by frequently performing in non-Jewish contexts. Along with Romani musicians, Jewish performers were recognized as highly skilled artists and frequently performed for affluent patrons during much of the nineteenth and early twentieth centuries. As American jazz made its way to Europe, klezmer bands took the lead in popularizing the new style in major urban areas throughout the continent.

The Holocaust, however, stifled the activity of European Jewish and Romani musicians as the Nazi regime exterminated millions from these communities during World War II. Some klezmer musicians fled to the United States but found little demand for their talents. For the next two decades, Jewish musicians performed styles typical of their adopted homeland. By the 1970s, however, the tragic memories of the Holocaust had receded enough that a nostalgic interest in klezmer inspired many young Jewish musicians to seek out older cultural bearers of the tradition and to revive the music.

Although the majority of these new musicians hailed from New York City, a group of young enthusiastic performers from Berkeley, California, who dub themselves simply "The Klezmorim," are often credited with spearheading a renewed interest in klezmer music, thanks to their mid-1970s recordings of early-twentieth-century styles. Other groups soon followed and, by the 1980s, began to combine the klezmer sound with other genres. The Klezmatics have proved to be among the most successful by fusing the traditional roots of klezmer music with current popular styles and avant-garde jazz. The resulting mix of irreverence and skilled musicianship appeals to a broad Jewish audience, and the group has achieved international acclaim since the 1989 release of their first album, *Shvaygn = Toyt* ("Silence = Death" in Yiddish). While their music is largely meant for a concert stage, their continued visibility has encouraged the popularity of klezmer ensembles in traditional settings to provide music for celebration.

LEARN MORE
on www.mymusickit.com
Chapter summary
and exam

SUMMARY

In this chapter, we explored popular world-music genres from several parts of Europe. The Eurovision contest is an important means of promoting popular artists from around the continent and some, such as the 1974 winning group ABBA, have achieved mainstream success as a result. Celtic musicians, such as Enya and the group Clannad, have also found a niche in the mainstream media by updating folk music for modern audiences. This mixing of old and new ideas is also prompting new audiences to undertake an exploration of the various styles of flamenco music.

However, many music styles in Europe remain popular without adapting their music to modern technological innovations or the current trends in mainstream popular culture. Fado and morna singers have found growing audiences that appreciate the intrinsic beauty of the music, while polka and klezmer bands remain steadfast entertainment for social occasions throughout the continent.

Pathways

- **Internet:** www.eurovision.tv/
  - Official Web site for the Eurovision song contest.
- **Internet:** www.abbasite.com
  - Official Web site for the Euro-pop group ABBA.
- **Internet:** www.riverdance.com/
  - Official Web site for the Riverdance tours and associated media.
- **DVD:** *Celtic Tides: A Musical* Odyssey. MPI Home Video, 1998.
  - A documentary about Celtic music, from its roots to the modern era.
- **Internet:** www.clannad.ie/
  - Official Web site for the Irish music group Clannad.
- **Internet:** www.enya.com/
  - Official Web site for Irish/New Age musician Enya.
- **Internet:** www.thechieftains.com/
  - Official Web site for the Irish music group the Chieftans.
- **DVD:** *Amália Rodrigues: The Spirit of Fado.* MVD Visual, 2006.
  - A documentary about fado performer Amália Rodrigues.
- **Internet:** www.cesaria-evora.com/
  - Official Web site of morna singer Cesária Évora.
- **DVD:** *Gipsy Kings: Tierra Gitana/Live in Concert.* SBME Import, 2005.
  - A documentary film about the flamenco rumba group Gipsy Kings.
- **Internet:** www.gipsykings.com/
  - Official Web site of the flamenco rumba group Gipsy Kings.
- **Internet:** www.jimmysturr.com/
  - Official Web site for the polka musician Jimmy Sturr.
- **Internet:** www.klezmerconservatory.com/
  - Official Web site of the klezmer group the Klezmer Conservatory Band.

Keywords for Additional Music Examples

- "Refrain," by Lys Assia (first winner of the Eurovision Song Contest)
- ABBA
- *"Ne Partez Pas Sans Moi,"* performed by Celine Dion (1988 winner of Eurovision Song Contest)
- "Hard Rock Hallelujah," performed by Lordi (2006 winner of the Eurovision Song Contest)

- Riverdance
- Enya
- Clannad
- Sound track from the Broadway musical *Hair*
- The Chieftans
- Other Irish music artists
  - Banshees in the Kitchen
  - Altan
  - Natalie MacMaster
  - Ashley MacIsaac
  - The Prodigals
- Flamenco artists
  - Pepe Marchena
  - Paco de Lucia
  - Tomatito
  - Vicente Amigo
  - Niño Josele
  - Camarón de la Isla
  - Ojos de Brujo
- Gipsy Kings
  - "Volare"
  - "Bamboleo"
  - "A Mi Manera"
  - "Hotel California"
- Original version of "Volare," by Domenico Modugno
- Modinha
- Fado artists
  - Amália Rodrigues
  - Mariza
- Morna artists
  - Cesária Évora
  - Tito Paris
- Polka music
  - Lawrence Welk
  - Beer Barrel Polka
  - Jimmy Sturr
  - Atomik Harmonik
  - Weird Al Yankovic
- Klezmer music
  - Klezmorim
  - Klezmatics
    - *Shvaygn = Toyt* (1989)

Sub-Saharan Africa: Icons of Afropop

INTRODUCTION

African popular music, commonly referred to as "Afropop," is often different in local contexts than what is commonly marketed in the international arena. Many readers may be surprised to find Western idioms, primarily jazz, as the fundamental aspect of many local genres. International audiences attending a world-music performance have come to expect something "ethnic," suggesting the inclusion of traditional instruments, overt polyrhythmic performance, and a predominance of African dialects. Those artists who achieve the greatest notoriety successfully blend a modern sound with elements from such identifiable indigenous musical roots.

MBUBE AND ISICATHAMIYA

Mainstream popular music has found inspiration in traditional world music since the late 1960s, when, for example, the Beatles were inspired by Indian music. Yet few would argue that the turning point for widespread interest in popular world music came with the success of American singer/songwriter Paul Simon's 1986 album, *Graceland* (see Chapter 1). Though the album and subsequent tour featured a variety of South African music styles and artists, the a cappella vocal group Ladysmith Black Mambazo found the greatest success in the aftermath of its popularity.

Ladysmith Black Mambazo had long been a powerful voice on the local music scene in the Republic of South Africa. Early members of the group were primarily relatives of the lead vocalist, Joseph Shabalala (b. 1941), who sang together as children in the 1950s. After performing with local groups in Durban, a port city in eastern South Africa, Shabalala formed his own choral group, Ezimnyama Ngenkani (The Black Ones) in 1960. Though the group was successful, he had a dream in 1964 of a new group that would "cut down" its rivals in local music competitions through a different kind of singing. The group's name was formed by combining the name of its hometown (Ladysmith), the word "black" from the black ox (a symbol of strength), and the Zulu word *mambazo* (meaning, "axe"). Through disciplined rehearsals that raised the group to professional standards, Ladysmith Black Mambazo soon outrivaled their competitors in almost every contest they entered throughout Durban and Johannesburg.

Their success earned them regular performances on the burgeoning Radio Zulu broadcast and eventually landed them a recording contract with Gallo Africa, the largest recording company in South Africa. This first recording, *Amabutho* (1973), proved extraordinarily successful: It sold more than 25,000 copies, achieving gold-record status and making Ladysmith Black Mambazo the first group of all-black musicians from South Africa to earn this award. Along with their follow-up album, *Imbongi* (1973), the group was successful enough to tour the country as professional musicians. By the early 1980s, their fame had spread internationally, and they were invited to perform in Germany as part of a festival promoting South African music traditions.

After their appearance on Simon's *Graceland* album, Ladysmith Black Mambazo catapulted to the forefront of the international music scene, where they have remained a fixture for the past twenty years. The members have changed, due to retirements and deaths, but the group continues to garner international acclaim, earning several SAMAs (South African Music Awards), two Grammys (in 1987, for *Shaka Zulu*, and 2005, for *Raise Your Spirit Higher*), and an Oscar nomination for the short documentary *On Tiptoe: Gentle Steps to Freedom* (2000). They have performed for many famous international figures, such as Nelson Mandela (b. 1918), Pope John Paul II (1920–2005), and Queen Elizabeth II (b. 1926). The group continues to tour internationally for several months each year.

Ladysmith Black Mambazo is the best-known vocal group from South Africa today, but their style of singing, referred to as **isicathamiya**, has been a part of the music scene in South African townships for more than a century. When diamonds and gold were discovered along the Orange River in the latter decades of the nineteenth century, many Europeans flocked to the region in search of riches. As the mining industry developed, numerous young men left rural farmlands to find better-paying work in growing urban areas. Those who worked in the mines typically resided in all-male hostels and were bused to their work each morning. The strenuous hours of hard labor, coupled with long periods of absence from their families, encouraged community bonding among the men, who frequently passed the time engaging in musical activities.

A tradition of choral singing developed that was primarily rooted in the call-and-response polyphonic singing of the Zulu people, along with harmonic influences of Christian hymnody. By the early twentieth century, performances were organized into informal contests. Called "nightsong," they took place regularly on Saturday evenings—the end of the workweek—and ran through the night. The vocal groups incorporated choreography

⊙▶ EXPLORE MORE
on www.mymusickit.com
Interactive Globe

Isicathamiya   the "c" represents a tongue-click, pronounced *ISI-"click"-A-THA-MEE-YA*

Ladysmith Black Mambazo, South African vocal group.

inspired by traditional dances, such as a high-stepping stomp, as well as ragtime marches popular of the period. Outside the camps, similar small-group choral performances were commonly found at various events, particularly in minstrel shows and for family celebrations, such as weddings. Western notions of harmonic progression, ragtime syncopation, and subdued dance choreography were more influential in these latter contexts.

By the 1920s, the urban areas of Cape Town, Johannesburg, and Durban were growing exponentially. Black South Africans continued to flock to these industrial centers for menial work as laborers in factories, the service industry, and the mines. As the populations grew, so, too, did the wealth of musical talent. In 1926, Eric Gallo (1904–1998), an Italian immigrant, established the country's first recording studio in Johannesburg and produced an associated record label, Gallo Africa, which remains the largest recording label in South Africa (it is known today as Gallo Record Company). In 1939 Solomon Linda (1909–1962), a company employee, made the label's most historically significant recording, "Mbube" (Lion).

"Mbube" became hugely popular throughout the country and transformed Linda and his group, the Evening Birds, into local celebrities. A decade later, American musicologist Alan Lomax (1915–2002) discovered the recording and recommended it to American folk musician Pete Seeger (b. 1919). Seeger's popular folk group, the Weavers, used the song as the basis for their recording "Wimoweh," (1951) and a later live version (1957) that was covered by another well-known folk group of the period, the Kingston Trio. Both groups acknowledged the African roots of the song in their live performances, but this connection was largely lost to the general public after the 1961 recording by the Tokens, which included original lyrics based loosely on the "Sleeping Lion" theme, which Seeger purported to be the meaning of the song. It has since been covered by more than a dozen artists and was featured in the 1994 Disney film *The Lion King*. The Tokens's version is a mainstay of oldies radio stations in the United States, and the song was the subject of the Emmy-award-winning PBS documentary *A Lion's Trail* (2002), which traced the roots of the song and its present manifestations in popular culture.

At the time of Linda's 1939 recording, this choral style of performance did not have a specific name. "Mbube," as the performance was named for Linda's record, was derived from a wedding song normally sung by female groups in rural areas. The success of the recording, however, encouraged people to adopt the word *mbube* for this type of a cappella singing when performed in nonritual settings for entertainment, such as the migrant workers' nightsong competitions.

During the 1940s, mbube groups experimented with new arrangements and vocal harmonies that further emphasized the low range of voices. In the late 1940s and '50s the practice known as "bombing" became common, in which singers performed wide descending melodic slides to imitate the sounds of bombing raids heard on World War II newsreels. This led to more emphasis on a "powerful" performance, with volume becoming an important asset to winning, which took precedence over witticism in the lyrical content and accuracy of pitch.

The migrant-worker performances became increasingly popular and evolved into concertlike shows where many of the choirs consisted of factory workers and miners from the country's various regions. These nightsong events were often advertised, and the informal gatherings became increasingly competitive once prizes began to be offered to winning choirs. Young men viewed participation in a successful mbube group as a badge of honor and a means of improving their social status within the community.

When Joseph Shabalala formed Ladysmith Black Mambazo in 1964, he essentially returned to the style of choral singing more common of vocal groups in the 1930s and early '40s, such as Solomon Linda and the Evening Birds. He emphasized accuracy of rhythm and pitch through quieter, lush harmonies, in contrast to the louder styles that by the 1950s dominated the nightsong competitions. He also modified the choreography to reflect the softer sound by "tiptoeing" through a performance, rather than stomping loudly on the ground. Ladysmith Black Mambazo soon bested their competition with this "new" sound, which was labeled *isicathamiya*, meaning, "walk stealthily" (i.e., to tiptoe). They became so successful that other groups eventually refused to compete against them.

The isicathamiya style is rooted in Zulu traditional singing but incorporates influences from other music that has been popular in South Africa since Shabalala first formed Ladysmith Black Mambazo. The most obvious traditional element is the dance choreography utilized by Ladysmith Black Mambazo and other mbube choirs, which is characterized by a high leg kick with outstretched arms, a movement borrowed from Zulu warrior dances. Ladysmith Black Mambazo uses the Zulu language for the majority of their songs, though English features prominently as well. The call-and-response organization follows in the Zulu choral tradition but often reflects the influence of Christian hymnody and other Western genres, including barbershop quartets.

FOCUS EXAMPLE
MBUBE/ISICATHAMIYA

"HELLO, MY BABY," PERFORMED BY LADYSMITH BLACK MAMBAZO
Focal Points

((• **HEAR MORE**
Download the
iTunes playlist link on
MyMusicKit

- **Voice:** All-male a cappella choir, with emphasis on lower range voices.
- **Melody/Harmony:** The vocal lead provides melodic content, with the backing choir singing in harmony.
- **Form:** The overall form is in two sections based on rhythmic differences, whereas the interior organization is based on call-and-response.
- **Rhythm:** The opening section is primarily in free rhythm but includes short phrases with a rhythmic pulse. The second section follows a duple meter until the closing phrase, which returns to free rhythm.

TIME	DESCRIPTION
0:00–0:23	Lead voice, with choral response in free rhythm.
	Hey, baby, hey.
	Hey, beautiful…
0:24–0:38	Choral section (no "call") with regular pulsation.
	Come along… (8 beats)
	(Uh!) Don't you… (9 beats)
0:39–0:48	Choral section in free rhythm.
	Come along…
0:49–1:01	Call ("controller") and response ("chord") organization returns.
	Don't you…
	I sent…
1:02–1:16	Choral section (no "call"), with regular pulsation as above.
1:17–1:27	Choral section in free rhythm, as above.
1:28–1:54	Call-and-response organization, with steady meter.
	Hello…
1:55–2:05	Group sings "Hello!" on each beat of the meter.
2:06–2:52	"Controller" improvisations continue as backing response sings, "Hello, my baby," with a steady meter.
2:53–3:09	Final phrase in free rhythm.
	Don't you…

This song, "Hello, My Baby," is a favorite among barbershop quartets in the United States and around the world. Barbershop singing is challenging because of the complexity of harmony and rhythm. These a cappella quartets rehearse many hours, without the aid of a conductor, to perfect their vocal phrasings. Each of the four members (tenor, lead, baritone, bass) sings a different pitch to create harmony. Variations in volume are a common feature of a performance, but the volume of each vocalist remains balanced unless a particular part is being emphasized. These groups frequently compete in organized events for international audiences.

Many of these traits are also common to the mbube choirs, such as the use of complex harmony and rhythm, variations in volume, and a competitive atmosphere. Mbube choirs, however, are much larger and include multiple persons singing the same part. The low-range voices are emphasized, usually including three or four vocalists, compared to one or two in the upper ranges. The lead vocalist (Joseph Shabalala, in this example) sings in a higher range to provide contrast with the choir and often sings alone as the call to the group's responding harmony.

Ladysmith Black Mambazo's version of "Hello, My Baby" is different from a typical barbershop rendering. One obvious difference is the text, which changes the basic lyric from "Hello, my baby" to "Hey, baby, hey" until the second section of the song. Throughout the performance, the lyrics have little in common with the original song. The simplicity of the lyrics in mbube and isicathamiya songs keeps the focus on the musical aspects of performance. This is typical since judges of the nightsong competitions today render their decisions with little consideration for lyrical witticisms or story lines. Mbube lyrics typically express a single idea, which the vocalists then render in their distinctive choral style. The themes common to the music of Ladysmith Black Mambazo revolve around peace, unity, and love as universal ideals.

Polyrhythm musical organization using multiple rhythms playing in relationship to one another rather than by a meter.

The music of sub-Saharan Africa tends to be rhythmically complex compared to music from other parts of the world. While instrumental music is frequently organized into layers of different rhythms (i.e., **polyrhythm**), vocal organization is typically based on call-and-response patterns. Call and response usually has a single lead vocalist, followed by a unison group response. This can be heard in the opening material (0:00–0:23), except that mbube choirs sing in harmony, not in unison. Polyphonic singing is often a feature of group responses in traditional settings as well. The specific use of major and minor chords is a Western influence, but the idea of polyphony is indigenous to the region. The lead vocalist in the mbube tradition is known as the "controller," and the group is referred to as the "chord," suggesting the use of harmony.

Although the opening material has no steady pulsation (i.e., free rhythm), the second phrase follows a steady beat. The line "Come along, come along, to kiss me, before I'm going" corresponds to eight beats and then repeats. The next line starts with a vocal grunt ("Uh!") and follows a nine-beat pattern with the lyrics "Don't you kiss me nice, nice, before I'm going," before returning to free rhythm with the final phrase (0:39). This variation of rhythm is an important feature of mbube performance. The lyrics, quite different from those in the barbershop version, are meaningful to an audience of South African migrant workers who must leave their families to earn money.

Call and response musical organization in which a lead call is followed by a group response.

The performance returns to the musical material of the opening verse, with a variation of lyrics in the **call-and-response** section. An important element to notice in the harmony is the emphasis on low-range voices, which is inspired by traditional Zulu singing. Loud, low-range vocals are thought to give a performance more power, an idea that transferred to the mbube competitions. The isicathamiya style has a quieter volume than typical mbube singing, though the predominance of low-range vocals continues to be a feature of the music.

The second section of the performance (beginning at 2:06) follows a steady duple meter until the final phrase (2:53). The lead vocalist ("controller") improvises between the choral response ("chord"). The harmonic progression moves consistently from the tonic (I) to the subdominant (IV) to the dominant (V) chords (see Chapter 2) through four measures, as follows:

| I | I | IV | V |

The "chord" rhythm changes in the middle section (2:06) to sing just the word "Hello!" on each beat of the meter; it then returns to the longer phrase "Hello, my baby." This I–I–IV–V harmonic progression is reflective of the influence that Western culture has had on South African choral singing in urban settings.

Mbube choirs still perform at weekly nightsong contests in Johannesburg and elsewhere in South Africa. They are often inspired by popular and religious music genres found in their country, whether indigenous or foreign. Ladysmith Black Mambazo's success has brought greater attention to local artists in other music genres, but few mbube choirs have achieved much international notoriety aside from Shabalala's group. Always spreading a positive message of peace in their music, words, and actions, Ladysmith Black Mambazo has become one of South Africa's greatest ambassadors to the world.

MARABI AND KWELA

Although mbube and isicathamiya frequently embrace popular music, the world-music industry typically labels this music as "traditional," perhaps because the performances are entirely vocal. The inclusion of modern instruments, such as electric guitars, is seemingly a requirement for a world-music artist to be considered "popular" by most music-business executives. If so, then South African musicians have much to offer in this regard as well.

Urban popular genres in South Africa today are generally a mix of indigenous inspiration and international influence. Traditional choral singing is sometimes a feature, as exemplified by the mbube groups, but is also found in other township styles. Short cyclical melodic phrases reflect traditional African music practices and are common to both instrumental and vocal music performance. The American influence on urban music in South Africa has been prominent since the 1880s, when fortune seekers from the United States streamed into the country in search of gold. American ragtime, minstrelsy, and gospel music became popular among both black and white communities, prompting some uniquely South African traditions.

Marabi is an early style of popular South African music that was initiated during this period and remained popular into the World War II era. The music began as an instrumental keyboard style, typically played on an inexpensive pedal organ, and was commonly heard in the *shebeens* (bars serving homemade liquor) found in the growing townships outside Johannesburg. Although the music used Western instruments and harmonies, the repetitiveness of the melody reflected a South African musical sensibility. The music was meant for dancing; extended solos were minimized so that the focus remained on the patron's activities, rather than on the musicians. By the 1920s, marabi had become the dominant musical style in the urban ghettoes and incorporated a variety of instruments, such as piano, violin, banjo, and drums.

American jazz was particularly popular during this era, influencing even the pennywhistle street music that was commonly heard in Johannesburg and other South African urban centers. Led by a tin whistle (also known as a pennywhistle) soloist, these small groups played a marabi-style repeated chord progression supplied by an accompanying acoustic guitar. By the 1940s, this improvisatory "happy" style had piqued the interest of radio broadcasters and record-industry talent scouts.

Success in the mainstream media helped to legitimize this street-corner music, which was labeled *kwela*, a slang reference to the police vans that patrolled the townships in Johannesburg looking for illegal shebeens. (Pennywhistle musicians frequently acted as lookouts to warn patrons of the approaching authorities by shouting, "*Kwela-kwela*.") Several groups added jazz drums and occasional piano to the instrumentation, but the pennywhistle remained the outstanding feature. Among the most successful kwela artists was Spokes Mashiyane (n.d.), who achieved notoriety with his 1954 recordings "Ace Blues" and "Kwela Spokes." He sustained his popularity throughout the 1960s and '70s, fronting his own bands and frequently performing with Miriam Makeba (1932–2008), who is arguably South Africa's most famous solo musician.

Miriam Makeba

Makeba, often dubbed "Mama Africa," became popular as a jazz singer in South Africa during the 1950s. Her appearance in Lionel Rogisin's underground documentary *Come Back, Africa* (1959), about the struggles of black South Africans under the apartheid political system, brought her to the attention of international audiences. This prompted her to leave her home country in pursuit of more creative freedom and financial reward. She frequently incorporated traditional music elements into her style, such as male backing vocals inspired by the mbube choirs, and sang modern versions of indigenous songs in her native tongue, Xhosa, which is distinctive for its several "clicking" phonemes. With the help of American musician and social activist Harry Belafonte (see Chapter 3), Makeba recorded several albums in the United States during the 1960s that featured songs in both English and Xhosa, most notably "The Click Song" and "Pata Pata."

Makeba's international notoriety came as not only a musician but also a cultural activist opposed to the segregationist policies of the South African government. In 1964, she presented to the United Nations General Assembly against the **apartheid** system and was subsequently banned from reentering her homeland. Her recordings were also banned, though she remained a recognized cultural icon of the antiapartheid

Apartheid a government policy of segregation that persisted in South Africa through the end of the twentieth century.

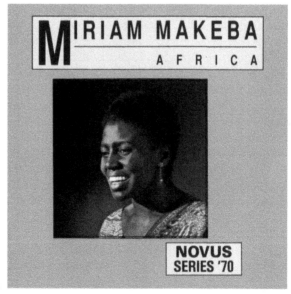

Miriam Makeba,
South African vocalist.

movement. During her concerts and speaking engagements, she continually educated the public about indigenous South African culture and the government's oppressive policies. In 1968, she married Stokely Carmichael (1941–1998), a Trinidadian American political activist who, in association with the Black Panthers, was a primary figure during the civil rights movement of the 1960s. The controversial union stifled Makeba's career within the United States, though she maintained modest appeal abroad.

After moving to Guinea, in West Africa, in 1969, Makeba continued to tour extensively throughout Europe, Africa, and South America. In 1974 she was invited to serve as a delegate of her adopted home to speak again to the U.N. General Assembly in opposition of apartheid. In 1986 she won the Dag Hammerskjold Peace Prize, awarded by the United Nations, and regained international popularity the following year as a participant in Paul Simon's *Graceland* tour, which allowed her to return to South Africa for the first time in more than two decades.

Her autobiography and subsequent comeback recording, *Sangoma* (1988), a collection of South African folk songs she knew as a child, reestablished her role as "Mama Africa" in the eyes of the general public. She appeared in the 1992 film *Sarafina*, starring Whoopi Goldberg, as well as the 2002 documentary *Amandla! A Revolution in Four-Part Harmony*, about the role of music in the struggle against apartheid. While the majority of protest songs from the apartheid period between 1948 and 1990 are infrequently performed today for lack of social relevance, they and the many musical activists associated with the struggle, such Vuyisile Mini (1920–1964), Hugh Masekela (b. 1939), and Vusi Mahlasela (b. 1965), along with Makeba, are revered for their historical significance as vital inspiration for achieving liberty from the prejudicial political system. Makeba returned to reside in South Africa in 1990 at the encouragement of African National Congress (ANC) leader Nelson Mandela (b. 1918), who had just been released after having served twenty-seven years in prison. She died in 2008 at the age of seventy-six.

MBAQANGA

Makeba is sometimes described as an early *mbaqanga* singer, though internationally she is regarded as a South African jazz vocalist. Her exile from South Africa in 1959 preceded the establishment of mbaqanga, which began in 1964 with the Makgona Tsohle Band, an instrumental group. These musicians drew from the popular American R&B sound, fusing it with the cyclic structure of marabi and improvisational solos featured in kwela music to create a distinctive style that featured electric instead of acoustic instruments. The saxophone became a common solo instrument, and a prominent bass-drum beat characterized the new *mbaqanga* (meaning "mish-mash" or "porridge") style.

Within a few months of forming, the Makgona Tsohle Band was teamed with vocalists for a studio recording for Gallo Records. The vocalists included several females, dubbed the "Mahotella Queens," and a lead male "groaner," Simon Mahlathini Nkabinde (1938–1999), whose deep, powerful voice and onstage dance performances reminded the group's urban audiences of their rural roots. During their concerts the group capitalized on this nostalgia by wearing clothing inspired by traditional styles, and they soon became famous throughout South Africa. Mahlathini became known as the "Lion of Soweto" (Soweto is a township outside Johannesburg), and the group, now called Mahlathini and the Mahotella Queens, recorded several successful albums, which were released locally throughout the 1960s and early '70s and included varying personnel in the female lineup.

"Township jive," as the popular music from the urban ghettoes of South Africa was often labeled, dominated the country's music scene for much of the late 1960s and '70s. The interweaving electric guitars influenced by Congolese soukous and funky bass

Mahlathini & The Mahotella
Queens

gave the music a modern sound that was original and not merely imitative of Western styles. The music was loud and full of energy, keeping audiences dancing until the early morning hours. Mahlathini and the Mahotella Queens quickly rose to prominence, traveling throughout the country with their charismatic stage show. Mahlathini was admired for his powerfully low vocal lead, and the Mahotella Queens' cheerful harmonies and buoyant dance choreography entertained the hundreds of migrant workers who attended their performances. They labeled their peppy brand of jive as *mqashiyo*, meaning "to bounce," which was as much a call for their audiences to dance as it was a reference to the Queens' own effervescent stage presence.

FOCUS EXAMPLE
MBAQANGA

((•● **HEAR MORE**
Download the
iTunes playlist link on
MyMusicKit

"KAZET," PERFORMED BY MAHLATHINI AND THE MAHOTELLA QUEENS

Focal Points

- **Instruments:** Two electric guitars (high and low), electric bass, synthesizer, drum set.
- **Vocals:** Male lead, with low "grumbles" (Simon Mahlathini) and backing female vocals (Mahotella Queens).
- **Language:** Mostly sung in Zulu but also includes English.
- **Melody:** Interweaving electric guitar lines repeat throughout the performance.
- **Harmony:** The backing vocals sing with harmony. Note that the electric guitars do not "strum" chords.
- **Rhythm:** Though a steady duple meter is present, the rhythmic articulation of mbaqanga often varies.

TIME	DESCRIPTION
0:00–0:05	Synthesizer and drum machine introduction.
0:06–0:09	Midrange guitar, and then electric bass, enter.
0:10–0:19	High-range guitar enters, with contrasting melodic line.
0:20–0:27	Male vocalist enters, with main melody in Zulu language.
0:28–0:33	Female group response.
0:34–1:25	Call-and-response organization continues in Zulu.
1:26–1:48	The lead vocalist says, "Africa!" and then improvises his lyrics.
1:49–2:36	Female group response returns as music continues to vamp.
2:37–3:08	Male vocalists shifts to English language.
3:09–3:47	Female vocal refrain returns, with lead vocal "groans."
3:48–4:15	New vocal material.
4:16–5:38	Female choral refrain returns, with lead vocalist singing in Zulu.

The instrumental opening introduces each of the performers at different points. The bass drum provides a steady beat, but note that each of the remaining instruments start on an offbeat, except the electric bass. This emphasis on offbeats happens throughout the performance and is easiest to hear with the snare drum, but note that the keyboard, electric guitars, and even voices enter on an offbeat.

	1		2		3		4		1		2		3		4	
Bass Drum	X		X		X		X		X		X		X		X	
Snare Drum		X								X				X			

((• **HEAR MORE**
on www.mymusickit.com
Mbaqanga Drum patterns

Certainly, this is not true of every mbaqanga song, but the offbeat articulation is a frequent occurrence typical of the genre. Listen for the subtle influence of Jamaican ska (see Chapter 3) as the keyboard plays a continuous skank offbeat starting at 0:10, when the second guitar enters.

The interweaving of the guitar lines is also a distinctive feature of mbaqanga and a common element of several popular styles in Africa, such as soukous and juju. Although the midrange guitar appears first, its melodic run falls later in the measure, beginning with the offbeat of the second pulse, whereas the high-range lead guitar plays a similar melodic run on different pitches, beginning on the offbeat of the first pulse. When both guitars play together, a continuous overlapping melodic line is created; the guitars are not used to strum chords, as is typical in most Western popular music. Some mbaqanga songs will use guitar chords, but repeated melodic motives such as these are more common.

The lead vocalist (Mahlathini) sings in Zulu, a language indigenous to South Africa. The female harmonic response is also in this language. The exchange between the vocalists follows a call-and-response format. While the lead vocalist changes the lyrics, the women sing the same refrain throughout the remainder of the piece. The music continues to jive on the same melodic material, repeating every two measures (eight beats). This continuous repetition of musical material is characteristic of mbaqanga and is derived from the earlier popular music styles of marabi and kwela.

When Western mainstream media became enraptured with South African music in the late 1980s and early 1990s, Mahlathini and the Mahotella Queens were invited to record in Paris. Their 1987 album *Paris-Soweto* included the major hits from their earlier

South African recordings but was specifically aimed at international audiences. Mahlathini's inclusion of English lyrics reflects this new patronage for South African music.

As the music and vocal refrain continues, Mahlathini begins to "groan," a signature style that he helped to popularize among mbaqanga performers. This leads to new vocal material, but the instrumental accompaniment remains the same. Improvised guitar solos are minimal in mbaqanga, usually occurring in short phrases or as a contrasting line to the vocal melody, rather than as extended extemporaneous passages. Other percussion instruments, such as a scraped gourd or tambourine, as well as a solo saxophone are sometimes included, but the core ensemble of two guitars, bass, and drums remains the standard backing ensemble for this music.

Mbaqanga played an important role in maintaining cultural pride among black South Africans during the years of apartheid. Musicians frequently performed for little or no pay to enthusiastic crowds gathered in township halls. Their message was one of resistance through happiness. Dancing, having fun, and enjoying one another's company were considered peaceful ways to resist the era's social and political oppression. Antiapartheid activists would take a more confrontational attitude toward the end of the 1980s, but the idea that cultural pride could be maintained through musical performance persisted through the struggle for a free South Africa.

Though mbaqanga was superseded in South Africa during the late 1970s and early 1980s by American music styles, such as disco and soul, the success of Paul Simon's *Graceland* album introduced the sound to a broader international audience. Most of the original members of the Makgona Tsohle Band reunited with Mahlathini and the Mahotella Queens for international performances, prompting new releases, notably *Paris-Soweto* (1987), which includes our Focus Example. Although the mbaqanga style has waned in popularity since the death of Mahlathini, in 1999, the Mahotella Queens still tour with new members, inspiring younger generations of musicians to draw on their roots for new musical creations. Some artists, such as Busi Mhlongo (b. 1947), continue to develop South African music by mixing contemporary influences with the older popular genres, including mbaqanga.

KWAITO

Most significant among recent musical developments in South Africa is *kwaito*. Often naively described as South African hip-hop, kwaito incorporates many preceding music styles, including kwela and mbaqanga, as well as music from the apartheid era, such as *toi-toi* (a marching style used during protests), that appeal to the performer's artistic objectives. Though American and British hip-hop and house music are the primary outside influences, kwaito is distinctively South African and has become the musical voice of the country's post-apartheid generation.

The pioneers of kwaito, such as Arthur Mafokate (n.d.), spent their early years as children of the antiapartheid revolution that peaked in the late 1980s. After this segregationist system was abolished in 1994, the younger generation sought a musical means of celebrating their liberation while voicing their frustration about living in the impoverished townships of urban South Africa. They avoided themes that dealt with the historical past and wrote lyrics that were intentionally apolitical, promoting a lifestyle that indulged in their newfound freedom yet still rebelled against economic and social prejudice.

Essential to the local success of kwaito is its use of indigenous South African languages and **Afrikaans**, a mix of Dutch and local dialects; English is often included to reach a wider audience. The colloquial language of the ghetto townships, known as

Afrikaans a South African language that mixes Dutch and indigenous dialects.

Tsotsi (Thug), is also commonly used and promotes the rough and rebellious image that kwaito artists typically portray. Kwaito uses all the modern studio technology typical of mainstream hip-hop in the Western world. Drum machines, synthesizers, samples, electric guitars/bass, sound effects, and similar elements keep the music current with modern international trends. The vocal delivery is modeled on the rapping style typical of Western hip-hop but makes more frequent use of call-and-response patterns (see Chapter 2). The lyrical themes of kwaito target the interests of South African youth culture, which is generally more interested in current fashions than politics. The music is primarily intended for dancing and mixes readily with international dance music from the Western world and elsewhere in Africa.

Among the most successful artists in the early twenty-first century is Bonginkosi Dlamini, better known as "Zola." His alias refers to one of the roughest neighborhoods of the Soweto Township outside Johannesburg, where he grew up. Zola is one of the few kwaito performers to emphasize serious subject matter in his music, and he has become an icon of the genre, hosting his own television show and appearing in films, such as the Academy-award-winning *Tsotsi* (2007), which featured his music on the sound track. Though the international mainstream media has paid little attention to the modern music of South Africa since the end of apartheid, the success of this film and an increasing interest among South African kwaito performers to use the music as a medium for social change are bringing greater visibility to the style, both at home and abroad.

WEST AFRICAN POPULAR MUSIC

While South African music has been especially popular on the international scene only since the late 1980s, West African musicians have garnered varying degrees of global success for several decades. Highlife, *juju*, and Afrobeat are genres well known to world-music enthusiasts. American jazz, funk, and, in the past two decades, hip-hop have been highly influential on West African popular music, but the most successful performers inevitably draw their inspiration from traditional performance practices, such as call-and-response singing and polyrhythmic instrumental organization. Often featured are local instruments, such as the *kora*, a 21-stringed lute-harp (chordophone), and many musicians are competent in the performance of both traditional and modern musical styles.

EXPLORE MORE
on www.mymusickit.com
Interactive Globe

Highlife

Perhaps the earliest successful popular music style emanating from West Africa is highlife. During the 1920s, highlife was essentially brass-band dance music for the social elites in British-occupied Ghana, then known as the Gold Coast. Performing waltzes, polkas, and other popular European dance music of the day for exclusive social events, the working-class populations came to consider the music as exclusive to those people "living the high life." Though the instrumentation duplicated that of European ballroom dance, some local musicians composed new music based on familiar folk melodies.

After World War II, Ghana's political climate changed as the country moved toward independence from British rule, which it won in 1957. Local traditions became increasingly influential on the dance-band repertoire, as did international genres, especially calypso, which had a similar historical evolution as dance-band music with a local flavor (see Chapter 3). American jazz, which then dominated the popular music landscape worldwide, expanded the audience for highlife bands as they incorporated jazz elements into their performances. During the 1950s, the optimistic attitude of the population toward the country's anticipated independence was reflected in the regular inclusion of indigenous rhythms, often played on traditional instruments, and lyrical content that addressed the changing political atmosphere.

A turning point in highlife's musical development came with the success of E. T. (Emmanuel Tettey) Mensah (1919–1996), a Ghanaian bandleader and trumpeter. Mensah had performed in various dance bands since the 1930s but established himself as an innovator in the post–World War II era with his highlife band, the Tempos. Unlike other highlife bands modeled after the large jazz bands of the swing era (1935–46), Mensah's group was pared down to just a few horns, an electric guitar, and a moderate rhythm section comprised primarily of Latin American percussion, along with some Ghanaian instruments. Calypso, samba, and rumba music was featured prominently in Mensah's style, which helped to liberate highlife music from its European mold. Polyrhythmic instrumental organization became a fundamental musical element, and the inclusion of local melodies in new compositions became common practice.

FOCUS EXAMPLE
HIGHLIFE

"GHANA-GUINEA-MALI," PERFORMED BY E. T. MENSAH
Focal Points

- **Instruments:** Saxophone, trumpet, trombone, electric guitar, acoustic bass, maracas, wood block, conga drums.
- **Vocals:** Male lead, with mixed male/female unison group response.
- **Language/Lyrics:** English language, with commentary about the independence of African nations.
- **Melody:** Hook melody on vocal refrain. Jazzlike trumpet solo.
- **Harmony:** Instrumental accompaniment provides background harmony.
- **Rhythm:** Follows a steady duple meter but incorporates Afro-Cuban polyrhythmic percussion.

TIME	DESCRIPTION
0:00–0:05	Opening guitar chords and percussion.
0:06–0:16	Saxophone solo on verse melody.
0:17–0:36	Trumpet and trombone enter on refrain melody.
0:37–0:47	First verse.
0:48–1:08	Refrain with mixed vocals on the song title melodic hook.
1:09–1:18	Second verse.
1:19–1:39	Vocal refrain repeated.
1:40–1:59	Improvised trumpet solo.
2:00–2:09	Third verse.
2:10–2:30	Vocal refrain.
2:31–2:41	Instrumental closing material.

The opening material introduces the instruments of the ensemble as well as the basic melodic and harmonic material. The saxophone plays the melody used later for the verse, while the entrance of the trumpet and trombone signals the hook melody used for the vocal refrain. The percussion instruments play with interweaving rhythmic patterns; most significant is the wood block (0:08) that sounds a reverse clave rhythm (2+3), revealing the influence of Afro-Cuban rumba music on Mensah's style.

Though earlier highlife music was mainly an instrumental tradition, social commentary became an increasingly important aspect of its vocal performances. Mensah sang in English as well as several indigenous languages, such as Ga, Fante, and Twi. His lyrics often focused on Ghana's independence and encouraged the unity of all African peoples against European colonial rule. His sound became particularly popular in Nigeria, where he often toured with a second band that he formed especially for his performances there. He also toured Europe and was successful enough to attract the interest of American jazz legend Louis Armstrong, who played with Mensah in 1956 in Ghana.

The vocal refrain highlights the song's title with a melodic hook. Mensah puts the group response on the line "Ghana-Guinea-Mali," ahead of the call provided by his vocal lead. This is the opposite of the usual call-and-response vocal organization of traditional music in Ghana, in which the call is first. The lyrics refer to Ghana's independence from colonial rule in 1957 and the subsequent independence movements in Guinea and Mali. The song reflects the optimistic attitude of Ghanaians during this period, who were hopeful that other indigenous populations throughout Africa would achieve similar political freedom.

The improvised trumpet solo is reflective of highlife's roots in American jazz music. The lyrical content continues with the independence theme of earlier verses. "Ghana-Guinea-Mali" became one of Mensah's most popular recordings His innovations inspired many highlife musicians to create a similar sound, though others kept with the standard big-band ensemble. Other entertainment styles, even palm-wine guitar, came to be regarded as highlife music so that the label was eventually used to describe a spectrum of stylistic features as diverse as jazz itself.

During the 1960s, highlife was superseded by Euro-American popular music genres as well as other African-based styles, mainly soukous (Congolese rumba) and later juju (see following section). Mensah continued to perform intermittently through the 1980s and was honored with several awards as one of West Africa's most important musical icons before his death, in 1996. Although highlife is less popular today, the genre is nevertheless recognized as historically important for the development of popular music in Africa.

Juju

In Nigeria, juju paralleled the development of Ghanaian highlife throughout the twentieth century. Dating to the 1930s, its early forms comprised only a few musicians playing a lute, such as a banjo typically played by the lead vocalist, a tambourine (known as *juju*), and a rattle (*shekere*). The percussionists often sang their vocal responses in partial harmony, usually parallel thirds, an influence of Christian hymnody. Because juju musicians often performed for local celebrations and important ritual events, Yoruba poetry figured prominently in the lyrical content.

As with highlife and many other traditions around the world, World War II and its aftermath greatly expanded the cross-cultural influences in juju music. Electric guitars and amplification systems appeared more regularly, which allowed musicians to add more instrumentalists without the worry of drowning out the vocalists. The Yoruba hourglass pressure drum, known as *dundun*, was commonly featured in later juju ensembles, as was an increasing number of traditional drums and other percussion. I. K. Dairo (1930–1996) and his band, the Blue Spots, were the most prominent juju musicians during the late 1950s and early 1960s, when nationalism was at its peak as Nigeria gained independence from the United Kingdom (1960). Dairo helped transform the juju sound from its modest small-ensemble roots to an exciting rhythmically intense ensemble that increasingly competed for audience appeal with the imported Ghanaian highlife.

As Euro-American rock music influenced popular-music culture around the globe, Nigerian musicians used new technologies to further distinguish juju from the music of

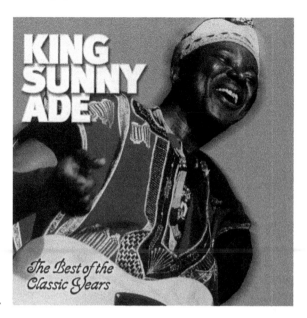

King Sunny Adé.

their West African neighbors. The oil boom of the early 1970s gave the Nigerian economy a boost that encouraged patrons to hire larger bands to raise their social prestige. The bands grew bigger and louder, as did their audiences. The most celebrated juju musician of this period was King Sunny Adé (b. 1946), known simply as KSA in his homeland.

KSA, a member of royal lineage from Ondo, in southwestern Nigeria, began his performance career in the 1960s playing in highlife and juju bands. Expounding on the innovations of I. K. Dairo, KSA formed his first band in 1966, dubbing them the Green Spots. He dropped the accordion that was often featured in Dairo's performances and introduced the pedal steel guitar, which added interesting aural effects in addition to its solo capabilities. The "talking drum" (dundun) became a mainstay of his performances, along with the electric bass. An expanded percussion section provided a complex polyrhythmic foundation rooted in Yoruba drumming traditions. But it was Adé's charismatic stage presence, distinctively nasal voice, "wizard" guitar skills, and creative use of sound effects on studio recordings and during live performances that earned him a steadily growing audience.

FOCUS EXAMPLE
JUJU

((• **HEAR MORE**
Download the
iTunes playlist link on
MyMusicKit

"JA FUNMI," PERFORMED BY KING SUNNY ADÉ

Focal Points

- **Instruments:** Multiple electric guitars, pedal steel guitar, synthesizer, electric piano, electric bass, various percussion, including dundun "talking" drum, shekere (gourd rattle), bell, conga drums, drum set. Electronic sound effects are a prominent feature.
- **Vocals:** Male vocal lead (KSA) and unison male group vocals.
- **Melody:** Short sung phrases with lead vocal, followed by group response. The melodic focus is on improvisational solos.
- **Rhythm:** Polyrhythmic percussion throughout the performance. Tempo gradually increases over the course of the performance.
- **Improvisation:** Extended improvisational solos, particularly on the pedal steel

guitar. Sound effects play a primary role in these passages. The dundun "talking" drum is often used as a solo instrument, though not in this example.

TIME	DESCRIPTION
0:00–0:13	Instrumental introduction.
0:14–0:47	"Ja Funmi" refrain.
0:48–1:03	Instrumental break highlighting lead guitar and dundun.
1:04–2:20	New vocal material.
2:21–2:45	Dundun improvisation is highlighted.
2:46–3:19	"Ja Funmi" refrain returns.
3:20–4:06	Vocal lead presents new material, with the lead electric guitar improvising between phrases. Note the falling portamento synthesizer sound at 3:54.
4:07–4:46	"Ja Funmi" refrain returns.
4:47–5:40	Pedal steel guitar solo.
5:41–7:08	Lead vocal with "Ja Funmi" refrain and improvised solos continue until the end of the performance.

Modern juju music typically begins with an instrumental introduction to establish the groove and initial tempo. This tempo may gradually increase throughout the performance, which is often several minutes long. The key features are the use of multiple electric guitars, polyrhythmic percussion, and distinctive indigenous instruments, such as the dundun.

Like South African mbaqanga and Congolese soukous, juju music uses two or more electric guitars playing repeated melodic motives from beginning to end. An additional lead guitar will sometimes contribute to the music in this way, or it will play improvised solos to complement the rhythm and regular melodic phrasing. Strummed chords are common but also play as a repeated harmonic motive, varying the pitches at different levels; this interweaving of guitar motives is an essential feature of juju. Our Focus Example includes three guitars, which are most easily heard when listening through stereo headphones. The midrange guitar playing a single repeated melodic line is heard in the right channel while a brighter timbre guitar plays an ascending chord pattern in the left channel. This leaves KSA to improvise in response to the instruments and vocal passages at a louder volume in the aural center.

Some juju music is sung in English, but the majority of lyrics are written in languages indigenous to Nigeria, such as Yoruba or Igbo. The lyric "Ja Funmi" means "fight for me" in Igbo and is a proverb intended to encourage the listener to think before taking action. The implied message is one of nonviolent resolutions to conflict, a notion unlikely to be conveyed to a cultural outsider.

The lyrics for juju often borrow from local poetry and traditional song. The vocalist may be telling stories of great events in an ethnic group's history, praising ancestral spirits, or relaying social and moral values through music. Such expressions are lost on non-native speakers, but the local populace understands the cultural inspirations for the lyrical content and the message the vocalist is delivering.

The dundun, a type of hourglass pressure drum found in West Africa, is often used for praising ancestral spirits or prominent figures in the local community. Its sound is distinctive for its ability to "bend" the pitch, which allows the performer to imitate the tonal inflections of the voice and speech rhythm patterns in order to "talk" with the drum. As with the actual language used in juju, understanding what the dundun musician is "saying" requires knowledge of the drum's "language" and how it is manifested in the performance. Juju music commonly features the dundun as part of the underlying rhythmic structure, but it may also appear as a solo instrument. Often, the dundun musician will "sing" the vocal refrain or recite the lyrics of a verse or other poetry. The musician may also improvise without trying to communicate a specific message. Recognizing the presence of the dundun is an important marker for identifying juju music.

Juju music evolved through the twentieth century and now includes influences from several popular world-music styles, such as calypso, jazz, and highlife. Mainstream popular-music trends during the 1960s and '70s also contributed elements that are heard in KSA's brand of juju, which is regarded as the highpoint in the genre's recent past. Aural processing effects were especially important to his performances during the 1970s and '80s, and these included prominent reverberation and echo effects along with electronic synthesizer sounds, such as the falling portamento pitch bend heard at 3:54.

KSA's most prominent contribution to the genre was his regular inclusion of the pedal steel guitar as a solo instrument. He found the distinctive timbre and characteristic "sliding" between pitches desirable and has included the instrument on many of his recordings since the 1980s. He has continued to experiment with other instruments, often adding traditional instruments from West Africa to his ensemble.

The presence of the dundun and pedal steel guitar, along with the interweaving guitar lines and polyrhythmic percussion, are helpful indicators in recognizing juju music. The soft-spoken vocal delivery that includes a group response, typically on the song's refrain, is also common to the genre. In addition, it is useful to notice the absence of instruments, such as trumpets, trombones, and saxophones. Although highlife influences are heard in juju music from the 1950s and '60s, juju today is primarily a guitar-based tradition. The novice listener is more likely to confuse the genre with South African mbaqanga or Congolese soukous than with Ghanaian highlife. But noticing the key elements highlighted previously should help even the first-time listener to recognize the distinctions between these often cross-influenced genres.

KSA made several recordings throughout the 1970s, renaming his band the African Beats in 1972. He is a household name in Nigeria and garnered international attention during the early 1980s after signing with Chris Blackwell at Island Records, the label that had successfully propelled Jamaican reggae artist Bob Marley to international stardom (see Chapter 3). Though Blackwell had aspirations of equally profitable returns, by promoting KSA as the "African Bob Marley," juju music did not appeal to Western audiences to the same degree as reggae had. KSA made only three recordings with Island Records before returning to Nigeria. Nevertheless, these recordings, along with his live performances, introduced juju to the world and established KSA's reputation as a pioneer of Afropop in the modern era. His popularity has remained steady within Nigeria, and he continues to record and tour.

Afrobeat

Afrobeat is another Nigerian musical style that fuses indigenous music with external genres. Paralleling juju and highlife, its rhythmic foundation is based on polyrhythmic percussion but is more heavily influenced by improvisational jazz. Afrobeat's creator, Fela Kuti (1938–1997), was born into a prominent middle-class family active in anticolonial protests while Nigeria was still controlled by Great Britain. Prior to the country's independence, Fela traveled to London in 1958 to study medicine but became enthralled with American jazz and instead learned music during his tenure in the United Kingdom.

Fela Kuti.

He returned to Nigeria in 1963 and worked to develop a new sound that fused his interest in improvisational jazz with West African highlife. In 1969, he traveled with his band, Koola Lobitos, to the United States, where he became enraptured with American funk, particularly the music of James Brown (1933–2006). He also found himself attracted to the political views of the Black Panthers during the height of the civil rights movement and increasing tensions over the Vietnam War.

Fela's American experience helped to shape the overt political commentary that infuses much of his music. His dozens of recordings throughout the 1970s and '80s are filled with criticism of the Nigerian government, its military dictators, and its corrupt politicians. These rebukes frequently provoked harassment and physical retaliation against him and his entourage. His scandalous lifestyle (such as having twenty-seven wives simultaneously), defiant lyricism sung in Pidgin English, and distinctive "endless groove" jazz sound intrigued Western audiences, earning him the attention of prominent record labels in Europe and the United States as well as frequent invitations to perform abroad. By the time of his death in 1997, Fela had recorded more than seventy albums and established Afrobeat as one of Africa's most prominent musical exports. His firstborn son, Femi Kuti (b. 1962), has since become one of the most successful musicians of the style.

The Praise Singers

While highlife, juju, and Afrobeat are established genres known throughout the world today, West Africa has also produced many globally recognized individual artists who fit less neatly into a specific stylistic category. Many of these performers hail from the westernmost countries of the African continent, such as Senegal and Mali. Traditional culture is highly influential on their repertoire and delivery of popular-music performances, most visibly noted in the use of traditional instruments, such as the *balafon* (xylophone) and *kora* (lute-harp). Active musical participation by the general population is common throughout the region, as it is in most of Africa, but the ethnic groups of these westernmost countries have also supported a caste of professional musicians, known as *jali* (plural *jalolu*), who maintain the oral histories of their people through praise singing.

The Western world has adopted the French term *griot* (wandering minstrel) to describe these professional artists and frequently applies the label to popular musicians who draw from their tradition. Musicians such as Salif Keita or Ali Farka Touré often borrow fingering techniques from the kora, the premier instrument of the jalolu. The vocal characteristics of these performers are also inspired by jali practices. Islam is widespread throughout West Africa, and the Muslim call to prayer and Koranic chant are considered influential on the melismatic vocal style of the griot musicians in both traditional and popular contexts.

Equally influential is the use of music as a means of telling stories, praising patrons, and educating the public on social issues. Nevertheless, the popular artists, such as Youssou N'Dour, have entertainment as their primary aim, so international influences, especially Latin music genres and Euro-American rock music, play important roles as well. Fusing these various styles while promoting the strong connection to their African roots has been the key to international success for the most famous of these griot musicians. After fame and fortune have been achieved abroad, many inevitably return home with an earnest sense of duty toward supporting their local communities.

SOUKOUS (CONGOLESE POPULAR MUSIC)

⊙➤ **EXPLORE MORE**
on www.mymusickit.com
Interactive Globe

While international audiences today are most familiar with Afropop from West and South Africa, many of the popular styles throughout the continent are indebted to music emanating from Central Africa, known generically within Africa as Congolese music and abroad as *soukous*. As with the early West African genres of highlife and juju, the roots of soukous began in the early decades of the twentieth century as radio and a burgeoning music industry within the French- and Belgian-colonized Congo region of Central Africa introduced African audiences to the current popular music styles from Europe and the Western hemisphere. These were dominated by jazz and, later, Latin music, particularly the Afro-Cuban rumba, which African musicians considered derivative of their own polyrhythmic traditions.

The earliest African rumba dance bands fused the Caribbean characteristics of the Afro-Cuban style with local music, such as palm-wine guitar, and sang in the widely known trade language of Lingala, which encouraged a nonspecific ethnic identity to appeal to the broadest audience possible. During the 1940s and '50s, commercial recordings of these dance bands became popular in many parts of sub-Saharan Africa. While the Euro-American influence was evident in the emphasis on a big brass-band sound, the Congolese sound incorporated a performance technique in which multiple guitars interwove short melodic phrases, which later influenced mbaqanga in South Africa and juju in Nigeria. The major difference was that this interplay was featured over the course of several different melodic phrases, rather than just one or two motives that merely supplied background support for the solo musicians and vocalists. The practice, known as *sebene*, was similar to performances on traditional melodic instruments, such as xylophones and lamellophones (e.g., *mbira*).

Sebene   the interplay of melodic motives in soukous music.

By the 1960s, these **sebene** sections, which concluded the song, had become the highlight of the music. Guitarists such as François Luambo Makiadi, (aka "Franco"; 1938–1989) and his band O.K. Jazz integrated rock music influences with extended guitar solos in their live performances, which carried on for twenty minutes or more. Audiences contributed to these energetic sebene sections with a variety of dances, the most popular being a hip-shaking frenzy known as soukous, that became ubiquitous by the end of the decade. While the big bands carried on, a trimmed-down version of the rumba bands appeared in the late 1960s and early 1970s, substituting synthesizers for the brass bands typical of ensembles in previous decades. These smaller troupes, led by the popular group Zaiko Langa Langa, became especially popular with teenage audiences, who were much more interested in a "rock" music sound than the "Latin jazz" sound that pervaded the earlier rumba bands.

Franco (François Luambo Makiadi), Congolese guitarist.

In the following decade, the political turmoil that had been mounting during the 1960s came to its peak when President Mobutu Sese Seko (1930–1997) initiated his "authenticity" campaign, intending to instill a unified sense of nationalism in the population. Many popular musicians, however, saw the new social edicts as a threat to their modern musical innovations and left the country. While most capitalized on the popularity of Congolese rumba in other African countries, such as Kenya and Tanzania, where the music was simply known as *Lingala*, others traveled to Europe in hopes of finding greater fame and fortune with European and American audiences.

Paris became a new center for Congolese rumba, and by the end of the decade recording-studio executives had begun to take notice. Needing a marketable label, the term *soukous* was applied to all the popular-music styles emanating from Central Africa. This included the slick studio versions recorded in Paris by artists such as Papa Wemba (b. 1949), who has been one of the most prolific performers of the various soukous styles since the 1960s. As new dances appear as part of the soukous scene, musical subgenres named after the latest dance fashion, such as *kwassa kwassa*, reinvigorate the Congolese rumba with each generation.

SUMMARY

In this chapter, we explored several of the most prominent music genres from sub-Saharan Africa that have attracted attention from international audiences. We began our journey in the townships of South Africa, the wellspring of some of the continent's most creative musical styles. These included mbube and isicathamiya choral styles, represented by the world-famous group Ladysmith Black Mambazo, as well as such instrumental styles as marabi and kwela that predate the powerful township jive, known as mbaqanga, represented by such musicians as the Mahotella Queens. We left South Africa with a brief introduction to kwaito, which reflects the musical trends of the country's current youth culture.

Traveling next to West Africa, we explored some older popular music styles, including highlife and juju, that still hold interest today, as well as Afrobeat, which achieved tremendous international acclaim during the 1970s. We acknowledged some of the great praise-singer artists, such as Youssou N'Dour and Salif Keita, who have

LEARN MORE
on www.mymusickit.com
Chapter summary
and exam

forged new pathways to popular world music on the international scene. Finally, we reviewed the eclectic mix of musical styles embodied in Congolese popular music, known as soukous.

Pathways

- **DVD:** *Ladysmith Black Mambazo: On Tip Toe.* Directed by Eric Simonson. 2000.
  - Award-winning documentary about Ladysmith Black Mambazo and the mbube choral tradition.
- **Book:** Erlmann, Veit. *Night Song: Performance, Power, and Practice in South Africa.* Chicago: University of Chicago Press, 1996.
  - Comprehensive review of the nightsong competitions in South Africa.
  - www.press.uchicago.edu/presssite/metadata.epl?mode=synopsis&bookkey=47071
- **Film:** *A Lion's Trail.* Directed by François Verster. Independent Lens, 2006.
  - A documentary film about the song "Mbube," recorded by Solomon Linda. Difficult to obtain but highly recommended.
  - *www.pbs.org/independentlens/lionstrail/index.html*
- **Film:** *Come Back, Africa.* Directed by Lionel Rogosin. 1960.
  - A documentary highlighting underground music activity in South Africa during the 1950s.
  - *www.lionelrogosin.com/default.php*
- **DVD:** *Rhythm of Resistance: Black South African Music.* Directed by Chris Austin and Jeremy Marre. Shanachie: Beats of the Heart Series, 2000.
  - A documentary from the 1980s that includes a variety of South African music genres.
- **Book:** Makeba, Miriam, and James Hall. *Makeba: My Story.* New York: Plume, 1989.
  - South African singer and activist Miriam Makeba's autobiography.
- **DVD:** *Amandla!: A Revolution in Four-Part Harmony.* Directed by Lee Hirsch. Artisan Home Entertainment, 2003.
  - A documentary about the role of music in the struggle to end apartheid in South Africa. Highly recommended.
- **DVD:** *Tsotsi.* Directed by Gavin Hood. Miramax Films, 2006.
  - A fictional film set in the townships of South Africa. Kwaito music is featured on the sound track.
  - *www.tsotsi.com*
- **Book:** Waterman, Christopher. *Jùjú: A Social History and Ethnography of an African Popular Music.* Chicago: University of Chicago Press, 1990.
  - A comprehensive review of jùjú music from its roots through the 1980s.
  - *www.press.uchicago.edu/presssite/metadata.epl?mode=synopsis&bookkey=59899*
- **Book:** Veal, Michael. *Fela: The Life and Times of an African Musical Icon.* Temple University Press, 2000.
  - A biography about the creator of Afrobeat music, Fela Kuti.
- **DVD:** *Baaba Maal: Live at the Royal Festival Hall.* 1998.
  - A documentary about the Senegalese musician.
- **DVD:** *The World of Youssou N'Dour.* 2001.
  - A documentary about the Senegalese musician Youssou N'Dour.
- **Book:** Ewens, Graham. *Congo Colossus: The Life and Legacy of Franco and OK Jazz.* Buku Press, 1994.
  - A biography about the soukous musician François Luambo Makiadi, aka Franco.

Keywords for Additional Music Examples

- Ladysmith Black Mambazo
  - Amabutho
  - Ladysmith Shaka Zulu
  - Ladysmith Raise Spirit
- Solomon Linda "Mbube"
  - Mbube Evening Birds
  - Wimoweh
  - Wimoweh Tokens
- Kwela
  - Kwela Spokes
- South African Musicians
  - Miriam Makeba
  - Hugh Masekela
  - Vusi Mahlasela
  - Makgona Tsohle Band
  - Busi Mhlongo
- Mahlathini and the Mahotella Queens
  - Paris Soweto
- Kwaito
  - Zola
- Juju
  - I. K. Dairo
  - King Sunny Adé
- Afrobeat
  - Fela Kuti
  - Femi Kuti
- "Praise Singer" Musicians
  - Salif Keita
  - Ali Farke Toure
  - Youssou N'Dour
  - Baaba Maal
- Soukous
  - Grand Kalle
  - OK Jazz
  - Zaiko Langa Langa
  - Papa Wemba
- Kwassa

South Asia and the Middle East:
Bollywood and Beyond

INTRODUCTION

Asian popular music undoubtedly covers the broadest array of sounds we will encounter in our excursion of popular world music. Though Asia comprises more than half the world's population, few musicians from this vast geographic expanse have achieved notoriety in the Western world. The twenty-first century, however, may well see an explosion of Asian pop stars on the international music scene, as the world's economic balance leans increasingly on Asian markets. As prospering populations fuel the music business in these arenas, the media machine, which now includes the Internet, will bring greater visibility to promising artists from the farthest reaches of the globe. Presently, however, the internationally recognized artists are typically those who perform classical or folk music rather than music that could be regarded as "popular." Some find themselves in demand in "world fusion" performances, whereas others are able to tour independently throughout the world with only their own musical interests in mind.

THE BEATLES

Throughout this book, our focus has been on artists and music styles generically labeled "popular world music." We could conceivably consider all music to be world-music, since it comes from somewhere in "the world." Using that criterion, the Beatles could be considered history's most popular world music artists. Even though the group disbanded in 1970, many of their songs are known the world over among young and old alike. Bands around the globe cover Beatles songs, and the faces of John, Paul, George, and Ringo are among the most recognizable on the planet.

Although their music continues to find new audiences with each generation, their lesser-known songs, such as "Within You, Without You," "The Inner Light," and "Norwegian Wood," are infrequently recognized by the general public. Many of these pieces feature the use of Indian classical instruments, such as the sitar and tabla, making the Beatles one of the first mainstream groups to fuse world music with modern popular music. The Fab Four's fascination with Indian culture is well known, but rarely does anyone consider them world-music artists. By today's standards, perhaps they are not, but during the 1960s the inclusion of world-music instruments on mainstream recordings (i.e., Euro-American popular-music records) was revolutionary. George Harrison (1943–2001), the group's youngest member, was the most seriously interested in Indian music, which is reflected in many of his contributions to the group's catalog as well as much of his solo work. His fascination with the sitar led him (and the other Beatles) to both musical and spiritual exploration of Indian music and culture.

Because of the Beatles' influence on pop culture in the Western world throughout the 1960s, many in the so-called hippie movement were influenced by Harrison's study of Eastern philosophy and music. In the mid-1960s Harrison befriended Pandit Ravi Shankar (b. 1920) and was instrumental in arranging the sitar maestro's appearance at the 1967 Monterey Pop Festival, considered a pivotal event in popular music history. Shankar also appeared at the legendary Woodstock concert event, in 1969, and in 1971 he and Harrison co-organized the Concert for Bangladesh, a charity event for relief of refugees from East Pakistan (today known as Bangladesh). The two men maintained their friendship until Harrison's death, in 2001, when Shankar was reportedly at his dying friend's bedside.

PANDIT RAVI SHANKAR

The association with George Harrison and many popular musicians of the 1960s and '70s made Pandit Ravi Shankar a household name in America and Europe for many years. Today's audiences, however, are probably more familiar with his daughters Norah Jones (b. 1979), an American folk-pop singer, and Anoushka Shankar (b. 1981), a sitar musician under the tutelage of her famous father. Nevertheless, he has long been at the forefront of promoting Indian music and culture to international audiences, first performing for Western audiences in the 1930s, as a dancer and musician in a traveling troupe led by his brother Uday Shankar (1900–1977). The elder Shankar's innovative theatrical presentations of classical Indian music and dance in Europe and the United States earned him great prestige as a celebrated choreographer and dancer in his homeland and abroad. These early experiences with the Western world's cultural elite undoubtedly aided the younger Shankar in his future aspirations to attract international audiences to his own performances.

By the 1950s, Ravi Shankar began writing the scores for Indian films and became music director for the country's national radio broadcast, All India Radio. His notoriety as a virtuoso sitar musician earned him many accolades both at home and abroad, where he was in great demand as a touring artist in Europe and, later, the United States. His recordings of Hindustani classical *raga* made during the early 1960s are considered among his finest studio works. Furthermore, he was strongly influential on jazz music icon John Coltrane (1926–1967), who named his son Ravi (b. 1965), after the Indian music emissary. By the time of Shankar's appearance at the 1967 Monterey Pop Festival, he was already a revered figure among world-music enthusiasts throughout the West.

Shankar continued to pursue his interests in cross-cultural collaboration, composing Western-style orchestral works that include traditional Indian instruments; in 1983 he was nominated for an Academy Award for his contributions to the score of the film *Gandhi* (1982). He has made numerous recordings of Hindustani classical music and continues to perform live, often with his daughter Anoushka. He has received many awards for his invaluable contributions to music and culture throughout the world and is generally recognized as one of the most influential musicians of the twentieth century.

BOLLYWOOD AND FILMI

The music played by Shankar and other classical artists has been the primary image of India's musical identity to outsiders. Yet, the popularity of Hindustani classical music within India (and among Indian communities abroad) pales in comparison to the much-adored music of the Indian film industry, known as *filmi*. India's film industry annually produces the largest number of movies in the world: more than one thousand in 2001,

◉➤ **EXPLORE MORE**
on www.mymusickit.com
Interactive Globe

George Harrison and Ravi Shankar, ca. 1968.

compared to roughly seven hundred from the United States. Although its worldwide revenues are far less (roughly $1.3 billion [India] versus $51 billion [U.S.]), India's film industry is becoming increasingly popular throughout many parts of the world, particularly in those experiencing a growth in Indian diasporas.

"Bollywood" is the label commonly used in the Western world to describe the whole of Indian cinema, though initially the term was only a colloquial reference to the burgeoning film industry in the modern city of Mumbai (formerly Bombay). Considered the Hollywood of India (Bombay + Hollywood = Bollywood), Mumbai is the second-largest city in the world, with a population of 13.8 million, and one of the most eclectic cultural centers in India. A rising middle class has brought increasing wealth and outside popular culture influences into the country as a whole, which has in turn affected the style and standards of Indian films. Once characterized as over-the-top melodramatic musicals, Bollywood films since the 1990s have garnered increasingly positive critical acclaim as well as a growing international reputation for better production quality and thematic variety. The success of *Slumdog Millionaire* (2008) at the 2009 Academy Awards, during which it won eight of its ten nominations, has certainly legitimized the industry's growing popularity.

The majority of Hindi films, as they are known in India, remain entrenched in the musical format, in which the plotline is often overshadowed by spectacular presentations of song and dance. Expecting the inclusion of playback singing and choreographed dancing is important to an appreciation of a Bollywood film on its own terms, just as you might anticipate musical performances in a 1950s- or '60s-era Hollywood film, such as *Singin' in the Rain* (1952) or *The Sound of Music* (1964), or more modern movie musicals like *Moulin Rouge* (2001) or *Across the Universe* (2007). Although the actors in Hindi films become famous in their own right, much of the interest in seeing the latest Bollywood production is due to the soundtrack, from which potential hit songs are often released well in advance of the film to pique interest (and sales) when the movie opens.

Where the actors in Western films are typically encouraged to do their own singing, filmi music rarely includes the voices of the actors who appear onscreen. Rather, they use **"playback" singers** who perform the vocals for the movie soundtrack. The same vocalist may be heard singing for different actors within the same film, sometimes even within the same song. This practice may seem peculiar to a Western audience, but

Playback singer
a singer in the Indian film industry whose voice is lip-synched by onscreen actors.

filmi fans appreciate the song as an entity separate from the film, and so the occurrence of differing faces backed by the same vocalist is accepted.

Audiences attend Indian films as much for the music as for the acting or story line. Playback singers often attain star status easily equaling and often surpassing their onscreen lip-synching counterparts. Many playback singers, particularly from the "golden age" of Hindi films (1950s–1970s) are known by first name alone, such as Lata (Mangeshkar) (b. 1929) or her sister Asha (Bhosle) (b. 1933). Along with male performers of the period, such as Mukesh (Chand Mathur) (1923–1976), these golden-age vocalists established the Bollywood style by which current playback stars, such as Alka Yagnik (b. 1966), still perform.

There are two basic types of filmi: sentimental songs and dance songs. The former have nostalgic or romantic themes, with an emphasis on melody and minimal inclusion of percussion instruments. The latter have strong rhythms and memorable melodic hooks. Each of our focus examples represents one of these categories. Though very different in mood, they share some common musical elements that help to identify each type of filmi music.

FOCUS EXAMPLE
FILMI

"SOJA RAJKUMARI," PERFORMED BY LATA MANGESHKAR

Focal Points

- **Instruments:** Listen for folk and classical Indian instruments, such as the sitar, sarangi, or tabla. Lush strings are typical of older filmi music, whereas in modern music synthesizers often supply similar orchestral effects. Modern instruments, such as electric guitars and drum sets/machines, are also common.
- **Voice:** The female voices tend toward a nasal quality, with a high range. Men's voices are often in a higher male range. Heavy reverberation is commonly used as an effect on the voices. Unison choral singing that emphasizes the upper female range is often featured as a response to the lead vocalist or to sing the melodic hook.
- **Language/Lyrics:** Typically sung in Hindi or English, though other native languages of India are found. Themes usually focus on romantic love or familiar contexts, such as a wedding ceremony or children's lullaby.
- **Melody:** A melodic hook is typical of the refrain, especially in dance songs. Melismatic ornamentations are common to vocal performance. String instruments tend to carry the main melody in instrumental sections.
- **Rhythm:** Dance songs have a heavy beat inspired by folk rhythms or Western popular music genres. Ballads often have varying tempos within the same piece and free rhythm passages.

"Soja Rajkumari," performed by Lata Mangeshkar

TIME	DESCRIPTION
0:00–0:20	String and piano introduction.
0:21–0:29	Female soloist (Lata Mangeshkar) enters.
0:30–0:45	String and piano accompaniment returns.
0:46–0:47	A sitar sounds.
0:48–1:27	Voice returns, followed by a tabla providing a steady beat.
1:28–3:07	The vocalist and accompaniment continue as before, but with some new melodic and harmonic content.

Western instruments have been a part of Indian musical culture since the sixteenth century; the violin is commonly used in folk, classical, and popular music. Filmi music frequently uses lush orchestral accompaniment that emphasizes the violin, particularly in sentimental songs, such as this children's lullaby. During the 1970s, live orchestras were often substituted with less expensive synthesizers. In today's industry, both are frequently used.

Lata Mangeshkar is among the most famous popular world-music artists. She has recorded thousands of songs in a career spanning more than forty years. Along with her sister Asha Bhosle, Lata established the archetype voice for female playback singers in the Indian film industry during the 1960s. Her vocal timbre tends to be nasal, particularly when singing in a higher range. She uses subtle melisma to ornament the melody, which is inspired by classical performance techniques that focus extensively on the use of ornamentation as a way to express emotion.

The use of classical and folk instruments in popular filmi music is very common and a distinctive element that helps with recognition. This, of course, assumes that the listener is familiar with the unique timbre of such instruments as the sitar and tabla. In this example, the sitar plays only a single sliding pitch to punctuate the end of a few melodic phrases throughout the performance (0:46/0:55/1:18/2:53). Sometimes such classical instruments will play extended solo passages, much like a guitar or saxophone might be used in mainstream popular music. Percussion instruments, such as the tabla, are also frequently heard playing the primary rhythmic component in filmi, as in this example.

This lullaby was first made famous in the 1940 film *Zindagi*, by Kundan Lal Saigal (1904–1947), one of Bollywood's early movie stars. Lata's version is consistent with the earlier recording, but advancements in recording technology have resulted in a higher production quality. Sentimental songs often draw on lyrical content from well-known songs or classical poetry. These songs are intended to stimulate an emotion in the listener and are sometimes based on musical rules related to the classical theory of *rasa*, which provides guidelines for how to express specific sentiments, such as love, sorrow, anger, or fear, through artistic mediums, like music or painting.

FOCUS EXAMPLE
FILMI

((• HEAR MORE
Download the iTunes playlist link on MyMusicKit

"CHAIYYA CHAIYYA," PERFORMED BY SUKHWINDER SINGH AND SAPANA AWASTHI

TIME	DESCRIPTION
0:00–0:05	Synthesizer string sound with wind chimes.
0:06–0:37	Female vocalist sings with melismatic opening phrase in free rhythm. Notice the electronic echo.
0:38–0:47	Electric guitar/bass, drum, and shaker introduce beat.
0:48–0:53	Male vocalist enters with "Chaiyya chaiyya" refrain.
0:54–1:09	Dance-beat rhythm begins.
1:10–6:53	The song continues with poetic verse and several repetitions of the "Chaiyya chaiyya" refrain.

"Chaiyya Chaiyya" was written by A. R. (Allah Rakkhha) Rahman (b. 1966), one of the premier composers of filmi music in the modern era. This song was written for a scene in the 1998 Hindi film *Dil Se* (From the Heart), starring Shahrukh Khan (b. 1965), one of Bollywood's superstar actors. The song was a big hit in India as well as in London, where Bollywood films are extremely popular and frequently open in major cinemas.

A. R. Rahman.

Many musical elements of "Chaiyya Chaiyya" are typical of modern filmi dance songs. The song opens with a synthesizer "string" sound, and the female vocalist, Sapana Awasthi (n.d.), has a somewhat nasal timbre that includes subtle ornamentation and short, sliding melismas added to her initial melodic line. Reverberation, with an extended decay time, enhances her voice, as does an echo of the final half of the phrase. The use of pronounced reverberation and echo is common in filmi music but is especially effective in this song, where it is coupled with the visual imagery of a train ride in the mountains (the context for its performance in the movie).

After the opening material, the music moves into a steady meter with a strong beat. In classic Bollywood films, a song's basic rhythm was often rooted in folk music traditions. In modern filmi music, the rhythms are often influenced by Western popular genres, such as rock and hip-hop. Other world-music influences, such as Afro-Cuban rhythms, are atypical in Indian popular music. The music follows formulaic techniques common to mainstream popular music as well, such as melodic hooks and the repetition of the vocal refrain several times throughout the performance.

Filmi songs often become popular in their own right, but their intended purpose is to accompany extended dance scenes in a movie. The choreography often incorporates folk and classical movements, along with a modern style of dancing. The performances typically include a dozen or more dancers executing the same moves simultaneously. The headlining actors usually play a central role in these dances and lip-synch to the sound track throughout the scene. The "Chaiyya Chaiyya" dance sequence was filmed atop a moving train in the mountains of southern India and is among the most memorable scenes in the history of Bollywood films.

Although Western audiences often discount the melodramatic acting and insertion of lavish dance numbers into the plotline, Hindi films have long been recognized for what movies are intended to be: an escape from the reality of life, if only for a few hours—and in the case of a Bollywood film, sometimes five or six hours! The actors are expected to be extraordinarily beautiful, as is actress and Miss World 1994 Aishwarya Rai (b. 1973), and the settings evoke an air of fantasy. Historical themes are becoming more common, but the majority of Hindi films are love stories with happy endings. Star-crossed lovers challenged by cultural obstacles, such as the practice of arranged marriages or socioeconomic disparity, typically provide the central plot.

Filmi dance sequences are intended to heighten this escapist perspective by taking on the qualities of a music video, where scenery changes can occur in seconds and the actors find themselves in some of the most beautiful places on earth. Expected cultural norms, such as no displays of public affection, are suspended for the length of the song, and the actors (in fact, the playback singers) can sing of desires that would be taboo in real life.

Directors of the past were keenly aware that their primary audience generally lived in poverty, so uplifting themes and fantasy imagery allowed for temporary relief of their viewers' everyday circumstances. As India's economy prospers, however, middle- and upper-class audiences, who are often influenced by Western cultural attitudes, have been an increasingly profitable market. So, too, are the thousands of nonresident Indians living in Europe, the United States, and elsewhere who watch Hindi films and provide an ever-expanding market. As such, some Indian filmmakers increasingly feature new story lines, scenery, and music, such as bhangra, that appeal to these growing audiences around the world.

BHANGRA

● ▶ **EXPLORE MORE** on www.mymusickit.com Interactive Globe

Indian filmi features vocals and melodic instruments, but the percussion-based bhangra style is often used for the dance sequences in today's Bollywood productions. Bhangra began as a folk genre from the Punjabi region of northern India and has evolved into one of the most significant types of popular world music on the global scene. Traditionally, bhangra was a celebratory dance performed by men and most commonly associated with harvest festivals. Today, folk bhangra is more often found at wedding and New Year celebrations. The musical accompaniment is dominated by percussion instruments, with the central instrument being a double-headed barrel drum, known as *dhol*. The dhol is held by a strap around the drummer's neck and played with two sticks. Several other percussion instruments are typically present, along with such melodic instruments as the *tumbi*, a single-stringed plucked lute that is often found in Bhangra pop styles as well.

Bhangra's evolution into a popular world-music style dates to the mid-1970s, when Punjabis from India (and Pakistan) began migrating in increasing numbers to London and elsewhere in Great Britain. As the Anglo-British mainstream largely ignored the expansion of the Punjabi population, members of the community established their own means of disseminating their cultural activities and products through new businesses, such as food markets and clothing stores. The latest Bollywood films were aired through BBC-TV Asian programming, and pirated cassette recordings of the hottest filmi songs were distributed through underground networks.

Though connections to home were important to the growing Punjabi community, the urban setting of London encouraged a modern perspective that reflected the diasporas' new cultural context. Soon music included lyrics that voiced their social struggles

Dhol drummer.

within British society, as well as nostalgic references to their South Asian origins. Since disco was the current musical trend, the London-Punjabi urbanites added synthesizer sounds and electronic drumbeats to the more familiar rhythms of bhangra to create a new style that was contemporary yet rooted in their traditional music. Early artists, like the Heera Group, experimented with the latest sounds while others, such as Apna Sangeet (n.d.), maintained the bhangra percussion as the centerpiece of the modern style. Dance clubs patronized by Punjabi youth increasingly included the latest bhangra hits along with the mainstream dance/disco music. By the mid-1980s, underground vendors were selling thousands of copies of modern bhangra recordings, which soon started finding their way back to India and Pakistan.

Malkit Singh, bhangra superstar.

Bhangra has evolved into a variety of styles, but the dance-oriented songs remain the most popular and are especially common at weddings and similar celebratory events. Modern artists, such as Jaswinder Singh Bains (aka "Jazzy B," (n.d.), incorporate drum machines, synthesizers, electric guitars, and a wide range of electronic effects inspired by mainstream popular music styles, such as rock and hip-hop. Among the most successful artists is Malkit Singh (b. 1972), who has more than twenty albums to his credit since the mid-1980s and was honored with the British MBE, presented by the Queen of England in 2008. While Singh's inclusion of modern sounds keeps his music up-to-date, he remains true to the roots of bhangra by using traditional instruments and bhangra rhythms as the core of his compositions.

FOCUS EXAMPLE
BHANGRA

"JAGO AAYA," PERFORMED BY MALKIT SINGH

Focal Points

- **Instruments:** Dhol drum, hand claps, tumbi (single-string chordophone), harmonium.
- **Vocals:** Lead male vocal, with mixed unison response.
- **Melody:** Strong, central tonality established by tumbi. Vocal melody is chantlike on just a few pitches.
- **Rhythm:** Strong, steady duple meter, with the standard bhangra rhythm (see the following figure).

TIME	DESCRIPTION
0:00–0:20	Instrumental introduction. Note the tumbi melodic hook at 0:06.
0:21–1:06	Lead vocal enters. Note the choral responses that repeat the lyric endings.
1:07–1:17	Tumbi melodic hook returns.
1:18–2:03	Vocal returns with some melodic variation.
2:04–2:12	Melodic hook returns, with addition of vocal effects.
2:13–3:04	Vocal returns, with melodic variation.
3:05–3:16	Tumbi melodic hook returns.
3:17–3:36	Harmonium instrumental solo.
3:37–9:02	Vocal returns, with continual reappearance of instrumental melodic hook breaks (4:17, 5:12, 6:14, 7:14). Note the steady bhangra rhythm throughout the performance.

Bhangra is dance music. The melody uses only a few pitches strongly centered on the pitch of the tumbi or other instrument that sounds throughout the performance. A male vocalist provides the text, which is mostly syllabic but will frequently include melisma on the last syllable of a phrase. In this example, a mixed male/female group with a filmi-like nasal timbre responds to Singh's vocal melody.

The key marker of bhangra, however, is the use of a regular rhythm. Tempos may vary from song to song, but the bhangra rhythmic pattern is what identifies the genre. The pattern is either played on traditional instruments or sounded by an electronic drum machine. The music follows a four-beat duple meter and includes three components: a continuous "anticipation" pattern, usually articulated by a high-pitched drum or a single-pitched melodic instrument, such as the tumbi; a strong, low tone on the first and fourth beats, usually provided by the dhol or a bass drum; and a higher tone drum or hand claps on the third beat.

Three components of the bhangra rhythm

	1		2		3		4		1, etc.
"Anticipation" Pattern	x	x	x	x	x	x	x	x	x
High Accent					X				
Low Accent	**X**						**X**		**X**

((•● **HEAR MORE**
on www.mymusickit.com
Bhangra Rhythms

These three components make up the basic bhangra rhythm typical of both the folk- and popular-music styles. Other features of the music may vary, but this driving rhythm is fundamental to identifying the genre.

In the mid-1980s, reggae influences began to find their way into bhangra music, prompting the success of such breakthrough artists as Apache Indian (b. 1967) and Bally Sagoo (n.d.), who by the early 1990s had found success with Britain's mainstream musical culture. Their achievements encouraged other Indian artists to pursue their own musical creativity in different genres. Pop-fusion artists, notably Sheila Chandra (b. 1965), attracted a wide audience and garnered international attention from fans and mainstream popular-music superstars, such as Peter Gabriel (b. 1950). By the mid-1990s, Punjabi artists performing in a variety of traditional genres, such as *qawwali*, which had been made famous by Pakistani musical icon Nusrat Fateh Ali Khan (1948–1997), were finding increasing international success by incorporating modern sounds and studio techniques. Many of today's contemporary artists of Indian descent, such as Canadian-born Kiran Ahluwalia (n.d.), continue to develop traditional genres, including *ghazal* (a poetry set to music), by mixing them with cross-cultural influences. The legacy of Indian music, both folk and classical, continues to shape the popular styles created by Indian artists throughout the world.

MIDDLE EASTERN POPULAR MUSIC

India's Bollywood may produce the most visible films of central Asia, but West Asian cinema has played an important role in promoting some of the Middle East's most prominent musical stars of the last century. Although music and dance are sometimes featured, they are not a ubiquitous centerpiece of the production, as in Indian films. Middle Eastern films are often critically acclaimed but do not achieve much notoriety in mainstream culture outside the region. Political circumstances have sometimes made it difficult for artists in music, film, and other industries to express themselves freely. Fundamentalist interpretations of the Islamic faith are often blamed, but these can also encourage the development of distinctive art forms by prompting a reaction to restrictive cultural policies.

Persian Popular Music

Among the most notable of popular music superstars from West Asia is Googoosh. Born Faegheh Atashin (b. 1951) in Tehran (Iran), Googoosh began performing with her father at an early age. The duo performed most often in cabaret clubs and for public programs and festivals, and their act was a mixture of acrobatics, dancing, and singing. During this early period in Googoosh's life, Iran was ruled by Mohammad Reza Shah Pahlavi (1919–1980), a monarch intent on modernizing the country to appeal to political powers in Europe and the United States. Several of his reforms, however, were controversial, most notably the banning of the *chador*, the outer garment traditionally

●→ **EXPLORE MORE**
on www.mymusickit.com
Interactive Globe

Googoosh performing in 2000 for the first time in the United States since she was decreed "decadent" and banned from singing in Iran after the 1979 revolution.

worn by women to cover their heads and body. Many women, such as Googoosh, readily accepted this break with tradition, but others considered the prohibition of the chador akin to forcing women to walk in public wearing only their undergarments, a cultural notion lost on many Western women who criticize the traditional attire.

Music of this period also reflected the uneasy melding of centuries-old customs with modern popular styles imported from the West. The most prominent musicians performed Persian classical music, whereas those playing popular styles were considered inferior. The first Iranian pop-music star to achieve respectable notoriety was Vigen (Viguen) Derderian (1929–2003). His success was due, in part, to his inclusion of traditional Persian instruments, such as the *santur* and *sehtar*, with Western-style instruments, including electric guitar, accordion, and the drum set. His vocal style maintained the characteristic melismatic text settings of traditional vocal performance, and his songwriters targeted a growing middle-class youth market through lyrics that were most often about unrequited love. Vigen's success initiated interest in the "new sounds" of the Western world, and his strong masculine image coalesced with Iran's patriarchal society.

In contrast, Googoosh represented the feminine image that the Shah's reforms were intent on promoting, especially with regard to equal rights for women. Unveiled and unafraid to follow the fashions of Western culture, she presented a cosmopolitan portrayal of the modern Iranian woman that was attractive to Iran's rising urban

Chapter 8 • South Asia and the Middle East: Bollywood and Beyond   **161**

middle class. She sang in Farsi, Armenian, Turkish, English, Spanish, and French, earning accolades abroad as well as in her native country. She acted in many films throughout the 1960s and '70s and was regularly featured on Iranian television, singing her latest recordings. Indeed, her fame was so widespread throughout Iran in the 1970s that people joked about hearing the name "Googoosh" as often as they heard the word "hello."

While her beauty and modernity added to her appeal among young Iranian urbanites, the essence of Googoosh's fame came from her voice. Seamlessly blending melancholy and grace, she expressed the poetry provided for her by Iran's leading composers with a heartfelt emotion that reflected not only her own personal challenges, but those of the Iranian population, which was growing increasingly discontent with the Shah's stringent rule. Throughout the decade he alienated nearly every segment of society through his public policies and personal actions, and by the end of the 1970s the country was poised for a revolution.

In January 1979 the Shah fled Iran, and soon thereafter the monarchy was dissolved. While in exile, he was permitted to enter the United States for medical treatment, which angered pro-revolutionaries in Iran who felt the Shah had been a "puppet monarch" of America throughout his reign. Protestors stormed the United States Embassy in Tehran and kidnapped fifty-two American diplomats, holding them hostage for 444 days, from November 4, 1979, to January 21, 1981. The hostage crisis fueled the influence of fundamentalist hardliners within Iran's new government and encouraged anti-American sentiment among its populace, conversely spurring anti-Iranian reactions within the United States and severing all diplomatic ties between the two countries.

The move toward modernism, which was viewed by traditionalists as "Westernization," ceased, and anything considered unacceptable by the influential Islamic clergy was abolished. Women were required to don the chador again or risk social ridicule, abuse, or imprisonment. Popular music, considered sinful and a result of Western influence, was banned and recordings were destroyed throughout the country. Women were no longer allowed to perform in public, and composers were often required to submit their lyrics to government censors, who ensured the text was morally acceptable according to their interpretation of the Islamic faith. To avoid such restrictions many artists left the country, as did a growing number of middle- and upper-class Iranians disillusioned by the failures of the revolution.

While many musicians left Iran and continued their careers by performing for the country's exiled communities, Googoosh remained. She was no longer allowed to perform in public, which she had done for nearly her entire life, and she was prohibited from recording new music of any kind. She adopted the traditional life of an Iranian woman and remained "silent" for more than twenty years. Googoosh's absence, however, only strengthened the adoration that exiled Iranians felt for her. Her songs, which so often dealt with longing for a lover's reunion, became a nostalgic symbol for Iranian expatriates wishing to return to their homeland. Even within Iran, at the end of the 1990s and early 2000s bootleg recordings of her music were in great demand within urban communities, particularly among young adults who were too young to remember the days of the revolution.

Musicians in Iran have long struggled to express themselves freely through their art. Even classical musicians have weathered periods of suppression that kept their performances hidden from the public. Depending on the attitudes of the local populace or current Shah, musicians played their music in secret for fear of persecution, performing only for close friends and fellow musicians in intimate settings, such as a family home. Although the social climate within Iran has changed for classical musicians, popular artists certainly can face similar challenges. Public performances may be monitored, but underground live performances do exist, and many artists find audiences by selling their music through the black market.

Googoosh's music remains popular within the country as well as among exiled Iranians nostalgic for their homeland. Her music represents an idealized past when Iran was on the brink of attaining international recognition as a first-world nation and global power. Freedom and prosperity were the expectations for the 1979 revolution, but instead the government instituted strict cultural and political edicts that discouraged many and spurred large numbers of Iranians to leave the country.

FOCUS EXAMPLE
PERSIAN POPULAR MUSIC

"GHARIB EH ASHENA" ("STRANGER, FAMILIAR"), PERFORMED BY GOOGOOSH

Focal Points

- **Instruments:** Stringed ensemble, electric bass, flute, *zarb* (goblet-shaped drum), *daf* (frame drum).
- **Voice:** Female vocalist (Googoosh) sings with frequent ornamentation and in a passionate tone.
- **Language/Lyrics:** Farsi (Persian) language. Romantic themes of emotional anguish are common.
- **Melody:** Minor scales predominate.
- **Rhythm:** Steady duple beat.

TIME	DESCRIPTION
0:00–0:06	Strings and electric bass begin, with descending chromatic melody.
0:07–0:13	Flute enters.
0:14–0:25	Percussion instruments enter.
0:26–1:12	First verse.

FARSI	ENGLISH
To az shahreh gharibeh bi neshooni oomadi.	You are from an unknown city with no sign.
To baa asbeh sefideh mehrabooni oomadi.	You come on a white horse of kindness.
To az dashthaayeh dooro jaadehayeh por ghobaar.	You are from a far-away desert filled with sand.
Baraayeh ham sedaayi ham zabooni oomadi.	You come with a voice like mine.
To az raah miresi por az gardo ghobaar.	You arrive covered in sand and dust.
Tamoomeh entezaar miyaad hamraat baahaat.	All the waiting and longing come with you.
Che khoobe didanet, Che khoobeh moondanet.	How good is seeing you, how good that you stay.
Che khoobeh paak konam ghobaaro az tanet.	How good it is when I wipe the sand away from you.

1:13–1:24	String interlude.
1:25–2:00	"Gharib eh Ashena" refrain.

FARSI	ENGLISH
Gharibeh aashenaa, Dooset daaram biaa.	Stranger, Familiar, I love that you have come.
Mano hamraat bebar, Beh shahreh ghesehaa.	Take me with you, to the city of fairy tales.
Begir dasteh mano, Too oon dastaat.	Take my hand, in your hands.
Che khoobeh saghfemoon, Yeki basheh baaham.	How good is our home, when there is someone with me.
Bemoonam montazer, Taa bargardi pisham.	Should I wait, until you come back to me.
Too zendoonam, Baa to man aazadam.	In my prison, with you I am free.

2:01–3:53	Return to opening instrumental material and repeat of verse and refrain.

Both Persian classical and popular music tend toward a melancholy mood. Chromatic and minor scales are more common than major scales, for the former better express the often sorrowful or nostalgic tone of the lyrics. This performance begins with a four-pitch descending chromatic scale; a descending scale is a compositional tool often employed to correspond with a sad emotion.

Western strings and a flute are coupled with percussion instruments typical of Iranian folk music. Popular world music frequently uses such combinations of Western and indigenous instruments, as we have seen in many of our Focus Examples, so it is important to become familiar with the different timbres of various instruments, such as the zarb (goblet-drum). This example also features the daf (frame drum), an especially common instrument in West Asia that has various labels and permutations throughout the Middle East.

"Gharib eh Ashena" ("Stranger, Familiar") is typical of many Persian songs in classical, folk, and popular contexts that deal with love lost, reminiscences of happy times in the past, and yearning for better days ahead through vivid poetic imagery. As much as these topics resonated with Iranians during the peak of Googoosh's popularity in the 1970s, exiled Iranian populations since the 1979 revolution have clung to such story lines as symbolic of their joyful memories, grief for their present exile, and hope for the future, when they will return to their beloved country. Though new Persian pop stars have appeared within Iranian diasporas, Googoosh's fame before the revolution and her decision to remain in the country afterward, relinquishing her public life in the process, endeared her to countless overseas Iranians who considered her courageous without measure.

Googoosh was unaware of her continued popularity during her twenty-year hiatus from public life. In 2000, she was permitted to leave Iran to act in a film directed by her husband, Masoud Kimiai (b. 1941). This prompted requests for her to perform a concert in Toronto's Air Canada Center, near the film production site. After accepting, she was quickly showered with other offers to perform, and soon the number of invitations amounted to an international tour that stretched over the next eight months. The outpouring of emotion from fans encouraged Googoosh to forgo her plans to return to Iran. She continues to perform her most cherished songs from the 1960s and '70s for audiences around the world, and she has recorded several successful albums since leaving Iran. Googoosh once again lives in the public eye as one of the many thousands of Iranians who yearn to repatriate someday without fear of social and political reprisals.

Arabic Popular Music

⊙➤ **EXPLORE MORE**
on www.mymusickit.com
Interactive Globe

In the Arab world, Islam is highly influential on musical production, but Euro-American popular styles are recognized as part of the region's musical soundscape. These outside traditions, however, are generally viewed as if they were a foreign language: good to know, but not a substitute for local music. Classical song maintains a strong "popular" appeal throughout the Middle East. While the instrumentation of the modern classical compositions is heavily laden with Western instruments, particularly strings (e.g., violin), traditional instruments, such as the *oud, kanun, ney*, and various percussion, are still fundamental to performance. Classical performers of these instruments continue to be highly regarded by the general public, and the names of iconic figures from decades, even centuries, ago are still recognized by people of all ages. Though contemporary artists have updated the popular styles with drum machines, synthesizers, and electronic sounds to cater to the youth culture and nightclub dance scene, the "classic" sound of purely acoustic instruments continues to be at the heart of the Arabic world's most popular music.

Although instrumental performance, particularly on the oud, is the medium for many successful musicians in the Arab world, poetic song is the most highly prized. This is due, in part, to the influence of Islam, whose members greatly admire the exquisite recitation of the Koran (which is not considered to be music). Many children study their religion by learning to chant the verses of Islam's holy book, and the performance of religious song at festivals throughout the region attracts large audiences eager to celebrate their spiritual beliefs through music, which the religion otherwise discourages.

Umm Kulthum

Imam a religious
leader in Islam

Most revered among the artists of the classical-popular style is Umm Kulthum (1904–1975). During her childhood, Kulthum was recognized for her vocal talents in reciting Koranic verse. Her father, an **imam**, sometimes dressed her as a boy so that she could perform for men in private venues. In 1923, she moved to Cairo, Egypt, where she was befriended by the local literati, several of whom wrote poetry for her to sing. Her diction was considered to be near perfection and her powerful voice and ability to improvise in the Arabic modal style, known as **maqam**, endeared her to classically trained artists as well as the general population.

Maqam the modal
system used in Arabic
music

As gramophones and radio became increasingly common throughout the Arabic world, Kulthum's popularity spread throughout the Middle East. She sang in several films during the late 1930s and '40s but did not pursue acting as a career. She preferred a live audience to inspire her performances, which regularly lasted three hours or more. Though she became quite wealthy, she remained committed to her humble upbringing and kept her private life hidden from the public eye. She was strongly patriotic and often performed to raise money for the Egyptian army. She was honored with many awards during her lifetime, and her monthly broadcast on national radio continues to air on the first Thursday of every month, featuring recorded performances of some of her most beloved songs. More than four million people attended her funeral in 1975, making it one of the largest recorded gatherings in human history.

Kulthum remains the watermark for female performers of Arabic classical-pop music throughout the Middle East. Many artists perform songs from her repertoire as tributes to the Egyptian diva, acknowledging her stature throughout the Arab world. "Inta Omri" is one of her best-known songs and has been recorded in many styles by dozens of artists. Some are upbeat "belly dance" versions with electronic instrumentals and processing effects, but the most respected are live performances that model Kulthum's classical style of singing. Our Focus Example is of the latter type, performed by Lubna Salame (n.d.) and the Nazareth Orchestra.

Umm Kulthum
on stage in Paris,
in 1967.

FOCUS EXAMPLE
ARABIC SONG

"INTA OMRI," PERFORMED BY LUBNA SALAME
AND THE NAZARETH ORCHESTRA

Focal Points

- **Voice:** Single female soloist.
- **Instruments:** Violins, acoustic bass, *ney* (flute), *dombek* (goblet drum), *riqq* (tambourine), and *kanun* (plucked zither), known collectively as a *firqa*.
- **Language/Lyrics:** Sung in Arabic. A single line of text may be repeated several times due to improvisation.
- **Melody:** Melody includes frequent ornamentation in both the voice and the instrumental accompaniment. The instruments play with a unison melodic line, imitating or matching the voice.
- **Rhythm:** Shifting tempos and variety of meter, often moving into free rhythm passages.

TIME	DESCRIPTION
0:00–0:40	Kanun and acoustic bass enter in free rhythm.
0:41–0:46	Strings enter.
0:47–1:03	Full ensemble enters, with main theme in duple meter.
1:04–1:37	New melodic material.
1:38–1:53	Ney joins the ensemble, with new melodic material.
1:54–1:59	Brief free rhythm passage.
2:00–2:28	Return to meter and new melodic material.
2:29–2:47	Ensemble shifts to free rhythm, with new melodic material.
2:48–3:51	Female vocalist enters.
3:52–4:02	Vocalist repeats the last two lines of the verse.
4:03–4:35	Rhythm shifts to duple meter, with continued improvisation on last two lines of the verse.

ARABIC (ROMANIZATION)	ENGLISH
Ragaa'ouni a'einaik el Ayam illi rahou	Your eyes took me back to my days that are gone.
A'alamouni andam a'ala El-Madhi wi gerahou	They taught me to regret the past and its wounds
Illi shouftouh kabli ma tshoufak a'inaih	Whatever I saw, before my eyes saw you, was a wasted life.
Omri dhayea' yehsibough izay a'alaya?	How could they consider that part of my life?
4:36–5:01	Vocal improvisation on the title lyric, "Inta Omri"

ARABIC (ROMANIZATION)	ENGLISH
Inta Omri illi ibtada b'nourak sabahouh	With your light, the dawn of my life started.
5:02–5:07	Applause.
5:08–5:58	Instrumental section.
5:59–8:27	Voice returns with instrumental accompaniment.

ARABIC	ENGLISH
Ad eyh min omri kablak ray w a'ada	How much of my life before you was lost
Ya habibi ad eyh min omri raah	It is a wasted past, my love.
Wala shaf elkalb kablak farhah wahdah	My heart never saw happiness before you
Wala dak fi eldounya ghair taa'm el-jiraah	My heart never saw anything in life other than the taste of pain and suffering.
Ibtadait bilwakti bas ahib omri	I started only now to love my life
Ibtadait bilwakti akhaf la ilomri yijri	And started to worry that my life would run away from me.
Kouli farha eshtakha min kablak khayali	Every happiness I was longing for before you
Eltakaha fin our a'ainaik kalbi w fikri	My dreams they found it in the light of your eyes
Ya hayat kalbi ya aghla min hayati	Oh my heart's life … You are more precious than my life
Leih ma kabilni hawak ya habibi badri	Why didn't I meet your love a long time ago?
8:28–8:40	Music shifts to free rhythm.
8:41–9:50	Music returns to a steady beat at a slower tempo.

The opening instrumental material reveals several characteristics of this classical style of popular song. The ensemble, known as a firqa, is a blend of Western stringed instruments and traditional instruments common to the Middle East. Because of their flexibility of pitch, stringed instruments such as the violin are easily adaptable to Arabic music (and other world music styles). The Arabic modal system, known as maqam, uses pitches not found in Western harmony; the violin, however, is capable of playing these frequencies because there are no fixed pitches on the instrument.

Another important feature of this opening is the use of varied melodic material. Repetitions of a melody may occur, but it is common to introduce new themes throughout a performance to make the music more interesting. Doing so also allows the vocalist more ideas with which to work in his or her own improvisations. Instrumentation may change in the performance of a melody, again to provide contrast rather than repetition, even if the melody is the same as in an earlier passage.

Variations of rhythm are also important. This instrumental introduction moves from free rhythm to duple meter. The beats are grouped into eight pulses, with the dombek emphasizing beats 1, 5 & 6. In later passages, this emphasis shifts to different pulses. This is common in Arabic music because of the use of rhythmic modes, known as **iq-at**, which may move the accent of pulses to different beats. Thus, the grouping of eight pulses here is accented on the 1, 5 & 6 beats, but later emphasizes beats 1 & 3 of a four-pulse grouping. Listening for the low tone played on the dombek is a good indicator of a shift in rhythmic mode.

The vocalist enters during the free rhythm passage (2:48). Her melodic line is ornamented heavily with a melismatic text setting. She moves through the lyrics at her own pace, with the orchestra providing support. Notice how the orchestra imitates some of her ornamentations, even though these are largely improvised. Vocalists and melodic instrumentalists abide by the rules of maqam, which is a modal system that includes an extensive number of fixed ornamentations that the musician must learn. During a

Iq-at   rhythmic modes in Arabic music

performance, the maqam will determine the pitches to be used during a performance (i.e., the scale) as well as ornamentations that can be included. Accomplished instrumentalists are often able to anticipate the improvisations of a vocalist because they draw from a similar pool of ornamentation possibilities.

Umm Kulthum was a virtuoso performer not only for her powerful voice but also for her extensive knowledge of maqam and the associated ornamentations. She prided herself on never singing a line of poetry the same way twice, and she would often repeat a lyric for several minutes with different melodic ornamentations. Less-accomplished performers may find themselves running out of improvised material, with only a few repetitions. Kulthum's live performances of a single song could extend to well over an hour, and often three or more.

An important consideration in appreciating the lyrical content of Arabic song is its association with Islamic poetry. Poetry has been an important cultural activity throughout West Asia for centuries. Much pre-Islamic poetry dealt with secular activities and spiritual beliefs that were frowned upon by early Muslim scholars. Converts to the religion began to write new poetry that espoused the spiritual and moral values of Islam. Sufi and Persian poetry influenced the tradition as well, using vivid imagery and symbolism as a means of expressing devotion to God.

Oftentimes, the lyrical content of a seemingly secular song is a thinly veiled expression of spiritual passion. Where a non-Muslim may view the passionate declarations of love and happiness as referring to affection for another person, a devout Muslim may interpret the lyrics as an exultation of spiritual ecstasy. This is especially true in the classical arts, where music is considered an effective means of expressing a person's passions. The lyrics of "Inta Omri" should be considered as a declaration of faith as much as a pronouncement of secular love.

After the applause for the opening section, the orchestra returns with new melodic material. Notice how frequently the melody consists of short melodic motives that repeat at different pitch levels. This is a common compositional tool in Arabic music that allows the composer to extend a passage without needing to create a new musical idea.

As the vocalist moves through the performance, note how the theme is similar with each verse, but never exactly the same. Even on the lines where the vocalist repeats the lyric, her ornamentations are unique. This variation of melodic content is essential for a successful performance.

"Inta Omri" contains several more verses that are not included in this performance, but the devotional theme remains similar. In the closing material of our example, the vocalist continues her ornamental improvisations of the basic melody. Again, it is important to recognize that melismatic singing is highly prized throughout West Asia, not just in Arabic vocal performance but in many classical traditions from Iran, Turkey, India, Pakistan, and elsewhere. This reveals a value system different from that of the Western world, where most music is sung with syllabic text settings. From the perspective of the Arabic classical musician, the inability to ornament a melody indicates a poorly skilled performer. That is in part why popular music from the Western world is considered inferior to classically inspired Arabic songs such as "Inta Omri."

Although Kulthum and many other classically trained Arabic performers are more highly regarded than those espousing a Western popular sound, musicians who do incorporate modern technology into their music frequently find great success. Islamic doctrine is critical of musical activity that stimulates emotional rather than spiritual intentions, but certainly not everyone in the Middle East is Muslim. Furthermore, open-minded Muslims recognize the decision to listen to secular pop music, native or foreign, as an individual choice. Only in regions where fundamentalist interpretations of the Koran are forced upon the populace is such secular music prohibited. Performers from non-Islamic backgrounds, such as Fairuz (b. 1935), who is Christian, or Ofra Haza (1957–2000), who is Jewish, have achieved international success and are much beloved in their homelands regardless of their listeners' religious backgrounds.

Although male pop performers are frequently successful, the aforementioned superstars (Googoosh, Kulthum, Fairuz, and Haza) are women, as are many others not noted here. Historically, throughout the Muslim world the role of entertainer has been played by women, who often perform as dancers accompanied by male or female musicians. Such secular performers were typically from the lower economic classes, marginalized ethnic groups, or non-Islamic religious backgrounds.

ALGERIAN RAI

Rai, an Arabic popular music genre that originated in Oran, Algeria, is a good example of a music that historically featured women of perceived "questionable" social status. Under Spanish rule (1509–1708), Oran was a heavily fortified port city and a popular destination for sailors looking to spend time with prostitutes kept by the local government. This stigma remained throughout the Ottoman occupation (1708–1830), when the city was beleaguered by earthquakes and suffered under military reprisals by the Spanish. By the time the French claimed it in 1831, Oran had fallen into disrepair, and its population was regarded as a disreputable lot. Over the next century, the population grew into a unique multicultural mix of Jewish, French, Spanish, and Arab communities, but the city never lost its sordid reputation.

> **EXPLORE MORE**
> on www.mymusickit.com
> Interactive Globe

The varied ethnic backgrounds provided for a wealth of musical resources. By the turn of the century, European and Arabic instruments were often found together in performance, and musicians frequently exchanged ideas about musical content. Improvised poetic song formerly associated with nomadic Bedouin shepherds found its way into Oran and was adapted to the new urban context by street musicians who performed with a variety of accompanying instruments. The lyrical content of these songs, known as *zedani* (or *hadhari*), dealt with the growing number of issues Algeria's underprivileged populations were experiencing under French rule. Poverty, crime, prostitution, and social discontent were common topics that concerned the zedani performers and their audiences.

The zedani singers were initially men, since female performances in public venues were limited to women-only events primarily because of social pressures that discouraged women from pursuing such activities. A woman who sang in public often sacrificed her social respectability, even if performing the *medh*, popular songs praising the Islamic prophet Muhammad. Consequently, most female performers were already poor or otherwise marginalized from the cultural mainstream. Some were content to perform for all-female audiences to maintain some vestige of perceived social acceptance, but others dismissed the expected cultural norms for women altogether and regularly performed in public for both sexes, typically in contexts considered disreputable by mainstream society. Nightclubs, bars, and brothels were the regular haunts for these rebellious women, who adopted as part of their stage names the honorific title *Cheikha* (*shaykhat*), quite aware of the irony inherent in the label.

By the 1930s, the Cheikha women were singing unabashedly about any topic that pleased them, often shocking their audiences with pointed poetry about the loss of virginity, pleasures of sex, indulgences in drinking, and discrimination against themselves and women in general. Their lyrics were mixed with bits of Oran street slang, French, and stock phrases borrowed from Bedouin poetry, such as the colloquial interjection "*rai*," translated roughly as "in my opinion," that allowed a singer time to consider the next lyric. This rebellious spirit, as exemplified by the matriarch of traditional rai, Cheikha Remitti (1923–2006), would prove a wellspring for later singers.

During World War II, American troops stationed in Oran brought with them jazz and popular music styles that influenced many Algerian musicians, including the rai performers. By the 1950s, the accordion was commonly featured in rai ensembles, though it was adapted to the Arabic modal system (maqam), which includes quarter tones not found in the Western tuning system. The rai musicians experienced a setback after Algeria won independence from France, in 1962, when the new government suppressed their performances, which were considered vulgar and counter to the country's new cultural policies aimed at portraying a "civilized" image to the outside world. Women performers suffered the most. They were banned from public performances, and the spotlight shifted to the genre's male artists. Even with such restrictions, many musicians, especially those in Oran, continued to perform and find inspiration in outside sources, such as the Beatles and James Brown. Several pioneering performers, including trumpeter Messaoud Bellemou (n.d.), believed that the future of rai depended on making the music danceable for general audiences.

By the 1970s, rai had become an amalgam of native and international influences. The vocal and lyrical prowess of the earlier cheikhs and cheikhas were still featured in the pop rai sound, but to these were added electronic keyboards, drum machines, and an assortment of other Western instruments, including the saxophone, trumpet, and accordion. As recordings became cheap and readily available during the cassette boom of the late 1970s the evolving pop rai sound quickly spread. Artists of this period adopted a new moniker, "Cheb" (meaning "young"), to distinguish themselves from the old-style rai performers. The popularity of the new rai rose within Algerian communities in France and soon spread into other Arabic-speaking countries.

By the mid-1980s, the government could no longer dismiss the popularity of this musical genre, and in 1985 it sponsored the first Festival of Rai. Although the event was outwardly intended to show the government's open-minded acceptance of a music that was frequently antiestablishment, an ulterior objective was to "clean up" the music by censoring lyrics and discouraging public dancing, particularly between men and women. The festival succeeded in bringing together many of the top performers but also prompted several artists to seek audiences outside Algeria, realizing that rai was destined to be stifled under government surveillance.

Most prominent among artists during this period was Cheb Khaled (Khaled Brahim, b. 1960), dubbed the "King of Rai" at the first Algerian Festival of Rai. Already a

Cheb Khaled, the "King of Rai".

well-known figure in the music community, Khaled left Algeria after the festival and re-established his career in Paris. In 1991, he signed with a prominent French record label to become the first rai artist whose music was distributed to an international market. Throughout the 1990s, he had several hits as a crossover artist in France and became wildly popular in India as well. His success paved the way for several other rai artists to reach global markets, most notably, Cheb Mami (b. 1966), whose contribution to the hit single "Desert Rose," by popular British musician Sting, has helped to introduce rai to many new global markets and American audiences, in particular.

FOCUS EXAMPLE
RAI

"DIDI," PERFORMED BY CHEB KHALED

Focal Points

((•● **HEAR MORE**
Download the
iTunes playlist link on
MyMusicKit

- **Instruments:** Two dombek (goblet drum), shaker, tambourine, synthesizer, saxophone, and drum set.
- **Voice:** Male vocalist (Cheb Khaled), with occasional use of melisma.
- **Melody:** Frequent use of melodic hook in both the vocal refrain and the instrumental breaks.
- **Rhythm:** Steady, duple-meter dance beat.
- **Form:** Verse-refrain-instrumental break repetition occurs throughout the song.

TIME	DESCRIPTION
0:00–0:04	Dombek introduction with shaker to establish tempo.
0:05–0:14	Synthesizer introduction.
0:15–0:31	Male vocalist enters.
0:32–0:41	Drums, tambourine, and "funk" bass enter, with strong dance beat.
0:42–0:52	Second verse and "Didi" refrain.
0:53–1:12	Instrumental hook phrase.
1:13–2:02	Verse-refrain-instrumental hook form continues.
2:03–2:30	Improvised saxophone solo.
2:31–5:02	Verse-refrain-instrumental hook form continues to the end.

The use of traditional instruments is common in rai, but they are generally either overshadowed by modern instruments such as the synthesizer, drum set, electric bass or guitar or may not be present at all. The use of synthesizers with a "brassy" sound already sets this style of pop music apart from the classically oriented style of Umm Kulthum, which emphasizes string orchestral accompaniment. "String" synthesizer effects are common in rai, but there is a tendency to sound more like a jazz band than an orchestra; thus, trumpets and saxophones are more typical than violins.

The vocal melody is repetitive, having a limited range. The text setting is mostly syllabic, though short melismas are often heard at the end of a phrase. Popular music is syllabic more often than are the classical arts, but the occasional prevalence of these ornamentations is indicative of popular music throughout West Asia. The lyrics are sung in Arabic, although, given the genre's popularity in France, French is also a common language for rai songs. Where classical song uses the expression of love as a symbol for spiritual devotion, in rai the love interest is entirely secular. In this case, the vocalist expresses his heartache for a woman he adores but who is not interested in him. The lyrics continue to evoke this basic theme throughout the song.

The tambourine, drums, and bass enter with a strong beat in duple meter. Rai is meant for modern dancing, so the music is heavily influenced by mainstream popular-music styles. The second verse concludes with the "Didi" refrain, which ends every verse. The instrumental melodic hook (verse-refrain-instrumental) rounds out the basic form and is repeated until the end of the song. The mainstream popular music format encourages this type of progression, frequently repeating the melodic hooks to make the song memorable and, consequently, to promote sales. The improvised saxophone solo briefly breaks up the pattern, again revealing the influence of rock and jazz music. The song returns to the verse-refrain-instrumental hook progression until the music ends.

Rai is one of the most successful popular genres to emerge from the Middle East. Its evolution from folk to modern presents an interesting case study of the influence of mainstream popular media on roots music genres. Today, the term *rai* represents a variety of styles, from the traditional sound of rai's original form still performed by cheikhs and cheikhas in Algeria, to the sentimental love songs of Cheb Hasni (1968–1994), to the hip-hop- and reggae-influenced pop mixes of contemporary artists, like Khaled (who dropped "Cheb" in 1992) and Cheb Mami.

SUMMARY

LEARN MORE
on www.mymusickit.com
Chapter summary
and exam

In this chapter, we reacquainted ourselves with pop culture's interest in Asian music and culture during the 1960s. Our exploration began with the Beatles and their fascination with India, as reflected in a few examples of their music. We learned about one of the most prominent figures in the world-music industry, Pandit Ravi Shankar, and then visited Bollywood to listen to filmi music, one of the most influential non-Western popular music styles around the globe. Our tour of Indian popular music finished in London with an introduction to the modernized version of bhangra.

Next we ventured to West Asia, a region dominated by Islamic culture, where we learned about Persian popular music and Arabic song, which is heavily influenced by classical music traditions. We wrapped up our discussion with a brief review of Algerian rai, which has become one of the most popular world music styles in Europe in the last few decades.

Pathways

- **DVD:** *The Complete Monterey Pop Festival.* Directed by D. A. Pennebaker. The Criterion Collection, 2002.
  - A documentary of the 1967 Monterey Pop Festival, considered a pivotal point in American popular music and culture.
- **DVD:** *The Voice of India: Lata Mangeshkar.* 2005.
  - A collection of film excerpts featuring the songs of famous filmi playback singer Lata Mangeshkar.
- **Book:** Manuel, Peter. *Cassette Culture: Popular Music and Technology in North India.* Chicago: University of Chicago Press, 1993.
  - A study of popular music and transformation of the music industry in India with the advent of cassette recording technology.
  - *www.press.uchicago.edu/*
- **DVD:** *Dil Se.* Directed by Mani Ratnam. 1998.
  - A fictional film starring filmi actor Shahrukh Khan. Features the song "Chaiyya, Chaiyya."

- **Internet:** "Welcome to Bollywood"
  - *http://ngm.nationalgeographic.com/ngm/0502/feature3/?fs=www7.nationalgeographic.com*
  - An online *National Geographic* article about the Bollywood film industry.
- **DVD:** *Googoosh: Iran's Daughter.* Directed by Farhad Zamani. 2000.
  - A documentary about Persian singer/actress Googoosh, prior to her return to public life in 2000.
- **DVD:** *Umm Kulthum: The Voice of Egypt.* Directed by Michal Goldman. 1996.
  - A documentary about Egyptian diva Umm Kulthum.
- **Internet: Keywords:** "Running with the Rebels"
  - An online article about Algerian Rai.
  - *www.echo.ucla.edu/Volume5-Issue1/al_taee/al_taee1.html#top*

Keywords for Additional Music Examples

- Pop culture interest in Indian music
  - George Harrison
  - Monterey Pop Festival, Ravi Shankar
- Filmi artists and music
  - Lata Mangeshkar
  - Asha Bhosle
  - Mukesh
  - Alka Yagnik
  - Soja Rajkumari
  - Chaiyya Singh
- Bhangra artists and music
  - Heera Group
  - Apna Sangeet
  - Jago Aaya Singh
  - Malkit Singh
  - Apache Indian
  - Bally Sagoo
- Other South Asian popular-music artists
  - Sheila Chandra
  - Nusrat Fateh
  - Kiran Ahluwalia
- West Asian pop artists and music
  - Viguen
  - Inta Omri
  - Fairuz
  - Ofra Haza
  - Cheikha Remitti
    - Cheikha Rimitti
  - Bellemou rai
  - Cheb Khaled
  - Cheb Hasni

East and Southeast Asian Pop: Karaoke Culture

INTRODUCTION

Despite the wealth of goods that East and Southeast Asian countries export to global markets, popular world music from these areas is probably the least familiar of all world music to general audiences outside the region. Ironically, the area's traditional genres, particularly those from Indonesia, Japan, and China, are a major focus for ethnomusicologists and world-music enthusiasts. Many traditional musicians, such as Tuvan throat-singer Kongar-Ol Ondar, have taken advantage of this outside interest by "updating" their performances, creating captivating music that mixes the most modern technological toys with some of the most ancient sounds on the planet

KARAOKE

Premier among these toys is the karaoke machine. Similar sing-along recordings have been common in the music industry since the early 1950s, but the advent of the karaoke machine in the 1970s created a revolution in musical entertainment that has since spanned the globe. *Karaoke* is a Japanese term usually translated as "empty orchestra." The implication is that only an instrumental sound track is heard, without vocals.

Early karaoke machines were a single unit that played a cassette recording of a popular song (without vocals) through an amplifier. Incorporated into the amplifier was a microphone input with a basic reverberation sound effect to give the amateur singer's voice a more studio-like quality. Later karaoke recordings took advantage of stereo channels by including a singer on one channel and only the backing music on the other. Consumers thus had the option of singing solo or with a vocalist to learn the words and melodic line, depending on the channel they selected. Technological advances and increased demand during the 1980s brought further innovations. Some machines had the capability of transposing the pitch of the music, the vocal input, or both, in an attempt to match the music to the singer's vocal range. Other machines tried to suppress the vocal line of any recording but produced poor overall sound quality, making them generally unpopular.

The debut of MTV (Music Television), in 1981, prompted an interest in karaoke videos. Scrolling the song lyrics across the bottom of the screen helped participants to sing along, even if they had never before heard the recording. Such video displays have become a mainstay of karaoke machines in both public and private settings, although purely audio karaoke remains more popular due to lower cost, larger song catalogs, and general interest in watching the performer rather than a video. The Internet and fiber-optic technology have enabled public venues that feature karaoke to gain near-instant access to an ever-expanding catalog of video and audio recordings. The video-game industry has also capitalized on the phenomenon, creating such titles as *Karaoke Revolution* (Konami, 2003) and spin-offs like *Guitar Hero* (Harmonix, 2005) in which the gamer uses an "instrument" controller to play the game.

The invention of the karaoke machine is a controversial topic, being credited to two individuals: Daisuke Inoue (b. 1940) of Japan and Roberto del Rosario (n.d.) of the Philippines. Inoue claims to have invented the first prototype in 1971 for what would later be known as karaoke, but he never patented his creation. Rosario is credited with patenting a similar machine, called the "Sing-Along System," derived from earlier prototypes he had invented in the late 1960s, though the official patent is dated 1983. Both men achieved a modicum of fame, though neither reaped the financial rewards of the karaoke craze that exploded in the 1980s.

No matter its origin, karaoke today is a global phenomenon. Though well-known in the Western world, it is most popular in East and Southeast Asian countries, where people of all ages join in the fun. In most of these nations, especially Japan, there is a cultural tendency to admire people with a reserved character. Public displays of emotion are discouraged, unless such behavior is expected within a specific context. Karaoke provides just such an acceptable context for greater freedom of expression and the surrender of cultural inhibitions.

Karaoke boxes (a small room with a karaoke video machine) are common in Japan because they provide an intimate setting for people to perform privately for their friends. Karaoke bars are also popular, since there is an expectation that most customers will sing regardless of their ability. The remaining patrons are expected to be supportive, encouraging the novice to be uninhibited. Such public venues are more commonly seen in the United States and Europe.

Although a friendly atmosphere amid informal gatherings is the norm, karaoke contests sponsored by local venues or advertisers are taken more seriously. Contestants will often dress in the style of the vocalist they are replacing and imitate that singer's stage demeanor. Prizes are sometimes awarded, and performers with aspirations of earning a living as a musician will often perform karaoke as a means of developing their stage skills. The most prestigious of these contests is the Karaoke World Championships, which was first held in Finland in 2003 and today includes participants from nearly thirty countries.

EAST ASIAN POPULAR MUSIC

East Asian popular music is primarily an export of Japan and Hong Kong, although mainland China and Taiwan occasionally produce successful artists as well. The Western world strongly influences the popular styles emanating from this region. Even so, many artists connect with their cultural roots through the use of traditional instruments, melodies, or lyrical content. Traditional music also thrives and is well respected by East Asia's youth culture, although most people consider it separately from music for entertainment (i.e., popular music). Traditional styles are used for spiritual purposes, rituals, or developing one's character, whereas popular music is primarily for pleasure.

EXPLORE MORE
on www.mymusickit.com
Interactive Globe

Enka

Among the most popular styles of music commonly found in an evening of karaoke, at least in Japan and Korea, is a genre known as *enka*. Enka dominated the popular music scene in Japan for much of the twentieth century and remains embedded in Japanese culture, even if its visibility has waned among today's youth. Enka is a soulful music, frequently likened to Portuguese fado (see Chapter 6) or early American country-western songs. The themes are typically nostalgic and sorrowful, revolving around forlorn love, homesickness, or personal tragedy.

Enka evolved from Japan's centuries-old tradition of street balladeers (*yomiuri*), who sang of current events and frequently poked fun at local authorities. During the mid-1880s, political activists adopted this public-performance practice to voice their discontent with the government and the lack of individual freedoms. The political speeches put into song became known as enka, formed from the words *enzetu* ("speech") and *ka* ("song"). Expressing their opinions through song in this accepted style afforded the activists some impunity from local law enforcement, which regularly arrested public speakers voicing political dissent.

By the 1920s, civil liberties had improved, and the lyrical content of enka shifted to more sentimental themes. Performers began to introduce musical accompaniment that often included Western instruments, such as the violin. By the 1930s, enka singers were backed by increasingly larger ensembles that included both traditional Japanese and modern Western instruments. Enka artists of this period also blended Japanese melodies based on pentatonic scales, with supporting harmony derived from Euro-American musical concepts. This combination resulted in a distinctive cross-cultural creation that adopted the modern sound without neglecting centuries of Japanese music tradition. In addition, female enka singers reflected this sentiment by sometimes wearing traditional kimonos during performances, whereas the members of their male backing ensemble typically wore tuxedos, business suits, or other forms of modern clothing.

Enka embodies the nostalgic respect the Japanese hold for their traditional culture while integrating the urban urgency of modern Japan. Pivotal in the genre's development was Hibari Misora (1937–1989), widely known as the "Queen of Enka." Hibari established herself as one of the nation's most prominent celebrities of the post–World War II era, recording nearly twelve hundred songs and appearing in more than sixty movies. Her music catalog includes enka as well as many standard jazz and popular songs sung in Japanese, reflecting the country's spirit of maintaining its own culture while accepting modern influences. Today's youth may prefer modern J-Pop and the sounds of the Western world to enka, but Hibari's music remains a mainstay of karaoke performances and is often covered by current enka artists.

Hibari Misora Museum, Kyoto, Japan.

FOCUS EXAMPLE
ENKA

"KANASHII SAKE" ("SAD SAKE"), PERFORMED BY HIBARI MISORA

Focal Points

HEAR MORE
Download the
iTunes playlist link on
MyMusicKit

- **Instruments:** Guitar, electric organ, orchestral background.
- **Voice:** "Trembling" female voice (Hibari Misora).
- **Language/Lyrics:** Sung in Japanese. Lyrics are sorrowful.
- **Melody:** Primarily pentatonic scales.
- **Rhythm:** Triple meter, with a slow tempo.

TIME	DESCRIPTION
0:00–0:16	Guitar introduction. Pentatonic scale using G, A, B-flat, D, and E-flat. (Resolution at 0:13 on pitch G.)
0:17–1:29	Female vocalist enters. Listen for the shift in tonal center and added scale degree (pitch C at 1:01).

JAPANESE	ENGLISH
Hitori sakaba de nomu sakewa.	The sake you drink alone at the bar.
Wakare namida no aji ga suru.	Tastes of tears parting.
Nonde sutetai omokage ga.	When you drink, the images you throw away.
Nomeba glass ni mata ukabu.	Float back up in the glass.

1:30–2:04	Vocals switch to spoken dialogue

JAPANESE	ENGLISH
Ah, Wakareta ato no kokoro nokoriyo,	Ah, the heart that's left after parting.
Miren nano ne,	The image of that person.
Ano hito no omokage	Lingers still.
Samishisa wo wasureru tame ni	You drink to forget the loneliness.
Non de iru noni,	Again tonight,
Sake wa konya mo watashi	sake makes me lonely
Wo kanashiku saseru,	It would be good to give him up.
Sake yo, dooshite, dooshite ano hito wo.	Sake, why, why that person.
Akirametara iino, Akirametara iino …	It would be good to give him up (repeat) …

2:05–3:29	Second sung verse.

JAPANESE	ENGLISH
Sakeyo kokoro ga arunaraba	Sake can put out.
Mune no nayami wo keshite kure	the troubles of your heart.
Yoeba kanashiku naru sake wo	If you get drunk, sake becomes lonely.
Nonde nakuno mo koi no tame	If you drink it, the tears are for love.

3:30–4:54	Third verse.

JAPANESE	ENGLISH
Hitori potchiga sukida yo to	Behind the heart that says.
Itta kokoro no ura de naku	It likes to be alone, I'm crying.
Sukide soenai hito no yo wo	Consumed with someone you can't have.
Naite urande yoga fukeru	The tearful, resentful night advances.

Translation by Anne Prescott, University of Illinois–Urbana-Champaign

Japanese classical and folk music are often based on pentatonic scales, meaning that only five pitches are used in a melody. Enka follows this tradition by using pentatonic scales for its own melody. The tonal center of the melody for "Kanashii Sake" is the pitch G. This is considered the pitch of resolution, where the music has released its melodic tension. The instrumental introduction begins on pitch A, finally resolving its melodic material at 0:13, on the pitch G. The entire pentatonic scale includes pitches G, A, B-flat, D, and E-flat.

Although Japanese traditional music does not use harmony, enka music often does. The pentatonic scale used for the melodic pitches suggests a G-minor harmony, which is appropriate since minor harmony is typically used to express sadness. The vocal line also uses the above pentatonic scale, starting on pitch D and resolving to G at the end of the second line of text (0:47). The melody then briefly shifts its tonal center to D and adds a sixth pitch (C) as a passing tone at the start of the word "*omokage*" (1:01). The tonal center returns to G at the end of the following line, "*mata ukabu*" (1:19). The prevalent use of pentatonic scales is one of the key markers for identifying enka music.

The story line describes a woman (or man) drinking her sorrows away by consuming *sake*, a rice wine commonly found in Japan. Hibari incorporates a stylized "trembling" vibrato, known as *kobushi*, during the sung sections on extended pitches. She further enhances the sorrowful theme during her spoken dialogue through breathy, desperate-sounding vocalization. During live performances, Hibari would often cry as she sang, with tears streaming down her face by the end of the song.

A brief appearance of saxophones before the second and third verses (2:00, 2:56) is a reminder that enka in the twentieth century was greatly affected by Western influences. Instrumentation is the most obvious Western element in the songs, but enka performers often sing jazz and popular ballads from the United States and Europe during their stage shows. Not only does this add a variety of styles, it also helps to change the mood since most enka songs have sorrowful themes similar to "Kanashii Sake."

Hibari is fondly remembered in Japan and elsewhere throughout Asia. Though several artists, such as Miyako Harumi (b. 1948), have found success as enka singers, none has achieved the broad appeal that Hibari did. She is regarded as a cultural icon in Japan, and her recordings are still in high demand. In 1994, a museum in her honor was opened to the public and has attracted millions of fans who pay tribute to her lasting legacy.

Modern J-Pop

Hibari Misora was also an important figure in the historical development of what is today known as J-Pop, or Japanese popular music, which traces its roots to Western popular music, primarily jazz. Jazz clubs first appeared there in the pre–World War II days but were banned by the imperial government during the war. Jazz returned, along with other American musical styles such as mambo, blues, and country music, during the early 1950s with the American occupation of Japan after the war.

By the end of the decade, rock music, which was sweeping the globe, also found an audience in Japan. Elvis covers were popular, but so were the "crooners" such as Paul Anka (b. 1941), who sang sentimental love songs similar in mood to enka performances. By far, the most successful J-Pop song of this period was "Ue o Muite aruko," better known internationally as "Sukiyaki." Topping the pop charts in the United States and elsewhere, the song, recorded by Kyu Sakamoto in 1963, has sold millions of copies worldwide and been covered by dozens of international artists, including A Taste of Honey. To date, no other Japanese song has found similar success in non-Asian markets.

Although J-Pop artists are little known in international markets outside Asia, some have found followings through exposure via other media, primarily the video-gaming industry and booming global interest in Japanese *anime* (animation). The video-game industry, in particular, has been an extremely lucrative Japanese export; most of the major players throughout its history have been based in Japan. Since the 1980s, Nintendo has been one of the most dominant companies, finding enormous success with arcade releases such as *Donkey Kong* (1981) as well as home console franchises, like *Mario Bros.* (1983), a *Donkey Kong* spin-off.

During the 1990s, Nintendo's *Pokémon* video game spawned a wealth of related merchandise that eventually became an international popular-culture phenomenon. Although earlier Japanese anime programs, notably, *Speed Racer* (1966–68), had achieved a modicum of popularity in the Western world, a television series and several movies based on the *Pokémon* characters quickly opened new markets for the genre. The popularity of *Pokémon* brought a watershed of interest in Japanese anime and related video games, such as *Final Fantasy, Dragon Ball* Z, and the Square Enix-Disney collaboration *Kingdom Hearts*.

J-Pop bands are frequently included on the sound tracks of those films, television series, and video games featuring Japanese anime. Most often, the songs fall more specifically under the industry labels of J-Rock, J-Hip-Hop, or techno. Some J-Pop bands have formed as a result of having composed music for video games and anime; one example is the Black Mages, who are best known for their contributions to the *Final Fantasy* series. Established artists such as Hikaru Utada (b. 1983), who is featured in *Kingdom Hearts*, have used these alternative media as a way to expand their international popularity.

From a musical standpoint, J-Pop and related genres parallel mainstream popular music found in the Western world. The influx of American culture has been quite pronounced since the end of World War II, and the economic prosperity of Japan, particularly during the 1980s, has been closely tied to U.S. markets. Japanese youth are as familiar with American pop-culture icons as are their English-speaking counterparts. The most obvious distinction between American popular music and that of Japan is the use of Japanese in song lyrics. Nevertheless, many of the biggest J-Pop hits are given English titles, even if the songs themselves are sung in Japanese. J-Pop songs with English lyrics are also common, though these typically have weak sales in English-speaking markets.

Two of the major musical tendencies in J-Pop are electronic instrumentals and strong melodic hooks with simple lyrical content. The karaoke phenomenon has been highly influential in this regard, since in these contexts J-Pop songs benefit from having catchy melodic lines and simple, repetitive lyrics. Image is essential for the success of a J-Pop star, and so inevitably the idols are attractive young men and women who are good dancers and have charismatic offstage personalities. A few such artists, including Namie Amuro (b. 1977), have achieved sustained, successful careers, but the majority have a brief shelf life that lasts only a song or two. Since this tendency is true of popular culture around the world, J-Pop icons generally accept their fleeting fame as part of the process of pursuing a career in the music industry.

◉→ **EXPLORE MORE**
on www.mymusickit.com
Interactive Globe

Cantopop (C-Pop)

Like J-Pop, C-Pop began with similar American jazz and pop music influences, but it developed along a much different path in the post–World War II era. From the late 1920s through the '40s, Chinese popular music centered in Shanghai was led by composer/performer Li Jinhui (1891–1967), who created a fusion style of American jazz and traditional Chinese music known as *shidaiqu* ("contemporary songs"). The music flourished during the 1930s and '40s but was banned in 1952, when the Communist government labeled it "yellow," meaning pornographic, for themes that the conservatives considered sexually suggestive. As a result, many Shanghai musicians left mainland China to continue their careers in British-controlled Hong Kong or Taiwan.

Hong Kong is located south of Guangdong province on the mainland. Its capital is Guangzhou, but the international community commonly refers to the city as Canton and the people of the province as Cantonese. Consequently, the major spoken dialect of the province, as well as in Hong Kong, is known internationally as Cantonese. Therefore, the popular music originating from Hong Kong is commonly labeled Cantopop, or C-Pop, and parallel styles emanating from Taiwan and Mandarin-speaking areas are known as Mandopop.

During the 1950s and '60s, shidaiqu persisted in Hong Kong alongside Western musical imports, such as Elvis Presley and the Beatles. Traditional music, such as Cantonese opera, also maintained a steady following but was stigmatized as being old-fashioned, a label applied by a growing number of young urbanites. Shidaiqu and Mandopop from Taiwan, sung in Mandarin (a second-language for most of Hong Kong's population), and the Western imports, sung in English (understood by many Hong Kong residents due to the British influence), were viewed as modern. This situation left an absence of homegrown modern music, a gap that Cantopop was destined to fill.

During the 1970s, television became increasingly common in wealthy households throughout Hong Kong. The era saw a rise in popularity of soap operas, which needed theme songs, and talent contests, which opened opportunities for singers and songwriters to entertain the local market by composing and performing music in Cantonese. The majority of these songs expressed sentimental themes sung in a melodramatic style, with an accompaniment of a small ensemble of modern instruments, such as electric guitars and synthesizers that produced heavy string effects.

As Hong Kong's economy prospered through the 1980s, so, too, did the local media industry. Artists and producers channeled their musical creativity into recording music that offered wide popular appeal rather than original sound. The karaoke boom also encouraged formulaic music that could be more easily sung by amateurs. To broaden their exposure, many artists, including Leslie Cheung (1956–2003) and Anita Mui (1963–2003), became film and television actors. Singing in other languages, mainly English and Mandarin, also helped to attract new audiences outside Hong Kong to the emerging Cantopop stars. Taiwanese Mandopop artists, such as Teresa Teng (1953–1995; see following section), reciprocated by recording songs in Cantonese, further expanding interest in the Hong Kong popular music scene.

By the 1990s, Cantopop stars were widely known wherever there were significant Cantonese and Mandarin-speaking communities, including in the United States and Europe. "The Four Heavenly Kings of Cantopop"—Jacky Cheung (b. 1961), Aaron Kwok (b. 1965), Leon Lai (b. 1966), and Andy Lau (b. 1961)—dominated the Cantopop marketplace throughout much of the decade, until the British handover of Hong Kong to China in 1997. After that date, Cantopop lost much of its momentum as many of its greatest stars immigrated to other countries or partially retired from the business. Mandopop stars from Taiwan and mainland China, along with American, European, and some Japanese imports, found increasing popularity as Mandarin was adopted as the official language of Hong Kong.

Mandopop (M-Pop)

Mandopop has roots similar to those of Cantopop, with both genres evolving from the 1920s–'30s shidaiqu music originating in Shanghai. Many popular singers during this era also appeared in films, contributing their singing talents to the productions. One of the period's most controversial figures was singer/actress Zhou Xuan (1918–1957), who acted in more than forty films and became one of the most popular Chinese singers of the gramophone era. Her personal life was unstable, marked by failed marriages, illegitimate children, suicide attempts, and, ultimately, her death in a mental asylum at age thirty-nine. Nevertheless, Zhou is nostalgically remembered by many Chinese, who cover her songs in karaoke performances or listen to modern versions of her music, to which have been added rhythm tracks, which are more popular with today's audiences.

Zhou and her mainland China contemporaries found audiences during World War II and the conclusion of the Chinese Civil War (1927–1950). Following the ban on popular music initiated by the Communist Party in 1952, Taiwan became the center for Mandopop musical production. Mandarin-language popular song was also prevalent in Hong Kong, but the majority of youth on both islands was more interested in Western musical imports. By the 1970s, Taiwan had established itself as an "Asian Tiger" economy, which encouraged the growth of the country's music industry. As in Hong Kong, Taiwanese television and song contests attracted many hopeful singers to the budding Mandopop scene.

The most popular Taiwanese singer of the 1970s and '80s was Teresa Teng (1953–1995), who recorded songs in Mandarin, Cantonese, Taiwanese, Japanese, English, and even Indonesian. Her music consists mostly of ballads and updated folk songs that feature modern instrumental accompaniment. Despite tensions between mainland China and Taiwan, Teng's music was widely broadcast in both countries, and her recordings sold with great success on China's black market. Her popularity even brought her an invitation to perform on the mainland, an event that never materialized.

⦿▸ EXPLORE MORE
on www.mymusickit.com
Interactive Globe

FOCUS EXAMPLE
MANDOPOP

((• HEAR MORE
Download the
iTunes playlist link on
MyMusicKit

"HE RI JUN ZAI LAI" ("WHEN WILL YOU RETURN?"),
PERFORMED BY TERESA TENG

Focal Points

- **Instruments:** Strings, electric bass, electric guitar, piano/synthesizer, drum set.
- **Voice:** Female vocalist (Teresa Teng).
- **Language/Lyrics:** Sung in Mandarin Chinese. Romantic love is typical thematic material for C-Pop and M-Pop songs.
- **Melody:** Strings provide a counter-melody to the vocal line. Note the frequent use of portamento.
- **Harmony:** Major harmonies predominate.
- **Rhythm:** Follows a steady duple meter.

TIME	DESCRIPTION
0:00–0:21	Instrumental introduction.
0:22–1:33	First verse.

MANDARIN CHINESE	ENGLISH
Hao hua bu chang kai	Flowers do not bloom forever
Hao jing bu chang zai	The beautiful scene will vanish
Qiudui jie xiaomei	Smiles give way to sadness
Lei shai xiangsidai	Love's yearnings end in tears
Jinxiao libie hou	After you leave tonight
He ri jun zai lai?	When will you return?
Hewanle zhe bei	Finish this cup of wine
Qing jin dian xiaocai,	Eat more
Rensheng nan de ji hui zui	In this lifetime
Bu huan geng he dai	One has so few chances to drink
Spoken:	
Lai, lai, lai.	Come, come, come.
Hewanle zhe bei zai shuo ba.	Finish the cup and we'll talk more.
Sung:	
Jinxiaou libie hou	After you leave tonight
He ri jun zai lai?	When will you return?
1:34–2:37	Second verse.

MANDARIN CHINESE	ENGLISH
Ting chang yang guan die	Finished singing, "Parting at Yanguan"
Chong jin bai yu bei	Again raise the white jade cup
Yin qin pin zhi yu	Talking sweetly
Laolao fu jun huai.	Holding each other tight.
Jinxiao libie hou	After you leave tonight
He rih jun zai lai?	When will you return?

Hewanle zhe bei	Finish this cup of wine
Qing jin dian xiaocai	Eat more
Rensheng nan de ji hui zui	In this lifetime
Bu huan geng he dai.	One has so few chances to drink
Spoken:	
Lai, lai, lai.	Come, come, come.
Zuihou yi bei. Ganla ba!	One last drink. All of it!
Sung:	
Jinxiao libie hou	After you leave tonight
He rih jun zai lai?	When will you return?
2:38–2:54	Closing instrumental.

Cantopop and Mandopop sound very much like "lounge music" to Western audiences. Strings typically carry the melody when the vocalist is silent. The bass plods along with a constant rhythm, and the percussion is subdued and steady. One distinctive feature to help identify the ensemble as being Chinese influenced is the frequent use of portamento in the string melody. Sliding between pitches is a common performance technique found on the *erhu*, a traditional fiddle found in Chinese folk music, particularly around Shanghai. Certainly, this technique is used in other parts of the world, but its prevalence in the popular music from Taiwan and China is a carryover from the folk style of erhu performance.

Cantopop and Mandopop stars invariably have silky, smooth voices well suited for pop ballads, which are standard in the repertoire. Though Western influences have brought harder-edged sounds into the rock and hip-hop genres, the distinctive feature of C-Pop and M-Pop is the soft, nostalgic character exemplified by performers like Teng.

Our Focus Example, "When Will You Return?" describes a scene (drinking in sorrow) similar to that of the enka song from Japan in the previous example, but the major harmony gives it a more encouraging spirit. The song was originally performed by Zhou Xuan, but with merely an accordion accompaniment (a popular instrument throughout China). Zhou's tone has a nasal quality reminiscent of classical opera singers, whereas Teng's voice is much fuller, as in the Western style of vocal performance.

For many older Chinese, the song has nostalgic associations with the Kuo Min Tang, the democratic political party ousted from mainland China by the Communist party after World War II. During the song's two popular renditions by Zhou and Teng, the theme "When will you return?" implicitly suggested a call for the Kuo Min Tang to return to power. In Zhou's era, this was due to the Japanese occupation of the country during World War II, whereas Teng's version was popular during the harsh period of the Communist Cultural Revolution (1966–76) in China (see the following section). Though the song never explicitly expresses political intent, its sentiment helped the troubled masses to cope with the hardships of these periods in Chinese history.

Teng's unexpected death of an asthma attack in May 1995 shocked her fans throughout the world. Many Mandopop stars have since paid her tribute, most notably Beijing-born music and film icon Faye Wong (b. 1969), who began her career performing Teng's music. She recorded a successful album of covers, *The Decadent Sound of Faye* (1995), to honor Teng only a few months after her death.

Chinese Rock

⊙→ **EXPLORE MORE**
on www.mymusickit.com
Interactive Globe

The history of popular music in mainland China is quite different from that of C-Pop. Although pre–World War II music followed the same path, the Communist takeover of China in 1949 resulted in the general population missing more than three decades' worth of modern musical influence due to the state's tight control over media outlets and musical imports. As mentioned previously, most popular-music styles were labeled "yellow," meaning that they were considered pornographic and counter to the state's philosophical objectives. Most Chinese people never heard of Elvis Presley or the Beatles until several years after these performers' fame took the world by storm. Only state-approved popular songs were broadcast, and the general population was inundated with "revolutionary" music that promoted the ideals of the Communist party. The Cultural Revolution (1966–76) was a particularly harsh period during which artistic activities deemed "liberal-bourgeois" were severely suppressed and outside influences tightly controlled by the government.

With the end of the Cultural Revolution came a brief period of liberalization, known as the Beijing Spring (1977–78), in which China's government permitted the general population to voice political and social frustrations. College students studying overseas returned to their homeland with new perspectives on the government and China's reputation in the international community. Outside cultural influences began to seep into the country, and many returning students brought with them fresh ideas about music, along with electric guitars, synthesizers, and portable amplifiers.

As Chinese students during the 1980s began criticizing their political leaders and the Communists' one-party control of the government, rock music emerged and bore a political edge. By mid-decade, restrictions against the broadcast of popular music on national media outlets had been reinstated, though approved songs were occasionally allowed on television and radio. In general, rock musicians were viewed as subversives and performed to limited audiences in bars and nightclubs, primarily in urban areas with large student populations, such as Beijing and Shanghai. Although most mainlanders preferred *gangtai* music, the "sweet and soft" styles emanating from Hong Kong and Taiwan as exemplified by Teresa Teng, pro-democracy student activists recognized the protest power of rock music as a means for rallying antiestablishment support.

During the April–June 1989 democracy movement in Beijing's Tiananmen Square, "Nothing to My Name," by rock musician Cui Jian (b. 1961), became the unofficial anthem, expressing the protestors' discontent with their lack of individual freedoms. Following the government crackdown of the protests, Chinese rock musicians became heroes of urban youth culture. Because overt political dissent was dangerous, some musicians adapted themes of revolutionary songs, such as "Nan ni wan," also performed by Cui Jian, and Communist propaganda slogans from the Cultural Revolution, subverting them into thinly veiled criticism of the government's civil liberties restrictions. The songs' original intent had been to promote Communist ideals—their themes often praised the populace overcoming the evils of authoritarian power—and the democracy activists now performed them as a rebuke against the Communist party, which they viewed as a suppressive regime. Traditional instruments, such as the *pipa* and *suona*, were sometimes included in rock-music ensembles, and well-known folk tunes occasionally provided melodic or lyrical content for a song as well. These additions gave the music a distinctively Chinese sound, but it was largely based on Western music-industry sensibilities.

For a few years, rock music in China maintained an enthusiastic following; performers gave concerts and toured the country with minimal government interference. Among the most popular groups of the period were Cui Jian's band ADO, as well as

Cui Jian, 2007.

Tang Dynasty and the all-female group Cobra. By the mid-1990s, however, fans became less inclined toward politically tinged performances and more interested in riding the tide of rapid commercialism. Western pop icons were preferred, and an influx of C-Pop and M-Pop stars from Hong Kong and Taiwan superseded the popularity of Chinese rockers. Though Cui Jian, the country's most successful rock musician, continued to tour at home and abroad, recognized by international audiences as a prominent figure of modern Chinese music and performing with such legendary Western rock bands as the Rolling Stones, most of his compatriots found it difficult to achieve notoriety as rock musicians.

Today's Chinese rock-music scene persists as hard rock/punk bands such as Brain Failure, Reflector, and Yoksa find underground audiences in major urban areas, where university students form the bulk of their fans. Yet, government censorship of the media, including the Internet, continues to thwart their popularity at home and abroad. Popular music in general is still viewed with suspicion by hard-liner members of the Communist party, who continue to exert their influence on popular culture by restricting programming deemed counter to the state's moral ideals, as evidenced by the cessation of the hugely successful talent competition "Super Girl Contest," broadcast from 2004 to 2006. As the country continues to expand its economic interests around the world, the influx of Western media will become increasingly difficult to manage, and future opportunities for Chinese rock musicians to find success are likely to emerge.

SOUTHEAST ASIA

As in East Asia, karaoke is an integral part of the popular-music scene in Southeast Asian countries, such as Thailand and Indonesia. Western pop stars are well known and often emulated by cover bands and Western-style pop artists throughout the region. C-Pop is also popular, especially among Chinese-descended populations, who are more prevalent in mainland Southeast Asia than in the region's island nations. The interest, however, is only one-sided, for it is rare that Southeast Asian artists find much success outside their home country.

Where Chinese and Japanese influence has "gone global" in many spheres, Southeast Asian countries remain less visible in worldwide media. The languages of indigenous music traditions, including pop, are understood primarily by local audiences. Overseas diasporas from Thailand, Indonesia, Vietnam, and other Southeast Asian countries are small compared to those from China, Korea, and Japan, and therefore exported recordings are less prevalent. The insularity of the region's music industry further presents a challenge for outsiders seeking to obtain recordings by local pop stars, particularly those performing such popular native genres as *luk thung* (Thailand) or *dangdut* (Indonesia), whose origins are inspired by folk traditions.

Popular Music from Thailand

⦿→ **EXPLORE MORE**
on www.mymusickit.com
Interactive Globe

Even though Rodgers and Hammerstein's notion of a polka-dancing Thai king in their 1951 musical *The King and I* is an unlikely scenario, Thai royalty have long held an interest in Western culture, particularly its music. The reigning king, Rama IX (Bhumibol Adulyadej; b. 1927), is a connoisseur of jazz and, in his youth, frequently played his saxophone for public and private audiences. He later performed with several of America's jazz legends, including Benny Goodman, Stan Getz, and Maynard Ferguson, and composed more than forty songs that are still played throughout Thailand. The king is not a "popular" musician, per se, but his interest in jazz has given Western popular-music idioms a legitimacy that has encouraged Thai citizens to adopt and adapt these genres as an integral part of the nation's musical soundscape.

One such adaptation is (*phleng*) *luk krung* ("city people songs"), a popular genre that flourished during the 1950s. Although Western music trends had been familiar to Thais since the mid-nineteenth century, musicians typically performed imported compositions or, occasionally, adapted Western melodies to compositions for Thai classical ensembles. Western orchestral and marching band music was popular, as were tango and early jazz, particularly after the end of the absolute monarchy in 1932, when the new government strongly promoted Western ideals and cultural idioms as a way to enhance its international image.

By the big-band jazz era of the 1940s, Thai composers such as Uea Sunthon-Sanam (1910–1981) and his band, Suntharaphon, were heavily promoted by the local government and encouraged to experiment with popular idioms, including creating jazz arrangements of traditional Thai melodies. Small and large jazz ensembles entertained the growing number of ballroom dancers found among Bangkok's social elite, often performing in hotels frequented by Westerners. To foster interest in the music, King Rama IX hosted weekly ballroom dance parties, and by the mid-1950s *phleng Thai sakhon* ("modern [i.e., Western-style] Thai songs," later known as *luk krung*) were among the most popular throughout the capital. The luk krung label became commonplace during the 1960s to distinguish the "city" sound from the developing "country folk" popular-music styles, known as (*phleng*) *luk thung* ("field people songs").

Luk Thung

Thailand's rural population consists primarily of rice farmers, particularly in the northeast and central plains, where luk thung originated. (*Luk thung* is the accepted transliteration of the Thai script, though it is often written incorrectly as *luk tung* or *look toong*.) Luk thung started out as a musical means of social criticism, primarily of the government and its officials during the World War II period and through the 1950s, when censorship of customs considered "vulgar," such as chewing betel nut, was extremely strict. Singers typically used the local dialect, not usually understood by the urban populations of Bangkok, and performed with simple ballroom dance bands for festivals, at temple fairs, and in the marketplace. They incorporated musical styles from Western idioms, such as mambo and country music, that were disseminated through film and radio broadcasts. As government restrictions eased during the 1960s, the lyrical content of luk thung shifted to more topical themes of daily life and romance. The period's most prominent singer was Suraphon Sombatcharoen (1930–1968), whose sentimental style became standard for the genre. His much-publicized murder was a temporary setback in the popularity of luk thung, which was superseded by an influx of American imports brought by the presence of the American military in Southeast Asia during the 1960s and early '70s, a result of the Vietnam War.

After the war, Thailand's economic prospects improved and its urban areas expanded rapidly as many rural Thais left the rice paddies to find work in the city. As unskilled laborers, the majority found jobs in factories, driving taxis or *tuk-tuks* (a motorized rickshaw), or selling goods in the open-air markets. Along with these "country folk" came cassette recordings of their favorite luk thung songs as well as traditional music, clothing, food, and other customs. Although Bangkok Thai were initially critical of this influx of rural workers, their constant presence soon encouraged a nostalgic empathy with the challenges of being "left behind" in a rapidly modernizing Thailand

One of the most important musical figures shaping the image transformation of rural Thais was Pompuang Duangjan (1961–1992), a young luk thung singer from Suphanburi, a small town in the central plains. Pompuang crafted an onstage persona that appealed to the fashion-conscious Bangkok urbanites while maintaining a pride in her upcountry roots that helped to dismantle social stigmas against those from the country's rural areas. She helped turn luk thung into an upbeat dance-oriented genre with several successful songs throughout the 1980s. Her "rags to riches" story inspired people of all ages and social classes, including King Rama IX, who attended her funeral in 1992, along with reportedly more than two hundred thousand mourners.

In the modern era, dozens of popular luk thung artists have found local success. Many make their living performing across the country, accompanied by large sound systems and troupes of dancing girls. Their tours draw hundreds of rural Thais together to attend the concerts, which bring the "big city" to the "country folk" who might otherwise never venture beyond their agricultural-based villages. Some luk thung artists enjoy mainstream success performing for large audiences in Bangkok as well as internationally for homesick Thai audiences, who relate to the music's sentimental themes and revel in the upbeat dance numbers that remind them of home. Among the most popular of these artists is Tai Orathai (b. 1980), whose rural roots, demure stage persona, and physical attractiveness, not to mention her charming vocal style, embody the quintessential elements of a luk thung singer, endearing her to thousands of Thai patriots across the globe.

Tai Orathai,
popular luk thung
singer.

 *FOCUS EXAMPLE*
LUK THUNG

((● **HEAR MORE**
Download the
iTunes playlist link on
MyMusicKit

"DUAK YAH NAI PAH POON" ("FIELD FLOWER IN THE CONCRETE JUNGLE"),
PERFORMED BY TAI ORATHAI

Focal Points

- **Instruments:** *Khaen* (free-reed aerophone), *wot* (end-blown flute), electric *phin* (plucked lute), electric guitar, electric bass, piano, drum set.
- **Vocalist:** Female vocalist (Tai Orathai).
- **Language/Lyrics:** Thai language. Lyrics focus frequently focus on daily life and sentimental nostalgic images. Lyrics follow meter and rhyme scheme of traditional *lam* poetry.
- **Melody:** Primarily syllabic text settings, with short melisma at the end of vocal verse. Intermittent instrumental hooks.
- **Harmony:** Primarily minor to express mild sadness, though many luk thung songs use major keys in dance-oriented music.
- **Rhythm:** Duple meter.

TIME	DESCRIPTION
0:00–0:15	Introduction with khaen, electric phin, electric bass, drum set.
0:16–0:29	Wot enters with instrumental theme.
0:30–0:58	Refrain.

THAI	ENGLISH
Hua jai tid din swam kahng keng yin kao kao	Her heart is of the earth [meaning that she is self-assured and nonmaterialistic], Wearing old jeans
Sai suea taw rawy kao kao kawd krapao bai dieow tid kahy	Wearing a 199-cent shirt, clutching a bag close
Krab la mae paw lang jahk rian job Maw Plahy	Farewell to Mom and Dad, after graduating high school

Lah tung dawk khun sai mah ah sahy pah pun	Farewell to the wind blown field of field flowers
	Move to the Concrete Jungle [meaning Bangkok]
0:59–1:27	First verse.
Aow raeng pen thun su ngahn ngern duean tam tam	It takes strength to invest in a low-paying job
Keb ngern khao ryan phahk kam	To save money for evening classes.
Kaw khwahm wang bon thahng puean fun	Hope is growing on the dusty road.
Sang khom mueang yai khahd khlaen nam jai juea jun	In the big city, people aren't kind or helpful
Chai khwam aud thon term thun hai yuen su hwai thuk wan	Be patient, stay strong to survive every day
1:28–1:57	Second verse. Note the harmony change.
Yu Mueang swan tae pen khon chan tid din	Living in the City of Heaven, but she's just a person of the earth.
Pen phu rab chai jon chin hu dai yin tae yin tae kham sang ngan	A lowly person, she hears orders often, she is used to being ordered around,
Tae yang yim dai praoh jai muean dok yah bahn	But she still can smile, because her mind blossoms like a field flower from the weeds.
Thung yu nai thi tam chan tae kaw bahn dai thuk weh lah	She might be lowly, but her mind is blossoming all the time.
1:58–2:27	Second refrain, with lyric variation.
Hua jai tid din swam kahng keng yin kao kao	Her heart is of the earth, Wearing old jeans
Sai suea taw rawy kao kao ta jai sahw bo doi rah khah	Wearing a 199-cent shirt, but inside her heart is not cheap
Wang wan nueng riyan johb chant hi fao raw mah	Longing for the day when her studies will finish.
Ja swam mong kut dok yah	When that day comes, she'll wear a crown of field flowers.
Tahy rup prin ya wan mah bahn rao	She'll take pictures of her graduation and return home.
2:28–2:57	Instrumental break (wot solo at 2:42).
2:58–3:26	Repeat of second refrain.
3:27–3:43	Instrumental conclusion (wot featured).

Luk thung ensembles use primarily Western instruments but will sometimes add traditional instruments, such as the *wot, khaen,* and *phin* heard in this example. These instruments are common to folk traditions from northeast Thailand and are strongly tied to the musical identity of the Isan (northeast) population. The khaen is a free-reed mouth organ, one of the few traditional world-music instruments that plays harmony. It sounds immediately after the cymbal crescendo at the opening of the song (0:02). The electric phin (and bass) also enter at this point. The recording separates the two, with the khaen predominant in the left channel and the phin in the right channel; therefore, listening with headphones can help to distinguish the instruments. The wot, which sounds like a flute, is perhaps the easiest to recognize (0:16), since it is frequently featured as a solo instrument. Many luk thung artists substitute synthesizers or modern instruments, such as a saxophone or guitar, particularly during live performances, but the appearance of these traditional instruments on a record is a hallmark of the region's musicians. The abovementioned instruments are heard at several places in our Focus Example, particularly at 2:28, when the instrumental break occurs.

Thai is a tonal language, meaning that the inflection of the voice on a single syllable can change a word's meaning. To speakers of nontonal languages, such as English, hearing the different tones can be challenging. Thai has five tones: middle, high, low, rising, and falling. The rising tones are generally most noticeable for non-Thai speakers—they may sound like mini-hiccups or one-syllable yodels. The tonal contour of the language is important to the singer's melody, for the sung pitches must correspond to the tones of the language; for example, if a word has a rising tone, the melody must go up.

Luk thung lyrics often draw from traditional singing by incorporating poetic meter and rhyming schemes common to the folk genres. A common practice is to use a word with the same phonemes but a different tone. In our Focus Example, you'll note the transliteration *"kao kao,"* which appears at the end of the first line and in the middle of the second. Its first appearance is spoken with a low tone, and thus the melodic line ends on a low pitch; this translates as "old" (0:35). The second appearance has a different tone—falling—that is also heard subtly in the melody; in this case *"kao"* translates as "nine" (0:39). Also, in spoken language, "199" would be said *roi kao-sib kao*), but here the *"sib"* is absent so that the words rhyme with the line above. The *"kao kao"* is thus a play on words as well as a play on tones. Similar rhyming schemes are found throughout the song. Such lyric sophistication is common to luk thung, but is a beauty largely lost on non-native speakers.

Luk thung lyrics typically deal with activities of daily life and have sentimental nostalgic themes. The karaoke video of our Focus Example depicts much of the song's lyrical content: It shows a young girl (Tai Orathai) meeting the challenges of life in the big city, working hard as a dishwasher, and attending college. The song was especially popular among the many Thai students who left their rural villages to attend universities in the growing urban centers throughout Thailand (Bangkok in particular), as well as with the many who studied abroad in the United States, Europe, and Australia. Thais are strongly nationalistic, and expatriates often find luk thung songs, such as our Focus Example, a comforting reminder of home, not only for the lyrical content but also for the use of traditional instruments uniquely associated with Thailand.

In 1970, the film *Monrak Luk Thung* (1970) was a huge hit throughout the country and prompted many Bangkok Thais, who felt alienated from their cultural roots, to reexamine their stereotypes of the country's rural culture, particularly that of the Isan (northeast) region. By the 1980s, regional culture was increasingly promoted to tourists, and academic institutions began incorporating folk studies into their curricula. Festivals, local literature, and a resurgence of interest in regional history and language flourished during the 1990s and continue today.

Each region has distinctive traditional styles, and the music from northeast Thailand remains the most successful of the popular regional types. Today, luk thung performers find popularity equal to that of their Thai pop counterparts, and crossover artists between the mainstream and luk thung are frequent. Luk thung shows, which regularly last four hours or more, tour the country and draw large audiences, even in remote areas. Luk thung artists permeate Thailand's media, adorning magazine covers, television shows, and print advertising, acting in films, and performing in music videos that are a staple of karaoke venues throughout the country.

Popular Music of Indonesia

EXPLORE MORE
on www.mymusickit.com
Interactive Globe

In terms of music, Indonesia is the most researched country in Southeast Asia. Since the late 1800s ethnomusicologists have been fascinated with the sounds of the *gamelan*, a traditional ensemble consisting of a variety of metal gongs and metallophones. Many of the field's best-known scholars, such as Colin McPhee (1900–1964), Jaap Kunst (1891–1960),

Rhoma Irama,
Indoneisan pop star.

and Ki Mantle Hood (1918–2005), focused their research on Indonesian music. Smithsonian Folkways, the premier world music label in the United States, dedicated its largest series—twenty volumes—to Indonesia. Numerous other recordings are readily available throughout the world, yet the vast majority of easily accessible Indonesian music is of traditional genres (i.e., folk and classical).

Indonesian popular music is certainly vibrant and important culturally. The second volume of the Smithsonian Folkways series is dedicated entirely to the popular genres of *kroncong* and *dangdut*. Indonesian popular music is readily available on the Internet; though purchasing CDs or cassettes is still difficult. Such recordings, however, are easily found by those lucky enough to visit the country, where cassette shops featuring national and regional popular music are plentiful at markets and urban malls. CDs are primarily enjoyed by the wealthy, but people living in the most rural areas of distant islands often have access to a radio or cassette player, so these media continue to be the most popular for the dissemination of Indonesian music.

Kroncong

The earliest style of popular music in Indonesia is *kroncong*, a reference to the sound of a small lute typically used in the ensemble. This instrument was brought to the islands by Portuguese sailors during the sixteenth century and became popular among the lower classes in the major seaport of Jakarta (formerly known as Batavia). This racially diverse population included people from the various parts of the globe where Portuguese sailors commonly traveled. Indian, African, Chinese, and European peoples mixed with one another and with the indigenous population to create a cosmopolitan city that has become one of the largest urban areas in the world, boasting more than 23 million inhabitants.

Kroncong absorbed a variety of cultural influences from the musical styles represented by Jakarta's varied ethnic backgrounds. By the 1930s, kroncong began to emerge from its socially disadvantaged roots to feature some of the brightest stars of the theater and budding film industry. By the end of the decade, a growing discontent with the Dutch colonial rulers, who had replaced the Portuguese in the seventeenth century, was increasingly expressed through patriotic anthems in the kroncong style.

After ousting the Dutch during World War II, the Japanese banned all foreign popular music, leaving kroncong as the major popular style. Filmmakers continued to use kroncong to attract wider audiences, and composers wrote music for the genre to encourage a unified national identity. With the Japanese surrender in 1945, Indonesia's leaders declared independence, resulting in four more years of armed struggle against Dutch attempts to reclaim the islands. Kroncong continued to be the primary musical medium for stirring patriotic sentiment among Indonesians.

Dangdut

As Indonesia's postwar urban youth came of age in the 1960s, they began to view kroncong as old-fashioned and preferred the rock and pop music emanating from the United States and Europe. The government, however, was less enthralled with these Western styles and proceeded to ban them. Nonetheless, these influences had already seeped into contemporary kroncong and could be heard in imported styles from other parts of Asia, particularly the music in Bollywood films (see Chapter 8), which were then and are today highly popular throughout the country. Malay orchestras, known as *orkes melayu*, capitalized on the urban youth's interest in these films, performing new music sung in either Indonesian or Arabic that blended Indian filmi music with urban Arabic styles accepted by the Indonesian government.

From 1965 to 1967, the nation's political leadership was in turmoil as revolutionary forces led by Suharto (1921–2008) ousted the increasingly Communist-sympathizing government of Sukarno (1901–1970) that had ruled since Indonesia's independence. Suharto's government was more favorable to Western influences, resulting in an influx of popular-music styles, mainly rock, that spawned a new musical genre known as *dangdut*.

Dangdut gets its name from the sound produced by the tabla (a pair of drums from India; see Chapter 8), which articulate the key rhythm of the music on the fourth and first pulses of the basic meter (thus, dang-*dut*). Many of the style's qualities are drawn from music played by the orkes melayu, mainly kroncong pop of the 1960s, with its Indian and Arabic influences. Many melayu artists, including Elvy Sukaesih (b. 1951), the "Queen of Dangdut," performed light and lyrical songs in the new style, but others found that the energy of rock music necessitated a harder edge. Essential to the development of this new rock-oriented form was Rhoma (formerly Oma) Irama (b. 1946), known as the "King of Dangdut."

Irama was also a melayu singer during the 1960s, when he performed alongside many of the era's female personalities, including Sukaesih. The new Suharto-led government allowed creative freedoms that Irama embraced, bringing with him a mass of young Islamic men who attended his concerts in increasing numbers as he incorporated more and more rock influences. As the cassette industry boomed in the 1970s, Irama's music was disseminated throughout the country, earning him unprecedented fame in the realm of Indonesian popular music. A devout Muslim, in 1976 he made the pilgrimage (*haj*) to Mecca, Saudi Arabia, returning with a new motivation to denounce social injustices and economic inequality, often criticizing the government in the process. His music also turned toward moralistic themes that espouse the virtues of Islam, a fact that often agitated conservative Muslims because of the popular-music context of his proselytizing. His fans, however, felt that he was the voice of their generation, speaking through a modern medium for a new era in Indonesia's history.

FOCUS EXAMPLE
DANGDUT

HEAR MORE
Download the iTunes playlist link on MyMusicKit

"QUR'AN DAN KORAN," PERFORMED BY RHOMA IRAMA

Focal Points

- **Instruments:** Electric guitar, electric bass, synthesizer, *krongcong* (small lute), saxophone, trumpet, drum set.
- **Voice:** Male vocalist (Rhoma Irama).
- **Language/Lyrics:** Indonesian (Bahasa). Lyrics are critical of Western decadence and the irreligious tendencies of people in the modern world.
- **Melody:** Two recurring melodic themes outline the form.

- **Rhythm:** Listen for the "dang-dut" rhythm emphasizing beats 4 and 1.
- **Form:** ABA–C–ABA.

TIME	DESCRIPTION
0:00–0:28	Instrumental introduction.
0:29–0:53	First melodic theme (Form A).

INDONESIAN	ENGLISH
Dari masa ke masa	From age to age
Manusia (manusia)	Man's
Berkembang peradabannya	Civilization develops
Hingga dimana-mana	By now everywhere
Manusia (manusia)	Man
Merubah wajah dunia	is changing the world

0:54–1:19	New melodic material (Form B).
Gedung, gedung tinggi	Tall buildings
Mencakar langit	Scrape the sky
Nyaris menghiasi	They adorn almost every country
Segala neg ri	In fact
Bahkan teknologi dimasa kini	technology in this day and age
Sudah mencapaikah masa sahmawi	Can reach into outer space.

1:20–1:42	Returns to first theme (Form A).
Tapi sayan disayang	But it's sad to say
Manusia (manusia)	Men
Lupa diri tinggi hati	have forgotten who they are and become arrogant
Lebih dan melebihi	They think they're
Tingginya (tingginya)	Even taller
Pencakar langitnya tadi	Than those skyscrapers.
1:43–2:15	Instrumental break—guitar solo.
2:16–2:53	New melodic material (Form C).

INDONESIAN	ENGLISH
Sejalan dengan roda pembangunan	As progress marches on
Manusia makin penu kesibukan	People get so busy
Sehingga yang wajib pun terabaikan	That they forget their duty
Sujud lima waktu menyembah Tuhan	To pray to God five times a day
Kar na dimabuk oleh kemajuan…	They are so drunk with progress
Sampai komputer di jadikan Tuhan	They think the computer is God
Yang benar aje (!)	You're kidding!

2:54–3:17	First theme returns (Form A).
Kalau bicara tentang dunia (dunia)	When they talk about the world
Aduhai pandai sekali	They're wonderfully clever
Tapi kalau bicara agama (agama)	But talk to them about religion
Mereka jadi alergi	And suddenly they're allergic

3:18–3:44	Second theme returns (Form B).
Membaca Koran jadi kebutuhan	Reading the newspaper is a necessity
Sedang Alqur'an cuma perhiasan	The Qur'an is just there for decoration
Bahasa inggris sangat digalakan	Everybody's crazy to learn English
Bahasa Arab katanya kampungan	But Arabic is considered backward
Ngak sala tuh (!)	They're wrong!

3:45–4:08	First theme returns (Form A).
Buat apa Berjaya di dunia (di dunia)	What good is success in this world
Kalau akhirat celaka	If it brings disaster in the next?
Marilah kita capai bahagia (bahagia)	Let us try to be happy
Di alam fana dan baqa…	Not only for today but for eternity
4:09–4:18	Closing material.

The opening instrumental material introduces the different instruments. The distortion effect on the electric guitar overshadows the kroncong, though both instruments typically appear onstage. The majority of instruments are of Western origin, but the important element that helps to identify this music as dangdut is the rhythmic emphasis on beats 4 and 1. This pattern is normally played by a tabla drum, but modern ensembles often substitute other instruments, such as the electric bass heard here. The pattern has a high pitch on beat 4 and a low pitch on beat 1 and also follows a long-short rhythm—long on the fourth beat, short on the first beat. The genre's name comes from an onomatopoetic rendering of this rhythm (dang-*dut*).

The opening verse introduces the two main melodic themes in an ABA form (ternary). A melodic hook is not used, though the recurrence of the initial theme helps unify the song. Irama's lyrics criticize the lack of spirituality in the modern world, which he views as increasingly materialistic. When Irama's fame was at its peak, others followed his lead by addressing similar moral issues.

Dangdut singers today are typically less concerned with weighty social or spiritual issues, opting instead for themes about love, dancing, and having fun. Dangdut icon Inul Daratista (b. 1979) has been the most visible of current stars, thanks to her controversial dance style that includes a steady hip swaying inspired by Balinese dance. Irama and other Muslim leaders have protested against her suggestive eroticism, but calls for the government to ban her music have only fueled her popularity among Indonesia's younger generation.

In the second verse, Irama's rebuke of modern society becomes sharper. His explicit references to Islam reflect his own spiritual beliefs, as well as the beliefs of many of his fans, who are predominantly Muslim men. He performs less frequently today, devoting himself to his religion as a prominent imam (Muslim leader).

During the 1980s, Irama collaborated with international artists, including Bollywood playback-singer icon Lata Mangeshkar (see Chapter 8). Irama used Indonesia's popular film industry to promote his own music by starring in several films, which are referred to as dangdut films for the prevalence of the music style in the score. Although critics felt that Irama had succumbed to the decadence of Western commercialization, his success solidified dangdut as a national popular-music style.

SUMMARY

LEARN MORE
on www.mymusickit.com
Chapter summary
and exam

In this chapter, we explored popular music styles from East and Southeast Asia. Karaoke is widespread throughout these regions and serves as a common medium for popular music entertainment. This includes older genres, such as enka from Japan, as well as modern J-Pop (Japanese pop). We heard the soothing sounds of C-Pop (Cantopop) and M-Pop (Mandopop, from Taiwan/China) and the harder-edged style of mainland China's rock music scene.

We then ventured to Southeast Asia, where folk music plays a more prominent role in popular music traditions. We listened to Thailand's luk thung, a country music with an urban sound, and then traveled to Indonesia to hear the eclectic ensemble of kroncong and its modern evolution, dangdut.

Pathways

- **Internet:** *www.ondar.com/*
  - Official Web site for Tuvan throat-singer Kongar-Ol Ondar
- **Internet:** *www.karaoke.com/*
  - An industry-supply provider for everything karaoke.

- **Book:** Drew, Rob. *Karaoke Nights: An Ethnographic Rhapsody.* Alta Mira Press, 2001.
  - A field study of karaoke culture that includes first-person experiences.
    - *www.altamirapress.com/*
      - Keywords: Karaoke
- **Book:** Yano, Christine. *Tears of Longing: Nostalgia and the Nation in Japanese Popular Song.* Harvard University Press, 2003.
  - A thorough review of Japanese enka history and artists.
    - *www.hup.harvard.edu/catalog/YANTEA.html*
- **Internet:** *www.misorahibari.com/?lang=en*
  - Official Web site (in Japanese) for enka singer Hibari Misora.
- **Internet:** *www.pokemon.com/*
  - Official Web site for Pokémon-related material.
- **DVD:** *Farewell, My Concubine.* Directed by Kaige Chen. 1993.
  - A fictional film about the life of two Beijing opera singers during the twentieth century, starring Cantopop icon Leslie Cheung.
- **Internet:** *http://teresateng.org/*
  - Fan Web site for Teresa Teng initiated by her younger brother, Jim Teng.
- **Book:** Lockard, Craig. *Dance of Life: Popular Music and Politics in Southeast Asia.* Honolulu: University of Hawai'i Press, 1998.
  - A thorough review of popular music in Indonesia, the Philippines, Thailand, Malaysia, and Singapore through the 1990s. Highly recommended.
    - *www.uhpress.hawaii.edu*
- **Internet:** *www.morlam-luktung.com/*
  - An introductory Web site to several of Thailand's most famous luk thung stars.
- **Internet:** *www.indonesianmusic.net/*
  - A Web site dedicated to Indonesia music merchandise.
- **Audio:** *Indonesian Popular Music: Kroncong, Dangdut, and Langgam Jawa.* Music of Indonesia series, Vol. 2. Smithsonian Folkways (SF 40056), 1991.
  - A collection of Indonesian popular music through the 1980s.
    - *www.folkways.si.edu/albumdetails.aspx?itemid=2298*
- **Book:** Wallach, Jeremy. *Modern Noise, Fluid Genres: Popular Music in Indonesia, 1997–2001.* Madison: University of Wisconsin Press, 2008.
  - A theoretically focused examination of the development of popular music in Indonesia at the turn of the century.
    - *www.modernnoisefluidgenres.com/*

Keywords for Additional Music Examples

- Modernized traditional Asian music
  - Ondar
- Enka
  - Hibari Misora
  - Miyako Harumi (not available on iTunes)
- J-Pop
  - "Ue wo muite arukou"
  - Cover of "Sukiyaki"
    - A Taste of Honey Sukiyaki
  - Black Mages
  - Hikaru Utada
  - Namie Amuro

- Traditional Cantonese opera
  - Cantonese opera
- C-Pop
  - Leslie Cheung
  - Anita Mui
  - Jacky Cheung
  - Aaron Kwok
  - Leon Lai
  - Andy Lau
- Mandopop
  - Zhou Xuan
  - Zhou Xuan Restoration Project
  - Zhou Xuan When
  - Faye Wong Sound
- Chinese revolutionary opera
  - Red Classics Peking Opera
- Chinese Rock Music
  - Cui Jian nothing
  - "Nan ni wan"
  - Cui Jian; Tang Dynasty
  - Brain Failure
  - Reflector
  - Yoksa
- Music from Thailand
  - King of Thailand music
  - Khaen Southeast Asia
  - Mor Lam
  - Siamese classical
- Music from Indonesia
  - Kroncong Segenggam
  - Elvy Sukaesih
  - Inul Daratista

Afterword

Your exploration of popular world music has just begun. We reviewed several music styles from around the world, but there are many, many genres and well-known artists that we overlooked for the sake of brevity. Furthermore, there are countless world-music traditions that fall outside the popular-music realm that were beyond our purview. Japanese *taiko* drum ensembles, for example, have a huge international following, but the music is regarded as "traditional" by the music industry. There are numerous composers who experiment with world-music traditions to create "world fusion" songs inspired by any number of musical locales. Folk and classical artists from around the world find themselves onstage with modern pop stars in ever-increasing numbers, as musicians around the planet use their artistic creativity to break cultural barriers and redefine the soundscape of our global village.

As you move beyond the pages of this book, remember that you live in an era in which the most distant parts of the globe can be seen in an instant through the Internet or satellite television. Beyond that, you can explore music in your own community or take a road trip to urban centers where diverse ethnic communities will teach you more about music and culture than you could ever glean from the pages of a book. Remember that music is only one lens you can use to examine our global culture. Whatever your interests—music, art, dance, athletics, politics, religion, business, medicine—these are all pathways to pursue new perspectives on life.

I hope you have found something in this book that piqued your interest to further exploration. Music is more than just listening; it is about living. Go and experience it. Find a concert, learn an instrument, take a dance class, or even just download a half a dozen new songs from different parts of the world. There are hundreds of books about world music that are readily accessible. I have recommended many resources throughout our journey; so pick a path and travel toward your own musical discoveries.

Music can take you to new frontiers, to places you never dreamed you would know. It can retrace history and show you the future. It can touch your spirit, stir your emotions, inspire your intellect, and bring joy to your life. As I said at the start, knowing music is knowing life and why people live it. Music may not be the meaning of life, but it can bring meaning to your life. If you love music, you already know this is true. If you have yet to experience this truth, put on your headphones, close your eyes, and just listen.

Pathways

- **Book:** Manuel, Peter. *Popular Music of the Non-Western World: An Introductory Survey.* New York: Oxford University Press, 1988.
  - A fundamental resource in the study of popular world music.
  - *www.us.oup.com/us/*
- **Book:** Miller, Terry, and Andrew Shahriari. *World Music: A Global Journey.* 2nd edition. New York: Routledge, 2008.
  - A survey of many traditional and popular world music traditions.
  - *www.routledge.com/TEXTBOOKS/WORLDMUSIC/2ndEd/*
- **Book:** Wald, Elijah. *Global Minstrels: Voices of World Music.* New York: Routledge, 2007.
  - A review of several world-music traditions, with an emphasis on the artist's perspective.
  - *www.elijahwald.com/global.html*

Glossary

Note: The definitions supplied are specifically oriented towards the commentary in this textbook. For standard definitions, please consult a general or specialized dictionary.

A

A cappella a vocal performance without instrumental accompaniment

A&R (Artist and Repertory) representative a person employed by a recording company to find and sign new artists

accent an emphasis on a particular musical sound

acoustic nonelectric instruments

afrikaans a South African language that mixes Dutch and indigenous dialects

afrobeat a music genre founded by Nigerian musician Fela Kuti (1938–1997), characterized by improvisational jazzlike solos and polyrhythmic percussion (see Chapter 7).

agogo a double bell common to African and Caribbean music

akonting a lute common in West Africa, often considered a predecessor to the American banjo

ANC acronym of the African National Congress, a political party from the Republic of South Africa noted for its antiapartheid stance during the 20th century

Anglophone an English-speaking person or population

anime a term most often applied to Japanese animated television or film

apartheid a government policy of segregation that persisted in South Africa throughout the 20th century

aristocrats the elite members of a society, generally consisting of the wealthy and powerful

Armageddon (Armagiddyon) a biblical reference to the end of the world, which Rastafari adherents accept as the current state of the planet (see Chapter 3)

arpeggio a chord whose pitches sound in succession rather than simultaneously

astrology the interpretive study of celestial bodies (stars, planets, etc.) and how they affect human and natural affairs

astronomy the scientific study of celestial bodies (stars, planets, etc.)

axé a popular-music style from Brazil (see Chapter 5)

B

b-boy/b-girl a hip-hop dancer

Babylon a label applied to governments and institutions that Rastafari adherents consider decadent and oppressive (see Chapter 3)

bacchanal a slang term used in Trinidad for a calypso singer's critical commentary (see Chapter 3)

Bahasa the official language of Indonesia

bailaoras/bailaores a dancer (Spanish), often from the flamenco tradition (see Chapter 6)

baile the Spanish word for "dance," forms one of the three components of flamenco, along with *cante* (song) and *toque* (instrumental) (see Chapter 6)

bairro a poor neighborhood in Brazil (see Chapter 5)

balafon a type of xylophone from West Africa (see Chapter 7)

ballad a sung narrative

ballroom dance a type of formal social dance

bandolin a small, high-range mandolin, with four double courses of strings, that is common to Brazil (see Chapter 5)

bandoneon a type of accordion typical of South America used especially in tango music (see Chapter 4)

banjo a lute common to North American folk music

bar mitzvah/bat mitzvah a coming-of-age ceremony in Judaism (see Chapter 6)

bateria a percussion ensemble typical of a samba school (see Chapter 5)

battles a singing or instrumental competition, especially in hip-hop music (see Chapter 2)

batuque an African dance transplanted to Brazil, characterized by a "belly bump" movement (see Chapter 5)

beat a regular pulsation implied or articulated in a music performance

Beatniks a subculture of young people during the late 1950s and early '60s (see Chapter 2)

betel-nut a mixture of plant and nut with other ingredients that turns the saliva a dark color; common in rural populations in Asia (see Chapter 9)

bhangra a folk and popular-music genre associated with Indian populations around the world, with roots in the Punjabi region of north India (see Chapter 8)

bhangraton a music genre combining elements of *bhangra* and reggaeton music (see Chapter 4)

Billboard Charts a music-industry magazine emphasizing music-recording rankings in terms of sales and popularity

black market an underground system of trade, typically dealing with illegal or scarce goods

bluegrass a folk-music genre common to the Appalachian region of the United States (see Chapter 2)

bodhran a frame drum common to Irish music (see Chapter 6)

body wave a dance movement common to hip-hop choreography (see Chapter 2)

Bollywood a reference to the Indian film industry, specifically to films produced in Mumbai (see Chapter 8)

bomba a drum commonly heard in samba music from Brazil (see Chapter 5)

bombardinos a reference to brass band instruments in Brazilian music, especially samba (see Chapter 5)

bombing a vocal practice heard in *mbube* competitions from South Africa (see Chapter 7)

boogie-woogie a style of blues characterized by a fast tempo and emphasis on piano bass lines (see Chapter 2)

boom box a portable cassette/CD player with internal speakers

bossa nova a popular-music style from Brazil characterized by an intimate atmosphere and small ensemble (see Chapter 5)

break dancing a style of hip-hop dancing that developed during the 1970s and early '80s (see Chapter 2)

break rhythm a rhythmic section in a song recording that is repeated to accompany hip-hop dancers (see Chapter 2)

breakin' a reference to hip-hop dancers performing solo choreography (see Chapter 2)

Brythonic a southern Celtic language family (see Chapter 6)

bubblegum pop a term frequently used to characterize formulaic music recordings (see Chapter 2)

Buddhism a religious tradition that emanated from Asia beginning in the 5th century B.C.

bumba-meu-boi a folk music and dance genre from Brazil (see Chapter 5)

C

C-pop (Cantopop) commercialized popular-music primarily emanating from Hong Kong (see Chapter 9)

cabaret a nightclub restaurant with live entertainment (see Chapter 2)

café cantantes a Spanish restaurant that offers live entertainment, particularly flamenco music and dance (see Chapter 6)

caixa a snare drum used in samba music from Brazil (see Chapter 5)

cajon a wooden box used for rhythm, often in modern flamenco music (see Chapter 6)

call and response a vocal organization in which a lead call is followed by a group response (see Chapter 7)

calypso a popular-music style from Trinidad characterized by witty social commentary (see Chapter 3)

candomblé an African-derived spiritual tradition primarily found in Brazil (see Chapter 5)

cantaora a flamenco singer (see Chapter 6)

cante the Spanish word for "song," one of the three components of flamenco, along with *baile* (dance) and *toque* (instrumental) (see Chapter 6)

cante chico a category of flamenco vocal style considered light in difficulty (see Chapter 6)

cante intermedio a category of flamenco vocal style considered intermediate in difficulty (see Chapter 6)

cante jondo a category of flamenco vocal style considered heavy in difficulty (see Chapter 6)

cantillation a liturgical chant, often associated with the Jewish ritual (see Chapter 6)

capo a clamp used by guitarists to change the pitch range of an instrument

capoeira a martial arts and dance tradition from Brazil (see Chapter 5)

Carnival a pre-Lenten festival common to areas with a prominent Roman Catholic population (see Chapters 3 and 5)

castanets a pair of handheld wooden idiophones used often in flamenco performance (see Chapter 6)

cavaquinho a high-range lute common to samba music in Brazil (see Chapter 5)

ceili bands an informal music ensemble often heard in public houses (pubs) in Ireland (see Chapter 6)

Celtic a label applied to cultural activities from populations of Scottish, Irish, or Welsh descent (see Chapter 6)

cha-cha a ballroom dance style associated with Latin American music (see Chapter 4)

chador a traditional garment from the Middle East, typically worn by Muslim women to cover the body and head in public (see Chapter 8)

changui a Latin American music style (see Chapter 4)

chanson a French song (see Chapter 2)

chantwell an early term used for calypso singers (see Chapter 3)

charanga a Latin American music style (see Chapter 4)

cheikha/cheikh a title used by *rai* singers from Algeria (see Chapter 8)

chocalho a shaken idiophone common to samba from Brazil (see Chapter 5)

chord (1) the simultaneous sounding of three or more pitches to create harmony; (2) the supporting vocal harmony in South African *mbube*/isicathamiya performance (see Chapter 7)

choreography the sequence of movements and foot patterns associated with dance

choro a small acoustic ensemble from Brazil comprised primarily of guitar-family instruments and a lead wind instrument, for example, clarinet/flute (see Chapter 5)

chromaticism sounding all succeeding pitches in a tuning system in ascending or descending motion

chutney music a category of popular-music from Trinidad associated with performers from the Indian diasporas (see Chapter 3)

clarinet a reed aerophone common to European music traditions

classical a label applied to formal cultural activities

clavé rhythm a syncopated rhythmic pattern common to Latin American music (see Chapter 4)

claves a pair of wood sticks commonly used in Latin American music (see Chapter 4)

coimbra fado a subcategory of *fado* music from Portugal (see Chapter 6)

colonialism the practice of obtaining political control over another country and occupying it with settlers

Communism a political theory proposed by Karl Marx (1818–1883) that outlined a government system in which all property was considered publicly owned and every citizen was provided for according to their needs and contributions to society

comparsa a dance common in Latin America, which is characterized by fast hip shaking (see Chapter 4)

compás a term that denotes rhythm in flamenco music (see Chapter 6)

composition a preconceived musical work

concertina a small accordion-type instrument

conga dance a dance in which participants follow one another in a single line and "kick" on every fourth beat of the music (see Chapter 4)

conga drum a tall barrel-shaped drum common to Latin American music (see Chapter 4)

congo a region in central Africa (see Chapter 7)

conjunto a polka-based music style heard primarily in Mexico and the southern United States

controller the lead vocalist in South African *mbube*/isicathamiya performance (see Chapter 7)

cotillion a formal ball for upper-class patrons that usually includes ballroom dance (see Chapter 2)

counterculture cultural activities and beliefs that differ from the prevailing social norm

crescendo an increasing volume of sound

cuíca a friction drum common to South American music, especially samba (see Chapter 5)

Cultural Revolution a period of political upheaval in China (1966–76) when the government instituted strict social and economic reforms (see Chapter 9)

cumbia a dance and music from Colombia that is similar to salsa music (see Chapter 4)

D

daf a frame drum common to Middle Eastern music (see Chapter 8)

dancehall a popular-music style from Jamaica characterized by a heavy dance beat (see Chapter 3)

dangdut a popular-music style characterized by electronic instruments and a persistent drum rhythm, for example, Indonesian *dang-dut* (see Chapter 9)

danzón a music style from Latin America (see Chapter 4)

darabukka a goblet drum common to the Middle East (see Chapter 8)

dem bow the basic *riddim* used in reggaeton music (see Chapter 4)

descarga the extended improvisation during performance of *son montuno* (see Chapter 4)

dhol a barrel-shaped drum common to *bhangra* music (see Chapter 8)

diaspora the dispersion of any population from its original ethnic homeland

dirndl a woman's style of dress typical of Eastern Europe (see Chapter 6)

diva a famous female singer

dombek (dumbek) a goblet drum common to Middle Eastern music (see Chapter 8)

dominant a harmony considered an interval of a fifth above the root/tonic or "home" harmony of a composition

double entendre a word or phrase with more than one interpretation

double bass   an acoustic chordophone with a low range

downbeat   the first pulse of a measure in music

dreadlocks   a hairstyle characterized by long braids, commonly worn by Rastafarians and reggae enthusiasts (see Chapter 3)

dub (doubles)   an instrumental version of a reggae song or an instrumental recording in a popular style emanating from Jamaica (see Chapter 3)

dundun   an hourglass pressure drum common to West African music, including *juju* (see Chapter 7)

duple   a meter in which the number of pulses is divisible by two

dynamics   the volume in a music performance

E

electronic synthesizer   a keyboard instrument that produces electronic sounds

Emmy   an award given to members of the television industry

enka   a music genre from Japan characterized by sad themes (see Chapter 9)

erhu   a two-stringed bowed lute from China (see Chapter 9)

escolas de samba   meaning "samba schools," a procession of musicians and revelers during Carnival celebrations in Brazil (see Chapter 5)

Estado Novo   meaning "New State," the political and social reforms instituted by the government in Brazil and other Portuguese-speaking areas (see Chapter 5 and 6)

ethno-pop   an early reference to popular world music

ethnomusicology   an academic discipline that focuses on world music and its cultural associations

Euro-pop   commercial popular-music from Europe

Eurovision   an annual international song contest whose participants hail from Europe (see Chapter 6)

F

Fab Four   a colloquial reference to the popular-music group the Beatles (see Chapter 2)

fadista   a vocalist who sings Portuguese *fado* (see Chapter 6)

fado   a popular-music style from Portugal characterized by sentimental themes (see Chapter 6)

Fante   a West African language (see Chapter 7)

Farsi   the official language of Iran (see Chapter 8)

favela   the slums of Brazil, particularly those in Rio de Janeiro (see Chapter 5)

filmi   an Indian film (see Chapter 8)

firqa   a music ensemble from the Middle East generally comprised of both Middle Eastern and European instruments (see Chapter 8)

flamenco   a folk and popular-music style from Spain that is characterized by the use of guitar, passionate singing, and vibrant dance (see Chapter 6)

flamenco fusion   a subcategory of flamenco that mixes elements of flamenco with other musical styles (see Chapter 6)

flamenco proper   the traditional forms of flamenco music (see Chapter 6)

folk   common or ordinary people, as well as their cultural activities

folk festival   a festival dedicated to traditional arts and crafts associated with common people

form   the underlying structure of a musical performance over time

forró   an accordion-based music style from Brazil (see Chapter 5)

foxtrot   a type of ballroom dance (see Chapter 2)

free rhythm   music that lacks a consistent pulse

freestyle rap   an extemporaneous poetry style associated with hip-hop culture (see Chapter 2)

freezes   a break-dance movement in which the performer stops suddenly (see Chapter 2)

friction drum   a membranophone that uses a stick to pierce the drum face to produce sound (see Chapter 5)

full step   an ascending or descending motion from one pitch to another at an interval of two chromatic pitches in a musical scale

funk   a popular-music style characterized by vibrant bass lines and a dance-oriented rhythm from the United States

G

Ga   a West African language (see Chapter 7)

Gaelic   the cultural activities of Celtic populations in Scotland, Ireland, and Wales, particularly their language (see Chapter 6)

gagaku   a classical ritual music from Japan (see Chapter 9)

gamelan   a music ensemble from Indonesia characterized by the use of large gongs and metallophones (see Chapter 9)

gangtai music   a Chinese reference to Western music (see Chapter 9)

ganja   marijuana, which is often used in Rastafari rituals as a means of heightening spiritual awareness (see Chapter 3)

genre   a category of music that has similar characteristics of style, form, and subject matter

ghazal an Indian poem set to music, usually with themes about romantic love (see Chapter 8)

ghettoes an urban slum, generally dominated by an ethnic minority

gigs an informal reference to a music event

Gitano an informal reference to a Romani person (also, Gypsy) (see Chapter 6)

Goidelic a northern Celtic language group (see Chapter 6)

golpeador a pick guard found on a flamenco guitar (see Chapter 6)

graffiti art produced by with spraying cans of paint onto public or private property, such as buildings or subways (see Chapter 2)

Grammy an award given to members of the music industry

gramophone an early type of record player

Great Depression a period of economic despair in the United States and throughout the world during the 1930s

griot a French term for a wandering minstrel, frequently used to describe West African praise singers (see Chapter 7)

guajira a music style common in Latin America (see Chapter 4)

guaracha a traditional music style common in Latin America (see Chapter 4)

guiro a scraped gourd instrument common to Latin American music (see Chapter 4)

guitarra Portuguesa a plucked lute from Portugal, especially common to *fado* performance (see Chapter 6)

H

habanera rhythm a syncopated rhythm common to Latin American music (see Chapter 6)

hadhari a musical predecessor of Algerian *rai* (see Chapter 8)

haj the Islamic sacred pilgrimage to Mecca

half-step an ascending or descending motion of one chromatic pitch of a musical scale

Harlem a district in New York City with a predominant African American population that, during the 1920s and '30s, was noted as the source of important developments in jazz

harmony a blending of three or more different pitches; a chord

highlife a popular-music style from Ghana characterized by the use of European jazz instruments and clear melody (see Chapter 7)

hi-hat a pair of cymbals operated by a foot lever

H.I.M. (His Imperial Majesty) pronounced "him," refers to Halie Selassie I, whom Rastafari adherents accept as the second incarnation of Jesus Christ, that is, the Messiah (see Chapter 3)

Hindi film an Indian film (see Chapter 8)

Hindustani a term that denotes north Indian cultural activities

hip-hop a cultural movement that originated within African American and Latin American populations of New York City (see Chapter 2)

hippie a person who adheres to a subculture that rejects the social norms of the cultural mainstream, especially during the late 1960s

Hollywood a district in Los Angeles, California, considered the center of the movie industry

hymnody the performance or composition of hymns (religious songs) in the Christian tradition

I

I and I Rastafari adherents substitute the word "I" for "me" and "I and I" for "we" to indicate their belief that all humans are spiritually united and one with Jah (God) (see Chapter 3)

iconography the study of images or symbols in the visual arts

Igbo a West African language (see Chapter 7)

imam a religious leader in Islam (see Chapter 8)

improvisation spontaneous musical performance

instrumentals a composition without voice

interface a device or program that enables a person to communicate with a computer

interval the distance between two pitches

iq-at rhythmic modes in Arabic music (see Chapter 8)

Irish Gaelic the indigenous language of Irish people (see Chapter 6)

isicathamiya a popular-music style from South Africa characterized by unaccompanied choral singing (see Chapter 7)

iTunes an Internet interface that enables users to download music, movies, and other media

J

J-pop Japanese popular-music (see Chapter 9)

Jah (Yah) a Rastafari reference to God, derived from the Hebrew terms "Jehovah" or "Yahweh" (see Chapter 3)

jali/jalolu a West African praise singer (see Chapter 7)

jazz a music type that originated in the United States characterized by improvisation, syncopation, and the use of European wind instruments and vibrant percussion

jig   a type of music composition that accompanies a dance of the same name (see Chapter 6)

juergas   an informal gathering of flamenco enthusiasts (see Chapter 6)

juju   a popular-music style from Nigeria (see Chapter 7)

jump blues   a subcategory of blues music characterized by a fast tempo (see Chapter 2)

K

kaiso singer   an early reference to Calypso singers (see Chapter 3)

kanun   a plucked zither from West Asia/North Africa (see Chapter 8)

karaoke   an amateur performance of a prerecorded song that excludes vocals (see Chapter 9)

karaoke box   an entertainment venue where patrons sing karaoke in a private room with guests (see Chapter 9)

key   the prevailing harmony of a composition or improvisation (see Chapter 2)

khaen   a free-reed aerophone from northeast Thailand (see Chapter 9)

kick drum   the largest drum of a standard drum set, generally played with a foot pedal

kilt   a traditional skirt made of tartan, usually worn by Scottish men (see Chapter 6)

kimono   a traditional garment worn by Japanese women (see Chapter 9)

klezmer (*pl.* **Klezmorim)**   an instrumental music style and ensemble associated with the Jewish community (see Chapter 6)

kobushi   a stylized "trembling" vibrato associated with Japanese vocal performance (see Chapter 9)

kora   a plucked chordophone (lute-harp) common to praise-singer performance in West Africa (see Chapter 7)

Koran   the holy book of Islam

kroncong   a popular-music genre from Indonesia, as well as a lute common in the region (see Chapter 9)

Kuo Min Tang   a political party (Nationalist Party) from China based in Taiwan that emerged after the Chinese Communist Revolution of 1949 (see Chapter 9)

kwaito   a popular-music style from South Africa characterized by a heavy dance beat and raplike vocal delivery (see Chapter 7)

kwassa kwassa   a modern dance style found in the Republic of South Africa (see Chapter 7)

kwela   a street music style noted for the use of a pennywhistle playing the lead melody (see Chapter 7)

L

lam klawn   a traditional music genre from northeast Thailand (see Chapter 9)

lambada   a dance style from Brazil characterized by touching stomachs with a partner (see Chapter 5)

lamellophone   a type of musical instrument classified as an idiophone

laoud   a type of plucked chordophone found in Latin America (see Chapter 4)

largo   the opening composed section of a *son montuno* performance (see Chapter 4)

Latin jazz   a jazz style that often includes Latin American instruments, rhythms, and melody (see Chapter 4)

Latin pop   a popular-music style that incorporates elements of Latin American music (see Chapter 4)

Latino   a person of Latin American ethnicity (see Chapter 4)

Lent   the period preceding Easter in the Christian calendar

lexical   the understood vocabulary of a language

line dance   a choreography in which dancers follow one another in a line or are organized in a linear pattern

lingala   a trade language of central Africa (see Chapter 7)

Lisboa fado   a substyle of *fado* associated with Lisbon, Portugal (see Chapter 6)

luk thung   a popular-music style from Thailand characterized by the use of modern electric instruments and lyrical themes focusing on daily life and rural contexts (see Chapter 9)

lundun   a music style from Angola that influenced the creation of Cape Verdean *morna* (see Chapter 6)

M

Mafioso   a member of the Mafia

major   a chord or harmony with the interval of the third (pitch level) at four half steps above the root pitch (see Chapter 2)

mambo   a music and dance style popular in the United States in association with Latin jazz (see Chapter 4)

Mandopop (M-Pop)   popular-music from Mandarin-speaking populations, primarily those from China and Taiwan (see chaper 9)

maqam   the modal system used in Arabic music (see Chapter 8)

marabi   a popular-music style from South Africa characterized by repeated motives and the use of a piano (see Chapter 7)

maracas   a type of shaken rattle common to Latin American music (see Chapter 4)

Mardi Gras a secular celebration, similar to Carnival, that precedes the period of Lent in the Roman Catholic church

mariachi a music style associated with festive celebrations in Mexico and the southwestern United States (see Chapter 4)

maxixe a Brazilian dance style (see Chapters 2 and 5)

mbaqanga a popular-music style from South Africa characterized by a dance beat, electric guitars, and a "growling" lead vocalist (see Chapter 7)

MBE (Member of the British Empire) an award presented to honor civilians of Great Britain

mbira a musical instrument classified as a lamellophone common in central and southern Africa (see Chapter 7)

mbube a popular-music style from the Republic of South Africa characterized by an unaccompanied vocal group (see Chapter 7)

MC-ing abbreviation of master of ceremonies, the art of vocal improvisation in hip-hop music (see Chapter 2)

measure a unit of time corresponding to a set number of beats

Medh a religious ceremony in Islam that is common to West Asia and North Africa (see Chapter 8)

medium an object that produces musical sound, such as an instrument or voice

melismatic a vocal performance of more than one pitch per syllable (see Chapter 2)

melodic "hook" a memorable music motive, phrase, or lyric in a popular song

melody a succession of pitches forming a musical idea

mento an early style of popular-music from Jamaica (see Chapter 3)

merengue a popular-music and dance style from the Dominican Republic (see Chapter 4)

metallophone a musical instrument made of metal, generally using metal keys of different sizes

meter the grouping of a specific number of beats

microtone a pitch frequency that falls between the standard pitches of the Western tuning system

minor a chord or harmony with the interval of the third (pitch level) at three half steps above the root pitch

modinha an early music style common in Brazil and Portugal (see Chapter 5)

montuno (1) instrumental solo breaks common to salsa and Afro-Cuban *son*; (2) repeated ostinato pattern of the piano during a *son* or salsa music performance

morna a popular-music style from Cape Verde characterized by sentimental lyrics (see Chapter 6)

moshing a dance practice associated with hard-rock music in which audience members jump and collide with one another

motive a short rhythmic or melodic idea

MP3 abbreviation of MPEG-Audio Layer 3, an audio file type common to digital media

MPB acronym for Música Popular Brasileira, a general reference to popular-music from Brazil (see Chapter 5)

mqashiyo a substyle of *mbqanga* popular-music from the Republic of South Africa (see Chapter 7)

MTV acronym for the Music Television broadcast station

Muzak light background music typically played in public places, such as a shopping mall or doctor's office

N

New Age denotes a cultural movement towards alternative lifestyles in Western culture, emphasizing spirituality, mysticism, and environmentalism (see Chapter 6)

ney a vertical flute common to West Asia and North Africa (see Chapter 8)

nightsong a song performed for nighttime competitions among *mbube* choirs in South Africa (see Chapter 7)

nonlexical a nonsensical word used in vocal production

note a visual symbolic reference for a pitch or rhythm; also used synonymously for the term *pitch*

nueva flamenco a modern flamenco style (see Chapter 6)

nueva trova a type of political folk song from Cuba (see Chapter 4)

nuevo tango a modern tango style (see Chapter 4)

Nuyorican a New York City resident of Puerto Rican ancestry

O

octave an interval of two pitches with the same name but sounding at different frequencies

offbeat a pulsation sounded between the regular beat or on the second and fourth beats of a four-pulse measure

"one-drop" rhythm a rhythmic deemphasis of the first beat of a measure in reggae music (see Chapter 3)

orchestra a large instrumental ensemble

orchestration the arrangement of musical elements for an ensemble performance

orkes melayu an early popular-music style and ensemble from Indonesia (see Chapter 9)

ornamentation an embellishment of a melody or musical sound

orquesta típica an ensemble common to tango music performance (see Chapter 4)

Oscar an award presented to members of the movie industry

ostinato a short, repeated melodic phrase

Ottoman a member of the former Ottoman Empire centered in Istanbul, Turkey (Chapter 8)

oud a plucked lute common in West Asia and North Africa (see Chapter 8)

P

pachanga a traditional music style from Latin America (see Chapter 4)

palm wine a guitar-based music style from West and Central Africa (see Chapter 7)

palmas hand clapping in flamenco and other Spanish music contexts (see Chapter 6)

palos the subcategorization of flamenco music (see Chapter 6)

pandereta a frame drum with cymbals, that is, tambourine (see Chapter 4)

panpipe an aerophone made of several pipes of varying lengths (see Chapter 2)

pedal organ a pedal-operated keyboard instrument

pedal steel guitar an electric zither typically played with a slide to produce portamento (see Chapter 7)

pentatonic a scale of five pitches

perreo a "grinding" dance associated with reggaeton music (see Chapter 4)

Persia the former name of Iran

phleng luk krung "city" popular-music from Thailand (see Chapter 9)

phleng luk thung "country" popular-music from Thailand (see Chapter 9)

phleng Thai sakhon Western-style music performed in Thailand (see Chapter 9)

phoneme a distinct unit of sound in a language

phonograph an early sound-recording/producing machine

piano a keyboard instrument

Pidgin English a simplified version of the English language that incorporates indigenous dialects and unique idioms of the region where it is spoken

pipa a pear-shaped lute common to traditional Chinese music (see Chapter 9)

piphat a classical-music ensemble from Thailand (see Chapter 9)

pitch a sound frequency, as used in a musical context

pizzicato plucking the strings of a violin or other stringed instrument with the finger

playback singers a singer in the Indian film industry whose voice is lip-synched by onscreen actors (see Chapter 8)

plena a traditional music style from Puerto Rico (see Chapter 4)

polka a traditional music style from Eastern Europe characterized by the use of accordion (see Chapter 6)

polyrhythm an instrumental organization that uses multiple rhythms playing in relationship to one another rather than according to a meter

poppin' hip-hop choreography in which dancers make abrupt, stylized movements (see Chapter 2)

popular a well-liked modern music (in contrast to folk or classical music) that is used primarily for entertainment and disseminated through music-industry media outlets, such as a recording or concert performance

portamento a continuous progression from one pitch to another through all the between frequencies

Porteños a person commonly associated with the seaport, specifically in Buenos Aires, Argentina (see Chapter 4)

praise singer a class of musicians from West Africa who earn a living by singing praises to community members (see Chapter 7)

Prohibition a period in American history (1920–33) during which alcohol was prohibited by law

pub a "public house" where food and beverages are sold, commonly found in the United Kingdom (see Chapter 6)

puirt a beul vocal practice that substitutes vocables for instrumental melody (see Chapter 6)

Punjabi a person and/or language from the Punjab region in south Asia (see Chapter 8)

punk a popular-music style from Europe and the United States characterized by a loud, fast, aggressive sound

puxador lead vocalist of the samba-school processions at Carnival in Rio de Janiero (see Chapter 5)

Q

qawwali a devotional music associated with Islam, especially common to Sufis from Pakistan (see Chapter 8)

quadrille a type of couples square dance (see Chapter 2)

quarter-tone half of a semitone

R

R&B acronym for rhythm and blues, a predominantly African American popular-music style in the United States characterized by moderately fast tempos and electric instruments (see Chapter 2)

race record an early music industry label for ethnic music recordings, primarily of African American music (see Chapter 2)

ragga a popular-music style from Jamaica characterized by improvisational vocals and a heavy dance beat (see Chapter 3)

ragga-soca a popular-music style that mixes elements of Jamaican ragga and Trinidadian soca music (see Chapter 3)

raggamuffin denotes a ragga music enthusiast (see Chapter 3)

ragtime a late-nineteenth-century popular-music style considered a predecessor to jazz (see Chapter 2)

rai a popular-music style from Algeria characterized by a dance beat and secular themes (see Chapter 8)

rap an improvisational vocal style common to hip-hop music (see Chapter 2)

rasa a theory of emotion or sentiment from India in association with artistic endeavors (see Chapter 8)

rasgueado a performance technique common to flamenco music in which the performer rapidly plucks the strings of a guitar with each finger in succession (see Chapter 6)

Rasta followers of the Rastafari movement (see Chapter 3)

Rastafari a spiritual tradition that asserts that the second coming of Jesus Christ has already occurred; commonly associated with reggae culture (see Chapter 3)

reco-reco a scraped idiophone common to Latin American music (see Chapter 4)

reel a lively traditional music from Scotland and Ireland (see Chapter 6)

reggae a popular-music style from Jamaica characterized by an emphasized offbeat and moderate tempo (see Chapter 3)

reggaeton a popular-music style from Latin America characterized by the use of the *dem bow* rhythm (see Chapter 4)

repinique a high-pitched drum common to samba (see Chapter 5)

rhythm the organization of durations of musical sounds

riddim percussion rhythm and bass melodic pattern common to dancehall music from Jamaica and Latin America (see Chapters 3 and 4)

riqq a frame drum common to West Asia and North Africa (see Chapter 8)

risqué a slightly indecent remark, especially one that is sexually oriented

Riverdance an Irish dance troupe and show that helped to popularize step-dancing on the international market (see Chapter 6)

rock a popular-music style characterized by electric instruments and disseminated through popular media, such as concerts, recordings, television, or the Internet (see Chapter 2)

rock steady a precursor to reggae music characterized by an emphasized offbeat and moderately fast tempo (see Chapter 3)

rockabilly a label often applied to early rock music styles that mix rhythm and blues and country and western music during the 1950s, as exemplified by Elvis Presley and Buddy Holly (see Chapter 2)

Romani an ethnic population that originated in India and migrated through West Asia, North Africa, Europe, and the United States; commonly referred to as "Gypsies" (see Chapter 6)

Romantic languages a group that includes Spanish, Portuguese, French, Italian, and Romanian languages (see Chapter 4)

root the "home" or "one" pitch or chord in Western harmony (see Chapter 2)

rude boy a youth subculture in Jamaica during the 1950s and '60s (see Chapter 3)

rumba a dance and associated music style from Latin America, also common in Africa (see Chapter 4)

rumba box a type of idiophone (lamellophone) that plays a low range of pitches; common to Jamaican *mento* (see Chapter 3)

rumba catalana (also, rumba flamenco) a popular-music style that mixes flamenco musical characteristics with popular dance idioms (see Chapter 4)

rumba clave a syncopated rhythm commonly heard in Latin American music (see Chapter 4)

rumba flamenco (also, rumba Catalana) a popular-music style that mixes flamenco musical characteristics with popular dance idioms (see Chapter 4)

S

sake a Japanese rice wine (see Chapter 9)

salsa a popular-music style from Latin America characterized by complex rhythmic elements and influences from jazz and rock music (see Chapter 4)

samba a popular-music style from Brazil characterized by a syncopated rhythm and clear melody (see Chapter 5)

sambista a participant in the samba schools during Carnival celebrations in Brazil (see Chapter 5)

sans humanitae literally, "without mercy," the unguarded critical commentary of calypso artists (see Chapter 3)

santur an Iranian zither (see Chapter 8)

sarangi a bowed lute from India (see Chapter 8)

saudade a sorrowful sentiment associated with Portuguese *fado* (see Chapter 6)

saw U a two-stringed fiddle from Thailand (see Chapter 9)

scat vocal improvisation in jazz music that uses nonlexical syllables (see Chapter 2)

search engine   a computer program designed to retrieve information from a database or network, especially the Internet

sebene   the interplay of melodic motives in *soukous* music (see Chapter 7)

segregation   the enforced separation of people according to racial and/or ethnic background

sehtar   a plucked lute common in central and west Asia (see Chapter 8)

semitone   the smallest interval used in the Western tuning system

shah   the title of former monarchs from Iran (see Chapter 8)

Shaykhat (also, Cheikha)   an honorific title adopted by *rai* vocalists from Algeria (see Chapter 8)

shebeens   a liquor establishment that often features music and dance, especially in South Africa (Chapter 7)

shekere   a gourd rattle with an external beading (see Chapter 7)

shidaiqu   an early popular-music style from China (see Chapter 9)

sitar   a plucked lute from India (see Chapter 8)

ska   a popular-music style from Jamaica, usually instrumental, characterized by an offbeat emphasis and fast tempo (see Chapter 3)

skank   a rhythmic pattern that emphasizes the upbeat, common to Jamaican folk and popular-music (see Chapter 3)

slackness   a slang term for profanity and crude commentary during DJ vocal improvisations in Jamaican popular-music (see Chapter 3)

Slavic languages   Eastern European languages, including Russian, Ukrainian, Belorussian, Polish, Czech, Slovak, Sorbian, Bulgarian, Serbo-Croat, Macedonian, and Slovene

sleng teng   a *riddim* heard in dancehall music from Jamaica (see Chapter 3)

soca   a portmanteau of "soul-calypso," a popular-music style from Trinidad that emphasizes dance rhythms over witty lyricism (see Chapter 3)

som tam   a papaya salad from Thailand (see Chapter 9)

son   the Cuban popular-music style that parallels salsa music elsewhere (see Chapter 4)

son clave   a syncopated rhythm common to Latin American music (see Chapter 4)

son montuno   an early style of salsa music that emphasizes extended instrumental improvisations over a repeated vamp (*montuno*) (see Chapter 4)

song   generally refers to any composition but is specifically associated with a vocal performance of a poem or other words set to music, with special attention to the melodic correlation between text and music (see Chapter 2)

soukous   a hip-gyrating dance common in Central Africa and later used to label various popular-music styles from the region (see Chapter 7)

soul   a popular-music genre that combines elements of African American gospel music with rhythm and blues

sound-system battles   a dance party in which two or more DJs use loud speaker systems to compete for the audience's attention (see Chapter 3)

soundie   a short music film popular during the 1940s (see Chapter 3)

soundscape   the aural environment of any particular location or general reference to musical activity common to a region or population

Spanish Harlem   an area of Harlem, a neighborhood in New York City, consisting predominantly of Latin American populations (see Chapter 4)

square dance   a group folk dance common in the United States (see Chapter 2)

stanza   a recurring group of music lines, that is, verse, usually with variations of text

step-dancing   a type of Irish folk dance characterized by minimal upper-body movement and fast-moving footwork (see Chapter 6)

stride   a popular jazz-music style with wide intervals on the piano that emphasizes a regular bass pattern, (see Chapter 2)

string   a strongly Western influenced popular-music style from Thailand (see Chapter 9)

subdominant   a harmony considered an interval of a fourth above the root/tonic or "home" harmony of a composition

Sufi   a practitioner of Sufism, regarded as the mystical branch of Islam (see Chapter 8)

suona   a double-reed aerophone from China (see Chapter 9)

surdos   a type of bass drum from Brazil (see Chapter 5)

swing era   a period in jazz music (1935–46) that emphasized big-band performance

syllabic   a vocal performance of one pitch per syllable of sung text (see Chapter 2)

syncopation   accenting a normally weak beat or sounding between beats

synthesizer   an electronic keyboard instrument

T

tabla   a pair of hand drums common to classical music from India (see Chapter 8)

tango a ballroom dance and associated music that originated in Argentina (see Chapter 4)

tango cancion a subcategory of tango that includes a vocal performer (see Chapter 4)

tapas a variety of appetizer cuisine often served at restaurants and homes in Spain (see Chapter 8)

techno a popular-music style characterized by electronic instruments and strong dance beat

Tejano music a popular-music style associated with Latin American populations in the southern United States, especially Texas, and Mexico (see Chapter 4)

tempo the speed of the beat in a music performance

text setting the correlation between text and sung melody (see Chapter 2)

timba a popular-music style from Cuba that parallels rock and hip-hop music (see Chapter 4)

timbales a high-pitched pair of drums common to salsa music (see Chapter 4)

timbre the quality of a sound (see Chapter 2)

time code a coded signal on a video or film that supplies data information, such as time reference and frame number

tin whistle a flute aerophone common to Irish music, as well as pennywhistle music (Kwela) from South Africa (see Chapters 6 and 7)

toasting a rhyming narrative tradition from Jamaica (see Chapter 3)

toi-toi a protest dance from South Africa (see Chapter 7)

tom tom a midrange drum, typically struck with a stick

tonal center the "home" pitch or harmony, that is, tonic, of a music performance

tonality the character of a piece with reference to its predominant harmony

tone a term used synonymously for "pitch"

toque the Spanish word for "instrumental," one of the three components of flamenco, along with *baile* (dance) and *cante* (song) (see Chapter 6)

township jive popular-music styles emanating from township regions in South Africa (see Chapter 7)

Trenchtown a government housing project in Kingston, Jamaica (see Chapter 3)

triple refers to a meter that uses a multiple of three pulses per measure

troubadour a wandering minstrel from Europe, especially France, during the Renaissance period (11th–13th centuries) (see Chapter 6)

trombone a low-range brass aerophone

tropicalia a popular-music style from Brazil characterized by an eclectic mix of instruments and topical lyrics (see Chapter 5)

trumpet a high-range brass aerophone

tsimbl (also, cimbalom) a hammered zither common to Eastern Europe, performed especially by Romani musicians (see Chapter 6)

tsotsi a street language and culture from South Africa (see Chapter 7)

tuk-tuk a motorized rickshaw from Thailand (see Chapter 9)

tumbi a plucked lute common to folk and popular-music styles of *bhangra* (see Chapter 8)

twelve-bar blues progression a standard harmonic progression comprised of twelve measures, typical of blues and rock music (see Chapter 2)

twi a West African language especially common in Ghana (see Chapter 7)

two-step a dance movement typical of polka music (see Chapter 6)

U

uilleann ("elbow") pipes a type of bagpipe from Ireland (see Chapter 6)

upbeat a normally unaccented beat, typically following the downbeat, or first beat

V

vamp a short repeated musical segment, typically supplying accompaniment for an improvised solo

viola a midrange bowed lute from Europe

viola de fado a low-range bowed lute common to *fado* music from Portugal (see Chapter 6)

violin a high-range bowed lute from Europe

virtuoso a highly skilled musician

virtuousity highly dexterous performance technique

vocable a nonlexical word or syllable

Vulgar Latin informal Latin spoken during the classical era that evolved into the Romance language by the 9th century (see Chapter 4)

W

waltz a ballroom dance and associated music in a triple meter (see Chapter 2)

Welsh a language, person, and/or cultural activity from Wales (see Chapter 6)

windmill a dance move typical of hip-hop performance characterized by the dancer spinning on the ground with legs outstretched (see Chapter 2)

WOMAD acronym for World of Music, Arts, and Dance, an organization dedicated to promoting international artistic traditions, especially music

woodblock an idiophone made of wood

world beat an early industry label for popular world-music styles

World fusion an industry label for popular world-music styles that combine more than one music tradition

world music an industry label for a variety of international folk, classical, and popular-music styles

X

xylophone a struck idiophone that consists of a set of keys of graduated length intended to produce different pitches

Y

yomiuri a street balladeer from Japan (see Chapter 9)

Yoruba an ethnic group from Nigeria and Benin and their cultural activities (see Chapter 7)

Z

zapateado the choreographed footwork of a flamenco dancer (see Chapter 6)

zarb a goblet-shaped drum from Iran (see Chapter 8)

zedani the poetic song of Bedouin shepherds from Algeria and elsewhere in North Africa (see Chapter 8)

Zion a biblical reference to Ethiopia / Africa, often cited as the spiritual home of Rastafari adherents and all African-descended populations (see Chapter 7)

zouk a popular-music style found throughout the Caribbean, especially in French-influenced regions (see Chapter 4)

zydeco a popular-music style from French-influenced region of the United States characterized by the use of the accordion (see Chapter 6)

Credits

PHOTO CREDITS

COVER: Michael Ochs Archives/©Michael Ochs Archives/ CORBIS All Rights Reserved.

CHAPTER 1:   **p. 3** Courtesy of the Library of Congress.

CHAPTER 2:   **p. 11** Photofest; **p. 14** JAN PERSSON/Lebrecht Music & Arts Photo Library; **p. 20** David Mager/Pearson Learning Photo Studio; **p. 28** Al Pereira/Getty Images, Inc./ Al Pereira/WireImage.

CHAPTER 3:   **p. 52** Echoes/Getty Images, Inc./Echoes/Redferns; **p. 44** Terry Miller.

CHAPTER 4:   **p. 63** George Haling/AGE Fotostock America, Inc.; **p. 69** Eduardo COMESANA/Lebrecht Music & Arts Photo Library; **p. 77** Frank Miceiotta/Getty Images, Inc./ Frank Miceiotta/Stringer; **p. 84** Photofest.

CHAPTER 5:   **p. 90** Le Grand Protage Image/Creative Commons; **p. 91** Creative Commons; **p. 94** Anitfluor/Creative Commons; **p. 96** Photofest.

CHAPTER 6:   **p. 111** Photofest; **p. 114** Andrew Griffith/ Creative Commons; **p. 120** Feliciano Guimaraes/Creative Commons.

CHAPTER 7:   **p. 136** Grant Goddard/Getty Images, Inc./ Grant Goddard/Redferns.

CHAPTER 8:   **p. 152** Michael Ochs Archives/Getty Images Inc.—Michael Ochs Archives; **p. 155** Photofest; **p. 157** Creative Commons; **p. 160** Lucy Nicholson/Getty Images, Inc./ Lucy Nicholson/Stringer/AFP; **p. 165** Staff/Getty Images, Inc./Staff/AFP.

CHAPTER 9:   **p. 176** Creative Commons; **p. 185** Yangon/ Creative Commons.

TEXT CREDITS

CHAPTER 3:   **p. 37** RUM AND COCA-COLA Music by JERI SULLIVAN and PAUL BARON. Lyrics by MOREY AMSTERDAM Additional Lyrics by AL STILLMAN © 1944 (Renewed) LEO FEIST, INC. All rights controlled by EMI FEIST CATALOG INC (Publishing) and ALFRED PUBLISHING CO INC (Print) All Rights Reserved. Used by Permission of ALFRED MUSIC PUBLISHING CO, INC.; **p. 54** "Get Busy" Source: Performed by Sean Paul.

CHAPTER 4:   **p. 66** "Por Una Cabeza" ("By a Head") Source: Performed by Carlos Gardel; **p. 78** "Oye Como Va" ("Hear How It Goes") Source: Performed by Tito Puente.

CHAPTER 6:   **p. 106** "Waterloo" Source: Performed by Abba; **p. 109** "Theme from Harry's Game" Source: Performed by Clannad/EMI Music Publishing; **p. 119** "Coimbra" Source: Performed by Amàlia Rodrigues, music by Raul Ferrão, lyrics by José Galhardo.

CHAPTER 8:   **p. 162** "Gharib eh Ashena" ("Stranger, Familiar") Source: Performed by Googoosh; **p. 166** "Inta Omri" Source: Performed by Lubna Salame and the Nazareth Orchestra/EMI Music Publishing.

CHAPTER 9:   **p. 177** "Kanashii Sake" ("Sad Sake") Source: Performed by Hibari Misora/JASRAC; **p. 182** "He Ri Jun Zai Lai" ("When Will You Return?") Source: Performed by Teresa Teng; **p. 188** "Field Flower in the Concrete Jungle" Source: Performed by Tai Orathai; **p. 192** "Qur'an an dan Koran" Source: Performed by Rhoma Irama.

Index